Greed, Self-Interest and the Shaping of Economics

Since 2008, profound questions have been asked about the driving forces and self-regulating potential of the economic system, political control and morality. With opinion turning against markets and self-interest, economists found themselves on the wrong side of the argument. This book explores how the past of economics can contribute to today's debates.

The book considers how economics took shape as philosophers probed into the viability of commercial society and its potential to generate positive-sum outcomes. It explains how dreams of affluence, morality and happiness were built upon human greed and vanity. It covers the bumpy road of the construction and reconstruction of this dream, exploring the debate on the foundations, conditions and limitations of the idea of the social utility of greed and vanity. Revisiting this debate provides a rich source of ideas in rethinking economics and the basic beliefs concerning our economic system today.

Rudi Verburg was assistant professor in the history and philosophy of economic thought at the Erasmus University Rotterdam. Recently he joined the research project 'What Good Markets are good for' as part-time researcher at the Vrije Universiteit Amsterdam. He has published books and articles on topics ranging from values and institutions, social cohesion, solidarity and care, and the history of economic thought.

Routledge Studies in the History of Economics

Greed, Self-Interest and the Shaping of Economics

Rudi Verburg

Routledge
Taylor & Francis Group

LONDON AND NEW YORK

First published 2018
by Routledge
2 Park Square, Milton Park, Abingdon, Oxon OX14 4RN

and by Routledge
52 Vanderbilt Avenue, New York, NY 10017

First issued in paperback 2020

Routledge is an imprint of the Taylor & Francis Group, an informa business

British Library Cataloguing-in-Publication Data
A catalogue record for this book is available from the British Library

Library of Congress Cataloging-in-Publication Data
A catalog record has been requested for this book

ISBN 13: 978-0-367-66697-2 (pbk)
ISBN 13: 978-1-138-28537-8 (hbk)

Typeset in Bembo
by Swales & Willis Ltd, Exeter, Devon, UK

This book is dedicated to my father, Jan Verburg (1924–2017), who was a man of wisdom and integrity, whose modesty and liberality sharply contrasted with the greed and vanity of our times.

Contents

Preface

Greed seems to have its moments. In this vein Keynes acknowledged greed's useful function in delivering society from the problem of scarcity in his essay *Economic Possibilities for our Grandchildren* (1930). Failing to take the power of the desire for distinction into account, Keynes asserted that greed had outlived its purpose. He foresaw a return to more lofty standards: "The love of money as a possession . . . will be recognized for what it is, a somewhat disgusting morbidity, one of those semi-criminal, semi-pathological propensities which one hands over with a shudder to the specialists in mental disease". Such exclamations are rare within the profession. As a rule, economists use the term self-interest; its solidity, neutrality and explanatory power held to be self-evident. Indeed, there is a surprisingly small amount of literature on the first principle of economics, self-interest, and its founding passions self-love/pride and greed. This book aims to fill some of this void and I hope the reader will read the book with as much pleasure as I had writing it.

I am indebted to all those who have provided me with their advice, comments and support, as I struggled to turn loose ideas into this book, starting with the two anonymous referees of a journal who both suggested that my first attempt on the subject in the form of an article read like a book proposal. With the encouragement and support of Hein Klemann at the Erasmus University Rotterdam, I followed up on this suggestion. Most chapters have been presented at the annual ESHET Conferences, and I am most grateful for the valuable comments, suggestions and criticisms I received from colleagues and friends. I especially would like to thank Jimena Hurtado, Michel Bee, Tony Aspromourgos, Daniel Diatkine, Richard van den Berg, Renee Prendergast, John Davis and Martijn Lak. Remaining mistakes only prove my failure to listen to sound advice. Last but not least, I am most grateful to my wife Johanna and children Marc and Steven for their patience and support.

1 Shifting narratives and the emergence of political economy

Shifting narratives

The economic, financial and political upheaval following the Wall Street crash of October 2008 signified not only a system failure but also a crash of the system's belief system. Gone was the casual acceptance of the positive effects of the pursuit of self-interest in a free-market system. Gone too was the self-assurance with which the essential long-term benefits of globalisation were proclaimed. Heartfelt convictions and basic assumptions from which an optimistic worldview had been wrought were challenged. In the decades before 2008, the

> idea was that capitalism, democracy and technology would advance simultaneously – and global peace would be the end-product. In a world in which all the major powers embraced democracy and market economics – and globalisation and high technology drew people together – war might become a thing of the past. Consumerism and connectivity would trump conflict.
>
> (Rachman 2011: 5)

According to Rachman, the year 2008 separated the age of optimism from the age of anxiety, confronting us with an alternative much more gloomy narrative that emphasised political instability and the rise of defensive, protectionist attitudes. In the wake of stagnation and the disenchantment of the notion that all were to benefit from globalisation, a zero-sum logic surfaced that resulted in rivalry and strife.

A second narrative emerged where ideas of mutual benefit gave way to claims that some had gained at the expense of an ignorant majority, ruining the cheerful and comforting notion of the invisible hand. As Stiglitz (2003: 14) described the sentiment when all still seemed light and bright in *The Roaring Nineties*: "The invisible hand theory was a great relief to CEOs, for it told them that by doing well (for themselves) they were doing good (for society). Not only should they feel no guilt in greed; they should feel pride". When the unwholesome consequences of the unrelenting pursuit of self-interest became apparent, however, underlying motives of human behaviour were questioned. Self-interest, previously seen as the *sine qua non* of the benefits of the free market system and the common good, was exposed as greed. Re-interpreting events, Madrick (2012) qualified the pre-2008 age of optimism as the age of greed.

Along with the uncomfortable but growing realisation of the existence of a less self-congratulatory narrative that did not promise a happy end, many pointed an accusing finger at economics. Caught in a sterile world of formal, mathematical language, economists had failed to anticipate and prevent the 2008 crisis. Putting too much faith in the optimistic narrative, the queen of the social sciences had not been alert enough to forces operating in the other direction. While *The Economist* took an inquiring attitude ('What went wrong with economics'), others were more prone to condemn the lack of relevance (Hodgson 2009; Coyle 2012) or/and the deceptive nature of economics' claims about the world (such as the invisible hand; see Samuels 2011; Fox 2009; Evensky 2012). Alan Greenspan, the former chairman of the Federal Reserve of the United States, famously admitted in a congressional hearing that he was shocked to find that he had been wrong to assume the beneficial nature of self-interest and the free market.

If we crossed a threshold between one narrative to another in 2008, then we crossed that same threshold in the opposite direction in the eighteenth century. The view dominating before 2008 is reminiscent of a set of ideas developed in the eighteenth century, which Hirschman (1977) has labelled the *doux commerce* thesis. It linked the positive social function of the love of money and expanding trade and commerce to order and prosperity, inspiring Kant to expect eternal peace as a by-product of strengthening economic and socio-cultural ties among nations. In the eighteenth century, this narrative triumphed over the nationalistic and zero-sum nature of trade that had ruled the age of mercantilism. The confrontation between the two narratives resonated in the eighteenth century views on economics just like it does today. The rise of the *doux commerce* thesis against the narrative of corrupting luxury, self-destructive passions and state power was one of the foundational ideas of economics.

Perspective and aim

Since 2008, profound questions have been asked about the driving forces and self-regulating potential of the economic system, political control and morality. A growing pile of publications emerged on the true nature of capitalism, often seeking to differentiate between right and wrong, moderate and excessive, good and bad capitalism (Baumol et al. 2007). Others are more pessimistic about chances at governance and reform and, bringing Marx's idea of inherent destructive tendencies in capitalism back to life, predict the imminent demise of capitalism (Posner 2009; Mason 2015). Defenders of capitalism countered that capitalism is change, an ongoing process of 'creative destruction', as Schumpeter would have it, that one should look at the long-term achievements of capitalism (McCloskey 2007, 2010), and that the real problem is that, due to rent-seeking businesses and government policies, the market is not allowed to do its benign work. If only competition and innovation would rule.

A parallel debate focuses on the limits of markets (Bolderman 2007; Stiglitz 2010; Bruni 2012; Sandel 2013). On the waves of neo-liberalism, the market triumphantly extended its domain in the eighties and nineties of the past century, detaching itself from internal and external restraints by deregulation, privatisation, liberalisation and globalisation (Harvey 2007; Becchio and Leghissa 2017). In 2008, the free market fell from its pedestal as its inherent tendency to deliver the good was proclaimed an illusion. Events made it perfectly clear that markets can just as well feed destructive passions and corrupt society.

Along with markets, self-interest, often the driving force of economic behaviour, has come up for a less appreciatory job evaluation. The world that neo-liberalism helped to create nearly crumbled under the untrammelled pursuit of self-interest. If self-interest is given free reign, greed will show its ugly face before long. With opinion turning against free markets and self-interest, economists found themselves on the wrong side of the argument with economics often being dismissed as the science of greed.

Although there is plenty of reason for economists to be modest about their science's performance, it also has a lot to contribute to today's debates, or rather, its past has much to offer. After all, economics developed as a scientific discipline in debating questions of law, liberty and commerce. Revisiting this debate enriches our understanding, not in the least because it allows us to avoid polarisation. Nowadays capitalism, markets and self-interest are often considered to be either all part of the problem or essential building blocks of the solution. Society, however, is the result of opposing and contending forces, moving towards or away from positive-sum outcomes depending on the strength of both inherent tendencies. The science of political economy emerged from a discourse between competing narratives on the promises and problems of commercial society, focusing attention on the conditions for and pitfalls of a positive-sum society. Accepting that opposing forces are at work, the real question is about the mechanisms and conditions conducive to positive outcomes. That is the way philosophers in the eighteenth century discussed the nature and growth of commercial society, a perspective which political economists in the nineteenth century increasingly lost. This study aims to answer two questions. First, building from the same materials – human greed, vanity, pride and rivalry – that showed us their destructive powers in 2008, how did philosophers in the seventeenth and eighteenth centuries construct a narrative of a positive-sum world? Second, what happened to this narrative so that greed and vanity became obsolete and disappeared from the theoretical framework of mainstream economics?

The literature bearing on these questions has only bits and pieces of answers to offer. Sometimes greed figures in analyses as a sideshow to some related subject (such as self-interest, selfishness, self-love etc.). In *Greed, Lust & Gender* (2009), Folbre, for instance, discusses greed and its constraints in a gendered history of economic ideas, criticising economics for constructing a concept of self-interest that denies gender inequality. Consideration of the topic of greed may also be restricted to some particular author, as in the case of Wright's *Adam Smith and Greed* (2005). Sometimes it is restricted to a particular period of time. So the idea of self-interest is often discussed either as a new way of thinking about man and society in the seventeenth and eighteenth centuries (Hirschman 1977; Myers 1983; Saether 2000; Force 2003), or in the context of questions of market coordination and limits to laissez-faire in the nineteenth and twentieth century (Medema 2009). For good reason too. In *Self-interest before Adam Smith* (2003), Force argues that the first principle of economics, self-interest, was rooted in two contending philosophical traditions (neo-Epicureanism/Augustinianism and neo-Stoicism), each representing different views on human nature. However relevant to the eighteenth-century debate, Force's skeleton of the two traditions is too coarsely woven as a framework for tracing the changing relationship between greed and self-interest after Smith.

Greed also turns up in the literature as part of a more general exploration and assessment of commercial society or capitalism. In this respect, it is a pity that Hirschman's *The Passions and the Interests* (1977) and his *Rival Interpretations of Market Society* (1982) do not link up. Rather than continuing the story of the vicissitudes of greed and self-interest in the growth of political economy, Hirschman (1982) classified different views on the dynamics of capitalism and its moral foundations. Or take McCloskey's apology for capitalism and the middle classes in *The Bourgeois Virtues* (2006), the first volume of a trilogy emphasising that capitalism was built on and build up the bourgeois virtues. Not only has capitalism made us richer and live longer, it has also improved our ethics. Painting the beneficial effects of capitalism in glowing colours, McCloskey castigated economics for reducing the moral dimension of economic action to prudence only. Economists have economised on love, mistakenly thinking they could do it on prudence alone. Prudence, McCloskey asserted, needs to be set in the context of and balanced with love, or more generally, the (bourgeois) virtues, to account for the working and performance of capitalism. However, she was so keen to stay away from the idea that capitalism is greed that she tended to neglect the other side of the spectrum. Prudence/self-interest should be positioned somewhere between the opposites of love and greed. Ignoring the darker side of self-interest, McCloskey overbalanced in her hymn to the positive dynamics between love and prudence.

Although the literature often parades the same personae dramatis and revisits the same issues, the upcoming chapters have their own story to tell. It is about greed (linked up with pride/vanity), self-interest and economics. It is a conceptual history including times before and after Smith, and recounts the debate on the social utility of greed and pride in commercial society from pre-classical thought to the beginning of the twentieth century. It tells the story of the rise and shaping of economics as a tale of the evolving relationship between greed and self-interest. Although often used interchangeably, greed and self-interest should be distinguished (Wang and Murnigham 2011; Kirchgässner 2014; Seuntjens et al. 2015). Greed is usually defined as (1) an excessive desire, most often in relation to wealth or money, with avarice, acquisitiveness, avidity, covetousness, cupidity and rapacity as the most used synonyms. Greed (2) is excessive in not being limited by need; with wealth or money becoming an end in itself instead of a means. To be morally reprehensible, however, greed (3) willfully has to be harmful to others and to violate some norm of fairness in having or acquiring wealth or money at the expense of others. Greed links the greedy person's being better off to someone else's being worse off. Moreover, greed (4) is tied to feelings of pride and shame. Greed is held to be a moral deficiency and shameful, while its reward, wealth or money, is linked to sentiments of pride and superiority over others. Self-interest differs from greed in all of these aspects. Self-interest is not inherently excessive; it is reasonable as it seeks wealth or money for its potential to satisfy desires; self-interest may conflict with the interest of others but may also happily coordinate to mutual gain, and its exercise does not inspire sentiments of pride or shame. Self-interest is conditioned and disciplined greed.

Recounting the story of the rise and fall of greed and pride not only serves idle curiosity. Given that the seventeenth- and eighteenth-century debate on commercial society contains the very elements that drive the two narratives today, one cannot pretend that this debate is a relic of the past, a story featuring trolls, druids and giants which became extinct species with the advance of sound scientific explanation. The debate, then and now, is about passions and interests (compare Akerlof and Shiller's book (2009) on animal spirits), about trust and cooperation, about rules and conscience (codes of honour, corporate responsibility, integrity etc.). Istvan Hont (2015) emphasised the need to study contemporary issues and intellectual history together for good reason.

Most economists, however, are quite unaware of the debate on order and cooperation in which their discipline is rooted, and are unfamiliar with the language in which the debate took place. As it inspired intense debate on the principles of human nature, greed and pride, wealth and power, passions, human motives, institutions and moral sentiments, it is a fascinating build-up of reflections which accompanied the transformation towards commercial society. Indeed, trade and commerce, having been associated for ages with self-seeking behaviour at the expense of others, became the basis of the health and wealth of a society. This only works if people work together. Solving this incongruity means showing the social utility of man's passions in fostering social cooperation and trust, on which the advantages of commercial society depend. How can human greed and pride possibly be outfitted for this purpose? Fully aware of the existence of contrary forces in society and the multiplicity of human intentions and aspirations, the story-tellers carefully grafted onto their narration those conditions, qualifications and exceptions that needed to be taken into account when considering principles in operation.

The ascent of the positive-sum narrative

Two different narratives. Although we tend to switch from the one to the other, at any point in time society is the scene of contrary forces – towards cooperation and harmony as well as towards conflict and discord – and moves along the negative-positive sum axis depending on the strength of the forces. Naturally, profound changes in society redefining the whole setting require a reassessment of the nature, strength and interaction of the forces and their consequences. That is precisely what happened when medieval society gradually but irrevocably gave way to commercial society. Trade and commerce rose to dominance as the prime sources of wealth and power, (re)defining collective identities and views on statecraft. Established ways and world views were challenged. As a consequence, the sixteenth and seventeenth centuries were flooded by ideas, views and propositions to make sense of developments. Traditional views were stretched to understand and assess changing circumstances, and familiar concepts and ideas were fitted to accommodate new conditions and aspirations. In this blender of ideas, 'interest' developed as a new language to discuss the terms and conditions of change, to articulate and legitimise new aspirations and ideals that went with the transition from feudalism to commercial society. The emergence of political economy was inseparable from the rise of commercial society, utilising the new language of interest to state its insights.

From this perspective, Adam Smith's *The Wealth of Nations* should be taken as a milestone in the debate on commercial society first and as the kick-off of economics second. How to assess the forces at work in commercial society? How to create the conditions for allowing society to move towards positive-sum outcomes? With the rise and growth of commercial society, structures of incentives and pay-offs and the interplay of passions and institutions needed to be reassessed and readjusted to create and maintain order and progress. The events of 2008 have placed the very same issues on the agenda again. How did philosophers in the seventeenth and eighteenth centuries, using the same materials, reason their way towards the idea of the social utility of greed and a conception of a positive-sum world?

From passions to interests

Ever since Antiquity, moral philosophers had emphasised the destructive nature of man's passions (James 1998, 2012), and therefore the need for passions to be tamed. Usually wisdom and reason were recommended to discipline the unruly passions. When Machiavelli started his analysis from 'man as he really is' and eschewed the comfort of the assumption of the potency of reason, he put up the challenge of finding some alternative to control the passions. The idea of neutralising one passion by another was widely discussed. Acquisitive passion in particular was seen as having great potential to deliver mankind from the destructiveness of his passions and the feebleness of reason and virtue.

The acquisitive passion, greed or love of money was subsequently redefined as interest, which was to become the new buzzword in the seventeenth and eighteenth centuries.

This is not to say that greed was dressed up and remodeled from a vice into a virtue. The rise of commercial society redefined the terms and conditions of what constituted 'harmful' or 'beneficial' behaviour. The 'transformation' of greed into interest is part and parcel of societal change – increasing division of labour, interdependence and need for cooperation – and redefines what behaviour is permissible and what behaviour is not to be tolerated. The same goes for self-love, featuring equally prominently in the genealogy of self-interest (Weststeijn 2011; Force 2003). At the heart of fallen man's passions, self-love drives man towards the wicked pleasures of pride and vanity. Reevaluated as a positive image of self and natural desire for esteem, self-love, pride and vanity came to be seen as constituent elements of order and prosperity.

All these changes and reevaluations resonated in the rise of the language of interest. Employing the concept of interest to capture and understand commercial society, philosophers looked beyond the unpredictable, irrational and inherently destructive nature of the passions and the question of their repression. Passions received a more favourable reading and were reinterpreted on a positive note in terms of interest. From this perspective, the transformation of greed into self-interest is part of the story of the ascent of the positive-sum narrative, shifting gear between the two forces in society. The prevalence of the constructive forces, however, was never self-evident and the positive vibes of self-interest were widely recognised by eighteenth-century philosophers to be dependent upon conditions and limitations.

From motives to consequences

It was not that philosophers suddenly felt that human nature had been misjudged all along and was naturally inclined to the common good. They were quite aware that it is not only from reason or virtue that positive-sum outcomes in society were to be expected. In a society characterised by specialisation and social differentiation, positive outcomes may also result from the way decisions and behaviour interact, however unintended and unanticipated. Attention shifted from underlying motives of behaviour to the mechanisms through which such unintended consequences materialised. The notion of desirable consequences out of self-seeking behaviour is reflected in the gradual transition of the model of the body politic, in which the parts are geared towards the whole, to the mechanistic model, the machine, in which the interacting parts unconsciously work together to produce a desirable outcome. Although both metaphors were often used interchangeably, the mechanical model proved most useful in writings on economic issues. The eighteenth century advanced the idea of the interrelatedness of the economy organised by the institution of the market for purpose. The competitive market was presented as an instrument of control, creating "a social result that is independent of individual will and intention" (Blaug 1978: 62). In this context Smith used the well-worn notion of the invisible hand in *The Wealth of Nations* and much of his analysis is designed to work out how to achieve positive-sum results from such a mechanism. Terms and conditions were discussed to explain how greed and pride should be disciplined in commercial society to the effect of refraining from harming others and be reinterpreted as self-interest.

From a negative/zero-sum society to a positive-sum society

All this would not have made much of an impression if it had not been for the rise of the idea of trade and economic activity as a positive sum game rather than an exploitative game. In a society based on the division of labour and specialisation, people depend on each other in order to provide for their needs. Society develops into a network of relations of exchange and such a network only works if all benefit from participating (Witztum 2010). Hence the importance of the competitive market for dissecting outcomes from individual intentions and to prevent some from appropriating the fruits of cooperation. Moreover, this positive-sum nature of individual efforts offers the prospect of growth and raising everyone's living standards, whereby everyone has a stake in society. Thus a new narrative developed, emphasising interests rather than passions, beneficial consequences rather than wicked motives and positive-sum rather than negative/zero-sum outcomes.

Outline of the study

All of these elements played their part in swinging around perceptions about the direction in which the forces operating in society move. Optimism on the immanent tendency towards a positive-sum society was built on the firm conviction of the existence of fixed, discoverable patterns in processes of production, distribution and consumption. Had not Newton himself argued that it was possible to discover the laws of nature that govern social phenomena by using the same methods he had so successfully used in natural philosophy? Notwithstanding man's selfish inclinations and ill intentions, there is a mechanism operating in economic processes, a providential law of nature for the good of mankind. If allowed to work freely, the mechanisms could be expected to have positive outcomes for society at large. This is what bubbles up in the magic of the market, inducing people to pursue their self-interest in such a way that outcomes are efficient and to everyone's benefit. It was this exciting newly evolving narrative that philosophers pursued, elaborated and assessed in reference to the old narrative. Chapter 2 discusses the historical changes in economic and ideological conditions up to the eighteenth century, through which greed turned from one of the deadly sins into a passion from which society derived social benefits.

Not all threaded equally cautiously in redefining the (im)propriety and limits of greed and other passions. Chapter 3 opens with the views of Bernard

Mandeville, who became infamous for the way he sang the praises of pride and greed for the public benefits these vices helped to procure. Showing how cooperation (and hence society's advantages) emerged from the passions of pride and greed, his views became a well-established point of departure in reflections on commercial society. However outrageous and baneful his views were said to be, underneath his paradoxes Mandeville raised serious questions about commercial society. If society is the product of both destructive *and* constructive forces, and cooperation depends on the fickleness of opportunities for private gain to be derived from society, how will the cooperative strategy prevail? After establishing the basic framework, this chapter proceeds by examining the answers given by David Hume and Jean-Jacques Rousseau. Arguing the growing preponderance of one of Mandeville's contending forces in society, the two philosophers came up with opposing views: Rousseau's image of commercial society is the pessimistic mirror image of Hume's optimistic account.

Chapter 4 inquires how Adam Smith assessed commercial society in the face of these two opposing assessments. It relates how Smith grew more hesitant than Hume in proclaiming that self-interest came down on the side of virtue, acknowledging that man's vanity and greed may get the better of him and combine against virtue. Although he never shared Rousseau's condemnation of commercial society, Smith returned again and again to the questions Rousseau's analysis raised, aware that any balance between contending forces is precarious, given man's unsociable sociability and changing circumstances.

At the birth of the science of political economy, the concept of self-interest was part and parcel of a long debate on passions, interests, virtue and order that accompanied the transformation of society and its political organisation with expanding trade and commerce. The second part of the book discusses the way the concept of self-interest was customised to meet new challenges in political economy in the nineteenth century.

In response to controversy about society and progress, equality and reform in the wake of revolutionary developments towards the end of the eighteenth century, the young science of political economy sought to establish itself. Chapter 5 describes how classical political economy came to make corrections to the Smithian framework and remodel itself into an abstract-deductive science aiming to state principles concerning wealth. These changing aims and ways also changed the substance of the concept of self-interest, rewriting not only the relation of self-interest to passions and institutions but also its relation to greed and pride.

Steering clear from the science of morals and politics and the questions of virtue and happiness, political economy increasingly grounded the idea of the benefits of self-interest on the natural laws of competition. Myrdal (1969[1954]: 126) expressed the pivotal role of competition in John Stuart Mill's views as follows: "Free competition is the alpha and omega. He never doubted that it is beneficial 'in principle'". Chapter 6 covers the socialist critique of competition as a benign mechanism. This key idea was seriously disputed by socialists like Robert Owen and William Thompson, who sharply contrasted competition and cooperation. Engels and Marx continued along this road to prove political economy wrong on its own terms. Refashioning greed into self-interest and building up a positive-sum narrative had taken more than a century. Developing its counterpart from arguments taken from the classical frame of thought took another century.

Chapter 7 discusses the reformulation of the positive-sum narrative by neoclassical economics in terms of rationality, efficiency and equilibrium. The concept of self-interest was refitted and reinterpreted to denote rationality and utility/profit maximisation, severing its ties with greed and pride. The clash of perspective between neoclassical economics and Veblen's institutional approach only tended to accentuate the contrast between the positive- and negative-sum narratives, and the fact that greed had been left behind in the mainstream.

Chapter 8 puts the story together and summarises how the world of economic ideas that framed greed (and pride) as self-interest changed and soaked off self-interest from its founding passions. This story and its language have long lost their currency. Especially in the twentieth century, economics came to adopt the language of mathematics to tell its story, while cutting it short by stripping it of conditions and context in a process of increasing specialisation and abstraction. This study is an invitation to reacquaint ourselves with this intellectual journey in the course of which political economy emerged and was given shape. It is a tale full of passion and sentiments of cooperation and conflict and of opportunities and restraints. Tracing the vicissitudes of pride, greed and self-interest in political economy, the book reflects much of the aspirations, hopes and disappointments of those who shaped economics as a science.

References

Akerlof, G.A. and Shiller, R.J. (2009). *Animal Spirits: how human psychology drives the economy, and why it matters to global capitalism*. Princeton, NJ: Princeton University Press.
Baumol, W.J., Robert, E.L. and Schramm, C.J. (2007). *Good Capitalism, Bad Capitalism, and the Economics of Growth and Prosperity*. New Haven, CT: Yale University Press.
Becchio, G. and Leghessa, G. (2017). *The Origins of Neoliberalism: insights from economics and philosophy*. New York: Routledge.
Blaug, M. (1978). *Economic Theory in Retrospect*, third edition. Cambridge/London: Cambridge University Press.
Bolderman, L. (2007). *The Cult of the Market: economic fundamentalism and its discontents*. Canberra: ANU E Press.
Bruni, L. (2012). *The Genesis and Ethos of the Market*. Houndmills/New York: Palgrave Macmillan.
Coyle, D. (ed.) (2012). *What's the Use of Economics? Teaching the dismal science after the crisis*. London: London Publishing Partnership.
Economist, The (2009). What went wrong with economics? *The Economist*, 16 July.

Evensky, J. (2012). What's wrong with economics? *Journal of the History of Economic Thought*, vol. 34(1): 1–20.

Folbre, N. (2009). *Greed, Lust & Gender: a history of economic ideas*. Oxford/New York: Oxford University Press.

Force, P. (2003). *Self-Interest before Adam Smith: a genealogy of economic science*. Cambridge: Cambridge University Press.

Fox, J. (2009). *The Myth of the Rational Market: a history of risk, reward and delusion on Wall Street*. New York: Harper Business.

Harvey, D. (2007). *A Brief History of Neoliberalism*. Oxford: Oxford University Press.

Hirschman, A.O. (1977). *The Passions and the Interests: political arguments for capitalism before its triumph*. Princeton, NJ: Princeton University Press.

Hirschman, A.O. (1982). Rival interpretations of market society: civilizing, destructive, or feeble? *Journal of Economic Literature*, vol. 20(4): 1463–84.

Hodgson, G.M. (2009). The great crash of 2008 and the reform of economics. *Cambridge Journal of Economics*, vol. 33 (6): 1205–21.

Hont, I. (2015). *Politics in Commercial Society: Jean-Jacques Rousseau and Adam Smith*. Boston, MA: Harvard University Press.

James, S. (1998). The passions in metaphysics and the theory of action. In: *The Cambridge History of Seventeenth-Century Philosophy*, Garber, D. and Ayers, M. (eds), Cambridge: Cambridge University Press, vol. 1: pp. 913–49.

James, S. (2012). Reason, the passions, and the good life. In: *The Cambridge History of Seventeenth-Century Philosophy*, Garber, D. and Ayers, M. (eds), Cambridge: Cambridge University Press, vol. 2: pp. 1358–96.

Kirchgässner, G. (2014). On self-interest and greed. *Journal of Business Economics*, vol. 84(9): 1191–209.

Madrick, J. (2012). *Age of Greed: the triumph of finance and the decline of America, 1970 to the present*. New York: Vintage Books.

Mason, P. (2015). *Postcapitalism: a guide to our future*. London: Allan Lane.

McCloskey, D.N. (2006). *The Bourgeois Virtues: ethics in an age of commerce*. Chicago, IL: University of Chicago Press.

McCloskey, D.N. (2010). *Bourgeois Dignity: why economics can't explain the modern world*. Chicago, IL: University of Chicago Press.

Medema, S.G. (2009). *The Hesitant Hand: taming self-interest in the history of economic ideas*. Princeton, NJ/Oxford: Princeton University Press.

Myers, M.L. (1983). *The Soul of Modern Economic Man: Ideas of Self-Interest: Thomas Hobbes to Adam Smith*. Chicago, IL/London: University of Chicago Press.

Myrdal, G. (1969[1954]). *The Political Element in the Development of Economic Theory*. New York: Simon & Schuster.

Posner, R.A. 2009. *A Failure of Capitalism: the crisis of '08 and the descent into depression*. Cambridge, MA: Harvard University Press.

Rachman, G. (2011). *Zero-sum World: politics, power and prosperity after the crash*. London: Atlantic Books.

Saether, A. (2000). Self-interest as an acceptable mode of human behaviour. In: *The Canon in the History of Economics*, Psalidopoulos, M. (ed.). London/New York: Routledge, pp. 45–67.

Samuels, W.J. (2011). *Erasing the Invisible Hand: essays on an elusive and misused concept in economics*. New York: Cambridge University Press.

Sandel, M.J. (2013). *What Money Can't Buy: the moral limits of markets*. London: Penguin.

Seuntjens, T.G., Zeelenberg, M., Breugelmans, S.M. and Van der Ven, N. (2015). Defining greed. *British Journal of Psychology*, vol. 106(3): 505–25.

Stiglitz, J.E. (2003). *The Roaring Nineties: seeds of destruction*. London: Penguin Books.

Stiglitz, J.E. (2010). *Freefall: America, free markets and the sinking of the world economy*. New York: Norton.

Wang, L. and Murnigham, J.K. (2011). On greed. *The Academy of Management Annals*, vol. 5(1): 279–316.

Weststeijn, A. (2010). From the passion of self-love to the virtue of self-interest: the republican morals of the brothers De la Court. *European Review of History: Revue europeenne d'histoire*, vol. 17(1): 75–92.

Witztum, A. (2010). Interdependence, the invisible hand, and equilibrium in Adam Smith. *History of Political Economy*, vol. 42(1): 155–92.

Wright, J.B. (2005). Adam Smith and greed. *Journal of Private Enterprise*, vol. 21(1): 46–58.

2 The rise of greed in early economic thought

From deadly sin to social benefit[1]

Introduction

Many see greed, avarice or love of money as the driving force behind the 2008 financial and economic crisis. After decades in which greed was propagated as an essential ingredient of material success for the individual and society alike and almost elevated to a form of art, we now wonder how we ever could have been seduced by ideas that stressed the usefulness of greed. There is a pile of recent books explaining the rise of an economic and intellectual climate that hailed greed and made us look away from its destructive potential (Brassey and Barber 2009; Mason 2009). Most accounts acknowledge the shadow of Adam Smith in one way or another, duly noting the quote about the self-interest of the butcher, the brewer and the baker,[2] and the myth that has been built around his invisible hand in turning the selfish pursuit of material gain into a contribution to the common good. By the time Smith published *The Wealth of Nations*, however, the debate on the serviceability of greed had been more or less settled and the fire had already gone out. So we should turn to the age before Smith to understand how human greed was able to develop from one of the most reprehensible vices to an almost indispensable building block of human welfare. It is this question that Albert Hirschman sought to answer in *The Passions and the Interests* (1977). His inquiry is set against the background of the question of why western Europe proved such fertile ground for the development of capitalism. In the most general terms, the explanations centre on two sets of factors: (1) changes in population, technology, methods and organisation of production, role of government etc., and (2) changes in values, attitudes, views and motivations. Hirschman was primarily interested in changes in values and the motivational structure of society. In *The Passions and the Interests* he retraced the process of ideological transformation in the seventeenth and eighteenth centuries through which the case for the social utility of greed was constructed. Given the questions that the 2008 crisis raised, it is worthwhile to revisit Hirschman.

Hirschman begins his story with the Renaissance after the breakdown of the chivalric, aristocratic ideal and the downfall of the medieval values of honour and glory. Moralising philosophy and religious precept were increasingly seen as ineffective in restraining man's destructive passions. Acknowledging the need to take man 'as he really is', the search for more prolific ways to curb man's passions inspired three solutions resulting in the identification of the lust for money as a force capable of restraining the inherently destructive passions.

The first solution was repression. This solution assumed an authority *ex machina* that does not share in the same failings in human nature as those repressed and as such is contradictory to its own premises. The second solution was built on the idea of harnessing the passions. With the state as the civilising medium, the destructiveness of the passions was to be averted by transforming them into a constructive force working toward the public good (1977: 16). The magic of this transformation failed to convince but hinted at a third solution, Hirschman argued. This involved the idea of controlling the passions by playing off one against the other: the principle of countervailing passion.

The bold idea of pitting one passion against another to the benefit of man and mankind required the identification of the taming passions and the passions requiring taming. Why did love for money, greed or avarice fit the bill? Here the notion of interest proved potent. Developed as a political maxim, interest was increasingly credited with the qualities of predictability and constancy. As the meaning of interest progressed in the seventeenth century from "the council chamber to the market-place", as Gunn had it (2010[1969]: 42), and was applied to individual aspirations and actions, greed became identified with interest. Given the positive attributes of material interest or love of money, avarice came to be acclaimed as a calm and persistent passion capable of taming the wild passions. This ideological and semantic drift heralded interest as the building block of order and wealth.

This transition in ideas did not imply that greed or avarice was upgraded in a moral sense. Whatever new ideas developed on the serviceability of greed in the seventeenth and eighteenth centuries, there was no change in the assessment of greed as morally objectionable. It was the backdrop of greed rather than greed itself that changed and in its wake views on the consequences of greed. This observation raises the question of whether the developments Hirschman described are adequately explained by reconstructing changes in ideas alone or that such an explanation should allow for the interplay of socio-economic and intellectual change. Given Hirschman's exclusive focus on the role of ideas, his account is somewhat coloured in disregarding the economic environment. Aiming to touch up the colour of Hirschman's account, I argue that it was the transition from self-sufficiency to an economy geared towards development and growth rather than the fall of the aristocratic ideal of honour and glory that paved the way for the idea of the social utility of greed. The point elaborated in this chapter is that this transition toward a growth-oriented economy came to tear down the zero-sum conception of society. It is against this change of décor that greed came to be seen as useful, that restraints upon greed were relaxed and that, once again, questions about the moral permissiveness of the striving for material gain were raised.

In order to describe these developments that turned greed from one of the seven deadly sins into a passion from which society derived social benefits, three stages may be distinguished, each representing a different economic context. In contrasting these three contexts, some characteristics light up while others fade, distorting the picture of each context if taken separately. Indeed, any attempt at characterising an economic context is a rational reconstruction at best, especially over such a lengthy period as in the case of the self-sufficient community. Notwithstanding the limitations of the stylisation used here, it is the differences between the economic contexts, even if represented in their ideal or typical forms, that buttress the story of how attitudes to greed changed with the economic context. The transition from self-sufficiency to a growth-oriented economy may be used to differentiate between the first two stages. While sharing the preoccupation with growth, the second and third stages differ in the perception of the nature of the economic game. It is only in the third stage that the idea of trade and commerce as a positive-sum game rather than a zero-sum game was voiced. The three sections that follow focus on these three stages, revealing that although greed or avarice is seen as a personal failing in virtue in all stages, each stage differs in its assessment of greed or avaricious behaviour because of shifting ideas about the welfare effects of economic activity.

The first stage: the self-sufficient community

In the first stage, ranging from ancient Greek thought and the Church Fathers to the Renaissance, greed is taken as a moral deficiency of the individual, with consequences harmful to individuals and community alike. Greed originates in a misconception of the true purpose of wealth. Wealth is a means of satisfying *necessary* wants and a surplus, if any, was to be used for the exercise of moral excellence in hospitality, charity and almsgiving. Money beyond necessary wants was to "be used in the service of one's fellow beings, not to be hoarded, unused" as Chrysostom put it (Karayiannis and Dodd 1998: 181). Given the diminishing utility of wealth following from this purpose, its pursuit is necessarily limited. As soon as greed or the lust for money appears on the stage and money-making becomes an end in itself, such natural limits are violated at the expense of the individual and the community.

In a small and self-sufficient community, any distinction between the interest of the individual and the interest of other members or the community as a whole is meaningless. People simply share an interest in the continuance of an adequate supply of goods essential to the survival of the community. In such a community, obviously, efforts that aim at private material gain with a corresponding loss for the other are inherently destructive and with reason: the community is at the centre of conceptions of virtue. Greed clashes with the unity of individual and collective interests, virtue and reason. In such conditions, the pursuit of individual advantage, gain or profit at the expense of other members of the community in a static organisation of economic life geared toward reproduction of material wellbeing is conceived as irrational and contrary to virtue. Recurring themes in the literature in this first stage of the self-sufficient community are (1) a theory of limits to the acquisitive passion in a subsistence economy; (2) the negative consequences of greed; and (3) the condemnation of greed on moral and socio-economic grounds.

Greek philosophy already included all these key elements (Balot 2001). Economic necessity, it is argued, forces men to live together. Aristotle explained that associations are formed to circumvent the individual's lack of self-sufficiency by establishing bonds of mutual benefit at different levels of social organisation (see Aristotle's *Politics* Book I). The most basic unit of association is the family household through which the basic necessities of life are provided. *Oikonomia*, or the efficient management of the household, concerns the just and efficient ways of using the available means to safeguard the survival of household and community. The village, the next level of social organisation, is a collection of households serving each other's reciprocal needs by exchanging external goods that make life comfortable. The polis is the highest level of association, and it is at this level that 'goods of the soul' (such as statesmanship and public service) are produced. Aristotle emphasised the need for limits on the means of acquisition. Such limits are implied in the purpose of wealth "as a means of being able to foster excellence in human beings" (Campbell 1987: 38). Exchange to provide for basic needs and some comforts of life is natural, bounded as such acquisitive activity is by basic satiation. If these basic needs are satiated, people turn to psychic goods that have infinite utility in building a positive self-image and sense of worth. Given such natural limits on desire, Aristotle argued, the economy is stable.

> Plato's and Aristotle's economics is not the economics of growth. Their approach is guided by a belief in the desirability of establishing a relatively stationary state of economic activity at a level which ensures the maintenance of a moderate standard of material well-being for the citizenry.
> (Gordon 1975: 27; see also Lewis 1978)

Greed, the unlimited desire for wealth, upsets this state of stability and peace. If the art of acquisition is infected by greed (an opportunity offered by money as a store of value) and the disposal of surplus is motivated by the desire for increasing riches, wealth becomes an end in itself. Such misconception of the true purpose of wealth is a moral defect, which elicits disapprobation and shame. Given that the individual's interest is strictly tied to the interest of the community, such unnatural acquisitive activity is both irrational and inefficient. The search for private gain upsets the stable state of the economy and hurts the quality of communal life from which private happiness is inseparable. This idea of a stable equilibrium or image of balance is essential to Aristotle's theory of virtue as the golden mean between two opposing extremes. In this vein, greed and avarice are interpreted:

> In regard to giving and getting money, the observance of the mean is Liberality; the excess and the deficiency Prodigality and Meanness, but the prodigal man and the mean man exceed and fall short in opposite ways to one another: the prodigal exceeds in giving and is deficient in getting, whereas the mean man exceeds in getting and is deficient in giving.
>
> (Aristotle *Nicomachean Ethics*, 1968, Book II, vii. 4: 99)

To keep within the bounds of propriety, it is important to steer by the compass of reason and virtue. The Roman orator Cicero cautioned in his discourse on obligations that "there are times when one course is likely to appear expedient and another morally right. The appearance is deceptive; for our standard is the same for expediency and for moral rectitude" (Cicero *De Officiis*, 1975, Book III: 74–5, 44 BC). Inappropriate behaviour in this respect, Seneca argued in his *Dialogues* (first century), is the result of ignorance and confusion. Anyone who fails to lead a life in accordance with right reason is a fool and will fall victim to confusing passions. In the search for external means of happiness in riches, status and power, lurks the danger that the fool will surrender to avarice, lust and ambition. The wise man conquers his passions by conforming to reason and finds peace of mind and happiness in virtue.

Similar ideas are to be found in the writings of the Greek Church Fathers who set out to develop a philosophy of Christian thought in the light of Hellenistic philosophy. Equally predisposed against the unlimited pursuit of wealth, Chrysostom (c. 356–407) drew a distinction between economising behaviour (expenditures for necessary goods and almsgiving) and avaricious behaviour, especially of the rich in their use of wealth to purchase luxurious goods, the latter being unnatural, unjust and irrational. In emphasising the importance of spiritual and psychic satisfaction over material satisfaction, he reaffirmed Aristotle's theory of natural limits on desire. No scarcity would exist if everyone restricted consumption to necessary goods and if the surplus would be distributed to the (deserving) poor through charity and almsgiving. Problems of scarcity and poverty stemmed from the unjust accumulation of wealth at the expense of others: "When production levels are constant, a greater share for a few means a smaller share for others" (Karayiannis and Dodd 1998: 185). The Greek Fathers emphasised the disruptive consequences of greed. Unlimited accumulation of wealth was seen as the main cause of unjust and unfair economic actions, a cause of war, injustice and slavery, as driving men to pursue and attain false goals, creating economic and social struggles and leading to the destruction of social peace (*ibid.*: 183–4). By exceeding natural limits in going beyond necessary consumption, greed strikes at the root of self-sufficiency.

Influenced by the Greek Fathers, St. Jerome (c. 340–420) explicitly stated the idea of a zero-sum game in individual efforts to accrue the gains from economic activity, arguing that "one man does not accumulate money except through the loss and injury suffered by another" (cited in Gordon 1975: 101). As a consequence, riches necessarily involved injustice as it results from exploitation. Not everyone was prepared to condemn accumulated wealth in equally unequivocal terms. Following Plato and Aristotle in arguing that man is driven into civil society to provide for the necessaries of life, St. Augustine, a contemporary of St. Jerome, argued that the accumulation of wealth is to be understood as the means to live a happy life. Wealth is therefore to be assessed in terms of its uses and contribution to virtue. As St. Augustine insisted: "Men are not made good by possessing these so-called good things, but, if men have become good otherwise, they make these things to be really good by using them well" (Gordon 1975: 104(n)). Augustine's thought involves the element of time, recognising the possibility of development and progress towards a more rational organisation of economic activity and administration of justice, provided man learns to use wealth well. Augustine's recognition of the possibility of economic development, however, was neglected when his writings were studied by medieval schoolmen (*ibid.*: 109). The same point was made by Heilbroner and Milberg (2009: 31) when they wrote: "Medieval economic organization was conceived of as a means of reproducing, but not enhancing, the material well-being of the past. Its motto was perpetuation, not progress". More broadly, Zaratiegui characterised traditional (feudal) society in the middle ages as:

> there is a multiplicity of small communities, including kinship networks and dispersed ethnic groups. Between these communities market interchange is often restricted and economic life is regulated by local conventions. Markets may exist within such communities, but they are embedded in wider systems of non-market relationships, and the behavior of transactors is governed by complex moral codes and informal sanctions.
> (Zaratiegui 1999: 210)

Given such hierarchical, feudal relations of (inter)dependence enveloped by customary rights and obligations, prosperity and poverty were a communal affair; the individual's material condition was predetermined by the social relations of the community (Rowlands 1999). In this setting, trade and markets were seen as morally suspect for a long time (Newhauser 2000; Muller 2002). Trade was firmly linked with greed, lucre, lying and cheating and the breach of rules and regulations. The practice of buying low and selling high without adding any value was designated as sinful and sufficient reason to deny tradesmen entrance to heaven. The logic of buying low and selling high out of considerations of personal gain was seen as detrimental to the logic of moral codes and mutual obligations that tied the fate of the individual firmly to that of the community.

Change arrived with the (first) commercial revolution in the eleventh century when agricultural methods were improved, the population grew and commerce and industry expanded. Money and markets became more important and a class of merchants emerged. Such developments gradually came to change the static and self-sufficient feudal system. The more impersonal nature of economic activities beyond the own community and region, with their possible corrosive or even destructive effects, invited new ideas on the individual's opportunities and obligations. Probably because its destructive potential became less personal, avarice was awarded a more prominent place on the list of deadly sins. John of Salisbury proclaimed that "There is no worse vice than avarice". Similarly inclined, Alan of Lille explained near the end of the twelfth century: "Avarice weakens friendship, generates hatred, breeds anger, plants wars, nourishes controversies, and ruptures the bonds of children to their parents" (cited in Little 1978: 36). No wonder that, as Odd Langholm (1987: 117) remarked, "very much of scholastic economics consisted in preaching against worldliness and greed". It is no coincidence that Dante in his *Divinia Commedia* (1306–21) described how one of hell's circles is reserved for squanderers and misers. Virgil explained that these deplorable figures have neglected to keep within bounds in dealing with money. It would take until the seventeenth century before the balance in the case of avarice was to shift, but then only because of the idea of good that may be extracted from two evils.

Even though the condemnation of greed remained in full force, boundaries with respect to the moral permissiveness of economic activity shifted in the course of time. In the wake of the (first) commercial revolution, careful attempts were made to find justification for trade and commerce considering that commerce did not need to be identified and condemned with the odious practices of merchants.

This gradual reappraisal of trade and markets went hand in hand with revisions in views and attitudes towards poverty and riches (Wood 2002). For a long time, riches were precarious with a view to one's chances for eternal life and many moral precepts existed with regard to the treatment of the poor and the importance of charity. Charity was a matter of reciprocity: benevolence and charity in exchange for salvation for the rich. As Giordano of Pisa explained: "Why are the poor given their station in life? So that the rich might earn eternal life through them" (cited in Wood 2002: 43). During the middle ages, however, the status of poverty and riches changed. Poverty was no longer seen as a sign of devotion, no more than riches implied a ticket to hell. "Wealth and beggary are two extremes. The mean is sufficiency", Jean de Meun noted in the thirteenth century (cited in Wood 2002: 42). The exercise of virtue requires a certain level of material well-being, but wealth may also intoxicate, luring away from virtuous behaviour, breeding cupidity. One needs to strike a balance between wealth and poverty. As St. Thomas (1224/5–74) indicated, avarice is associated with immoderation, with direct and harmful consequences suffered by others:

> Covetousness may signify immoderation about external things in two ways. First, so as to regard immediately the acquisition and keeping of such things, when, to wit, a man acquires or keeps them more than is due. In this way it is a sin directly against one's neighbour, since one man cannot

overabound in external riches, without another man lacking them, for temporal goods cannot be possessed by many at the same time.

(cited in Viner 1978, from St. Thomas'
Summa Theologica: 62)

Riches were not to be desired for their own sake but to serve the use of virtue, a point of view that expressed the priority of the common good over the individual good. Aquinas cautioned against trade because such profit-seeking activity "awakens greed in the hearts of the citizens" and induces "each one to seek his own profit, despising the public good" (Worland 1987: 142). At the same time, Aquinas acknowledged the usefulness of the merchant to state and society, arguing that commerce can be morally justifiable. As Langholm wrote:

> Quite literally, in the medieval configurations of vice, avarice was the stem from which all specific economic vices branched off. In a subsistence society, the simplest inference is that one who gratifies his greed will deprive someone else of his bodily sustenance. In exhortations against the avaricious, considerations of the inner and outer aspects pull together: harming his own soul, he harms his neighbour's body. To the reflecting social philosopher, however, the problem is not that simple. In economic activity, one man's profit is not always another man's loss. Avarice is not only a psychological urge, it can sometimes be socially beneficial.
>
> (Langholm 1998: 446)

Trade and its practitioners performed a useful function for society. Consider for instance the necessity of trade in times of scarcity. Neither is trade necessarily a matter of fraud and exploitation. Risk, labour, transport (from areas of plenty to those of scarcity) were put forward as valid arguments to allow the merchant to sell above cost price and make a profit. Much depended upon the right intentions of the merchant. Not only is the merchant entitled to profit to compensate for work and risk, moderate profit is also justifiable to provide for the needs of his dependents or to contribute to charity and public service.

Another topic of reflection concerned private ownership of productive resources. Surely productive resources should contribute to the common good in enlarging possessions, but private ownership implies a powerful incentive for efficiency. Once productive resources were held in private property, however, would owners be prepared to share the fruits of their labour? How to manage the trade-off between the duty to share and the need for incentive with a view to the common good (Langholm 1987)? More broadly: to what extent would the growing importance of trade, markets and profit-taking to generate subsistence and means to support the poor in times of need erode the significance of moral and religious sanctions with respect to the obligation to charity? Such reflections suggest a clear understanding of the possibility of divergence between individual interest and the interest of the collective as well as an acknowledgment of the fact that 'one man's profit is not always another man's loss'.

Given that individual interest was no longer strictly tied to the interest of the community, justice was key to medieval economic thinking to prevent harm to others. Gray put it most succinctly when he wrote: "No one, under any circumstances, should take advantage of his neighbour. This is the sum and substance of mediaeval economic teaching" (1959: 46). This does not imply that profit-taking was always morally reprehensible. With the beneficial potential of trade and markets recognised and trade no longer condemned as inherently sinful, economic discourse focused on ways to regulate trade and markets to ascertain that their potential was used in a way beneficial to society (Langholm 1987). Explorations into the just price, usury, fraud and deception concerned the rules of the (zero-sum) game as well as the conditions under which one man may profit without corresponding loss for others. It is not all 'black-and-white': greed may come in different shades. Such reflections proved fertile ground for the growth of the notion of the social utility of greed in the second stage.

The second stage: the mercantile state

The first commercial revolution ended around 1350 when the Black Death began to spread, ravaging Europe in the fourteenth and early fifteenth centuries. The consequent fall in population and output resulted in a prolonged period of economic depression. It took until 1450 before recovery set in, kicking off the second stage of commercial growth. Economic activity increased. With relations of exchange expanding within and between regions, a network of markets developed. Increasingly, the breakdown of the manorial system, urbanisation and the monetisation and commercialisation of economic life changed society (Crouzet 2001).

Growth in a pre-industrial economy, however, was always constrained by the dependence on agriculture, low productivity and the use of crude technology. In pre-industrial societies, growth was extensive:[3] real income per capita as the ratio of population to resources (especially land) did not increase much. Eric Jones speaks of "static expansion" (1988: 29): negligible income growth per capita with total output and population increasing at a comparable rate. Nevertheless, markets widened as more goods were traded, trade networks in Europe were integrated and interaction between European regions expanded. Regions and nations became more dependent upon each other's produce and the division of labour increased. Trade, especially foreign trade, was the most dynamic sector of the economy, allowing for capital accumulation, investment and innovations. Given that growth was constrained by its nature, however, such efforts induced protectionism and conflicts over exclusive rights, giving rise to a process of state-building to promote self-sufficiency within borders and to achieve a position of strength and power in competition with other countries. Such changing conditions inspired new alliances (of commercial enterprise and state power) and objectives, changing the pre-industrial economy (Wilson 1984) and shifting the focus in economic thought from household management to the management of state and society.

It is generally acknowledged (Wiles 1974; Magnusson 1987; Heckscher 1994[1935]) that in the mercantile age, growth and development became a central objective in political and economic thought. In times of nation-building, political and economic success was measured by a nation's relative wealth and power. Economic growth was promoted to fund geographical expansion and enhancement of state power. Given the prevalent idea of the dependence of surplus creation on foreign trade, and the conditions of stagnation that prevailed during much of the seventeenth century, it was quite natural to think of trade and commerce in terms of economic warfare (Hont 2010). Economic thought in the second stage, or the mercantile age, struggled with this tension between the objective of growth by foreign trade and the zero-sum notion of trade. In the face of natural, institutional and geopolitical constraints on expansion and improvement, governments tried to enforce economic policies designed to encourage economic development, especially through the promotion of production and exports. Despite inherent tensions, it was this change of décor that paved the way for a less harsh judgement of greed that stressed its conditional usefulness rather than its unconditional condemnation. This idea of the utility of greed gained force as (1) it was realised that greed was not irrational in each and every case; (2) a new theory of limits to greed was developed; and (3) economic discourse began to emphasise growth rather than sufficiency, and efficiency and material ends rather than moral and religious ideals (justice, salvation).

First, greed looked better in a setting of material ends and growth or accumulation. This new setting changed the rationality of greed. Greed is irrational in an economy geared towards self-sufficiency and a static organisation of economic life. It does not make sense to pursue material gain at the cost of others if they belong to the same community and everyone's happiness and quality of life are intertwined. The moment this interdependence becomes faint and indirect, and one's happiness no longer depends on that of the others within the community, greed does not queer one's own pitch and is far less irrational. As soon as communality is broken, as soon as separate interests are identified and perceived to exist, the question arises of who (and in what measure) is to gain and who stands to lose. Hirschman observed that "moralizing philosophy and religious precept could *no longer* be trusted with restraining the destructive passions of men" (1977: 14–15; italics added). He gave no reason but it is plausible that the problem arises once the passion of greed could no longer be depicted as irrational. And if rational, what about its objectionable character? The unity of individual and collective interests, virtue and reason was broken, creating room for perceptions of differences between individual and collective interest, and between reason and virtue, with which new opportunities and combinations presented themselves.

Second, if an unlimited desire for wealth is not necessarily harmful to the community and quality of life, a new theory of limits is required. If greed is not controlled by internal motivations of the individual as stakeholder in the community, limits are to be put in place by an outside force. Given that repressing greed would stifle incentives, the idea developed of harnessing the passions; i.e., channelling man's self-seeking activities into socially useful directions. Following the timid attempts of the scholastic writers, philosophers started to reflect on the social utility of greed. It wasn't that greed was no longer seen as an individual moral defect. Rather, philosophers increasingly toyed with the idea that greed may have positive consequences besides negative ones. The individual sin of avarice may have consequences that serve national or collective interests. In his *England's Treasure by Forraign Trade* (1959[1664]: Chapter VII), Thomas Mun thus identified three types of gain: (1) the gain of the state or commonwealth at the expense of the merchant; (2) the gain of the merchant at the expense of the state; and (3) the gain of the king at the expense of both the merchant and the state. The pursuit of riches at the expense of the other is not necessarily against the interest of the state, opening up the possibility (denied by Cicero) of a separation of expediency and moral rectitude. Given the reformulation of objectives in terms of the wealth and power of the nation-state, considerations of expediency took precedence over ethical concerns in economic discourse.

Third, the transition from scholastic economics to mercantilism[4] signified a change of focus in economic analysis from sufficiency and justice to economic growth. In the mercantilist literature, minds are set upon economic development and growth as the goal of economic activity. This shift implied new ideas about economic surplus (Aspromourgos 1996). In the scholastic literature, surplus – what is available over and above basic needs (in accordance with social status) – was to be used for purposes of charity and almsgiving to help those in need. Such considerations faded away to be replaced by the idea that resources can be used more productively through investment and accumulation. This should not be taken to imply that the breakdown of the traditional, self-sufficient community led philosophers to shed the belief that someone's gain was necessarily the loss of another in exchanges. This idea was ingrained into the pre-industrial economy in its dependence on low-productivity agriculture and animate (solar-based) sources of energy:[5]

> The supplies of food, raw materials, and thermal energy all depended directly on the amount of available land and on the solar energy captures by that land. Moreover, all these uses of land stood in competition with each other. Increasing the area devoted to one use . . . required the contraction of another
>
> (de Vries and van der Woude 1997: 719)

Applying this zero-sum notion to national trading within a static view of economic development, mercantilists assumed in one form or another[6] that an increase in the wealth of one nation can be achieved only at the expense of the wealth of other nations. Even if it was recognised that the domestic economy might contribute to growth, attention focused on foreign trade. Given the prevalence of the idea of a fixed quantum of resources or wealth and the consequent notion that one nation's gain is another nation's loss, efforts focused on redistribution and rent seeking to increase the relative share of a nation in the world's wealth. The best-known policy to promote rent seeking, of course, is protectionism, through which wealth is redistributed from foreigners to the citizens of the country ('beggar-thy-neighbour' policies) while aiming at a self-sufficient nation-state to secure provision and evade dependence on rival nations.

It was in this context that the notion of the social utility of greed gained acceptance, at first in particular with respect to efforts to advance the national interests at the expense of other countries. Several sources contributed to its development, including writings from Machiavelli and Montaigne that drew a distinction between the public and private realms in society. Separating the princely interest or *raison d'état* from individual interest, they argued that different moral standards apply to the private and the public realms. What is more, virtue and vice are not easily distinguished even with respect to individual motivations, behaviour and outcomes. Apparently virtuous behaviour (judged by its appearance or consequences) may be motivated by vicious passions such as greed. Or take Poggio Bracciolini's *De Avaritia* (1428), which argued that man's desire for wealth is natural. In *Deux paradoxes de l'amité et d'avarice* (1598), Antoine Hotman recommended the pursuit of riches as being both natural (why would nature otherwise have given us so many emotions to acquire wealth?) as well as socially desirable. Greed is part of the basic make up of people, and, following Francis Bacon's motto, 'Nature cannot be conquered except by obeying her', the grand design is to build a society that leads such passionate energy into socially useful channels.

Another source of the notion of greed and avarice as a source of social good is the mercantilist literature. Toying with this idea, Antoyne de Montchrétien (1576–1621) in his *Traicté de l'oeconomie politique* (1615) emphasised the need to harness such passions by the aid of human authority to turn the pursuit of gain to public advantage. He argued that the prosperity of the realm depends on merchants who are motivated by their desire for gain, and that government should encourage them rather that treat them as vicious. As it is pointless to extort public spiritedness, why not direct individual efforts motivated by ambition and avarice into socially beneficial channels, aided by customs and human authority?

Similar views were pursued in Jansenist philosophy.[7] The underlying belief in Jansenist philosophy is that God's world of harmony and charity had been lost in the fall of man, and that man now struggles with himself in futile attempts to regain such unity and harmony. According to Blaise Pascal (1623–62), the most famous Jansenist, there are three distinctive and separate orders of human life (Pascal 1962[1669]). He distinguished between the order of concupiscence, the order of charity and the order of reason and intellect. Although human reason is capable of establishing the principles that govern the physical world, as soon as man starts to make judgements on the human design of that physical world, reason is corrupted by the passions. Reason, confronted with so many contradictions in human nature and with all the diversity of life, cannot manipulate the ropes with which to tie the world of concupiscence to the world of charity. Fallen man has set his heart on concupiscence, attractively presented in all the diversions of life, which drown every thought of man's true calling. In that madhouse, there is no room for true virtue; what passes for virtue is but vice in disguise. Man, unable to escape the domination of his basest needs, has created a sinful equivalent of the lost ideal: "men have devised a bastard morality from concupiscence itself, an inverted version of the order of charity" (Keohane 1980: 275).

The writings of another Jansenist, Pierre Nicole (1625–95) (James 1972), feature a certain admiration for the potentially positive consequences of *amour-propre*, which in its manifestations is held in check by the similar self-interested actions of others. Men motivated solely by the desire to maximise their own happiness do so by satisfying the needs of other men, the source and foundation of all commerce among men. To Nicole, greed is a fascinating though corrupt alternative to charity. Enlightened self-interest, Nicole argued in his *Essais de morale*, is capable of bringing about a well-ordered society meeting human need, presenting an appearance of "complete peace, security, and ease as if one were in a community of saints" (Viner 1978: 135). Greed even outdoes charity.

> What a piece of Charity would it be, to build for another an intire House, furnish it with all necessary Houshold-stuff; and after that to deliver him up the Key? Concupiscence does this cheerfully. What Charity would it be to go and fetch Drugs from the *Indies*, to submit ones self to the meanest Offices, and serve others in the most abject and painful commands? And this Concupiscence does without ever complaining.
>
> (Nicole *Moral Essays* 1696, vol. II:
> Of Grandeur, Part I, §29: 98)

If the consequences of greed and self-interest are indistinguishable from those of charity, and given its beneficial consequences in terms of public prosperity, greed was to be given more room to play. "There is therefore nothing whence Men derive greater benefits to themselves than their own Concupiscence". Nicole warns, however,

> that it [greed] may be disposed to do these Offices, there ought to be something to keep it within compass. As soon as i'ts left to it self, it flies out and keeps within no bounds. Instead of being beneficial to human Society, it utterly destroys it. There is no excess it will not run into, if not held back.
>
> (Nicole *Moral Essays* 1696, vol. II:
> Of Grandeur, Part I, §29: 98)

He points at the necessity of a political order that, supported by fear of punishment, artfully manages cupidity and directs it towards employments beneficial to society (see also Viner 1978; Keohane 1974).

The same themes are played by Jean Domat (1625–96), who argued that divine providence has given self-love, poison of the heart, its own antidote as the multiplicity of needs that self-love creates forces us towards commerce with others. However feeble such a foundation of society is, it works admirably and, however misguidedly, suggests the appearance of virtue. To ensure that the acquisitive passions are kept within the limits of their serviceability to society, the state is called upon to direct economic life by way of laws, regulations, controls, prescriptions, monopolies and privileges. As Davenant expressed it:

> There is hardly a Society of Merchants, that would not have it thought the whole Prosperity of the Kingdom depends upon their single Traffick. So that at any time, when they come to be Consulted, their Answers are dark and partial; and when they deliberate themselves in Assemblies, 'tis generally with a Byass, and a secret Eye to their own Advantage . . . And 'tis now to be apprehended, That they who stand possess'd of the ready Cash, when they discover the Necessities of other People, will, in all likelihood, prompted by their Avarice, make use of it very destructive to their Fellow-Subjects, and to the King's Affairs, if not prevented by the Care and Wisdom of the State.
>
> (Davenant 1698 *Discourses*, Part I, Discourse I (p. 30) and Discourse II (pp. 45–6))

If the first stage is distinguished from the other stages by its focus on self-sufficiency vis-à-vis growth, the second and third stages – in which the notion of the social utility of greed is brought to fruition – differ in their view on the nature of the economic game and in subsequent views on how to restrain greed while preserving its serviceability to society. Table 2.1 sums up the various differences between the three stages.

Given the goal of growth within a setting characterised as a zero-sum game, the literature in our second stage emphasises the need for public authority to ensure the social utility of greed. Nevertheless, some philosophers already hinted at the existence of some providential or natural order that establishes a balance or equilibrium because of self-enforcing limits that individuals impose

Table 2.1 The development of views on greed in relation to societal setting

Period	Middle Ages	1500–1700	Enlightenment
Social unit	Community	Mercantile state	Society
Economic goal	Self-sufficiency	Growth	Growth
Economic game	Zero-sum	Zero-sum	Positive-sum
Gain through	Fraud	Rent seeking	Production
Greed	Irrational	Social utility	Social utility
Limits to greed	Natural/satiation	Public authority	Interdependence and competition

on each other's behaviour. This natural order would increasingly appeal to the imagination once it was conjoined with the view of the mutually beneficial nature of trade and commerce. It was these two ideas that set the third and final stage.

The third stage in greed's rise to serviceability

The idea of a positive-sum game made its appearance towards the end of the seventeenth century, even though it took more than three quarters of a century before it found general acceptance. There is something about the last decade of the seventeenth century. It keeps turning up in descriptions of the transformation of thought as it progressed towards the Enlightenment. In *La crise de la conscience européenne 1680–1715*, Hazard (1963[1935]) argued that all ideas that were to characterise the Enlightenment were already present in rudimentary form at the end of the seventeenth century. Raab (1964: 237(n)) argued that it was in this last decade of the seventeenth century that the notion of interest acquired an economic meaning, changing the predominance of political objectives in reflections on state and society in favour of economic objectives. The same period is crucial to Wiles's claim that Heckscher's static interpretation of mercantilism in his monumental *Mercantilism* (1994[1935]) was inaccurate with respect to the writings of the later English mercantilists. Wiles (1974, 1987) argued that a dynamic view of the economy became adopted from the last decade of the seventeenth century onwards. It focused on the goal of economic development and growth through the mutually advantageous interaction between domestic development and international trade. Whereas Thomas Mun and Josiah Child forcibly argued that "[a]ll trade is a kind of warfare" (cited in Letwin 1963: 44), in 1696 Charles Davenant argued against the beggar-thy-neighbour policy of the Dutch, claiming "That their True Safety and Welfare depends upon the Strength and Prosperity of England" (cited in Wiles 1974: 63). Dudley North, in similar vein, wrote:

> Now it may appear strange to hear it said, That the whole World as to Trade, is but as one Nation of People, and therein Nations are as Persons. That the loss of a Trade with one Nation, is not that only, separately considered, but so much of the Trade of the World rescinded and lost, for all is combined together.
>
> (*Discourses upon Trade* 1691: 13)

In many ways this idea of the mutuality of gains or interdependence given expression here was to become crucial to Enlightenment thinking. After Hazard's crisis of conscience, thought broke away from a passivity that had dominated the ideas on man and society in the face of wars, famines and epidemics, and rejected the conviction that such catastrophes represented the inevitable condition of fallen man. This escape from passivity is probably most aptly described as a change in attitude, or as Gay phrased it, "a recovery of nerve" (1977: 6).

On two counts, philosophers believed that the future held a better lot in store for mankind. They built their hopes, first, around the conviction that Newton had pointed the way to reliable knowledge. If in the study of man and society a parallel course was followed, it would become possible to discover the laws of nature that govern social phenomena. Armed with such knowledge, and by adapting his actions and institutions to principles upon which he could rely, man would be able to press the laws of nature into the service of his attempts to better his condition.

Second, instead of stressing the imperfections in human nature (an outlook which had led to attempts to persuade man of his duty to God and the state and to respect institutional constraints on courses of action), the emphasis shifted to man's sociability as the directive orientation in human conduct. Man's sociability was no longer perceived as an enforced artificial device designed to ensure compliance with religious and political imperatives, but rather as being an inherent characteristic of human nature as much as selfish inclinations are. This led to a new perspective with which to assess the regulatory structures of society. Although not denying the existence of imperfections in human nature, Enlightenment thinkers deliberately turned away from attempts to remedy those individual defects. Instead the belief gained currency that the order and perfection of the whole were actually dependent on the imperfections of the parts (Lovejoy 1978[1936], Chapter VII). Perhaps the most provocative example of this claim can be found in Mandeville's *Fable of the Bees*: "Thus every Part was full of Vice, Yet the whole Mass a Paradise" (1988[1723]: 24).

Given these two sets of ideas, the key question concerned the mechanism and the (natural) laws that governed its operation through which movements of (economic) agents were mutually adjusted to the good of all. How did this mechanism work so as to create order and wealth in society, not thanks to, but despite the imperfections of the parts? The search for answers inspired a new perspective on the social utility of greed and a matching theory of limits. This section aims to show how, from the realisation of mutual gains from trade, the idea of a system of interrelated parts developed in which the social force of competition was assigned the role of bringing about the harmony of the whole.

Drawing attention to the role of the institutional environment in the rise of the industrial age, Joel Mokyr (2006) has argued that institutions – as expressed in the prevailing worldview, belief system, attitudes and formal rules – may be obstructive as well as receptive to change and innovation, holding back or reinforcing economic progress. He emphasised the importance of Enlightenment ideas and ideals in shaping the institutional reforms that created the susceptibility to technological change and innovations that initiated the industrial revolution. One such belief in the former sense was the zero-sum game between nations to accrue gains from trade and commerce, given that resources or wealth were assumed to be fixed. In breaking away from natural and institutional restraints upon development and growth, overcoming this belief proved crucial to the development of new ideas on the social utility of greed.

Spiegel summed up this static conception of development in mercantilism as follows: "When one country increases its share of [power, trade and/or treasure], another country is bound to suffer a corresponding loss . . . What is true of countries also applies at a different level to the economic relations among individuals" (Spiegel 1971: 115–16). In the 1690s this worldview was challenged with the rise of the idea of trade and commerce as a positive-sum game. Although interests may be opposed, they are at the same time mutual to a certain degree in that people in societies characterised by division of labour and specialisation depend upon one another in order to realise anticipated gains. As Daniel Defoe (1713) pointedly declared: "The Language of Nations one to another is, I let thee gain by me, that I may gain by thee" (cited in Wiles 1974: 64).

With the rise of the idea of trade and commerce as a positive-sum game in the 1690s and the concomitant notion of interdependence, profit-seeking activity gradually shifted from rent seeking to productive activity. This development was used by Ekelund and Tollison (1981) to characterise mercantilism as a rent-seeking society. The authors distinguished between rent seeking and profit seeking. Profit is taken as a normal economic rent in the sense that its presence signals resource owners where a more profitable allocation of resources is to be had, and as such profit seeking is part and parcel of a competitive market order. Rent seeking is understood as the "activity of wasting resources in seeking transfers" (*ibid.*: 19). The authors argue that in England rent seeking was a perfectly rational strategy from self-interested individuals in a monarchy, but that the cost-benefit structure changed with the victory of Parliament in 1688. Transaction costs increased sharply with multiple decision-makers, eroding the rate of return to rent seeking in comparison to the 'profitability' of productive activities (Mokyr 2006).

Changing ideas about profit in relation to trade and production give further credence to this development. Meek argued that competition increased in the eighteenth century, whereby efforts concentrated on the reduction of production costs rather than on attempts to keep up their monopolistic position in foreign markets. Moreover, it was gradually recognised that net profit on capital was a separate source of income in its own right. With the emergence of the idea of "profit as *originating* in the process of production and as merely being *realised* in the act of sale" (Meek 1951: 32; italics in original), views on the origin of surplus shifted from exchange to production. So when the rate of return between rent seeking and productive activity changed in favour of the latter, production became the dominant avenue through which gains were pursued. This ties in with the growing need toward the end of the seventeenth century "to expand the domestic market so as to find an outlet for increased production" (Perrotta 1997: 296).

In the decades that followed, more and more reasons were found to argue the mutual advantage of foreign trade.[8] It was argued that a country cannot hope to benefit from what it sells to others without buying things in return to provide those others with money with which they can buy domestic goods. Others started to draw attention to the importance of international specialisation.[9] Given differences in factor endowments between nations, international specialisation would further the growth of trade and encourage the spread of inventions and improvements. As such, development is a two-way street: a nation's advancement towards wealth and prosperity is intimately linked to, and even may be seen to depend upon, the economic development of other countries (Wiles 1974).

The development of this argument in the economic literature of the eighteenth century was coupled with a growing emphasis on the harmful consequences of rent seeking (Mokyr 2006, 2007). Increasingly, efforts to redistribute wealth and rent seeking were seen to distort incentives, misallocate resources by using resources to obtain privileges instead of using them productively, and raise costs. This would lead to inefficiencies, reduce the overall pie and stifle growth and innovation. Condemning the efforts of merchants to ward off competition and establish a monopoly, Turgot (1773) wrote:

> These fools do not see that this same monopoly which they practice . . . against their own fellow-citizens, consumers of the commodity, is returned to them by these fellow citizens, who are sellers in their turn, in all the other branches of commerce where the first in their turn become buyers . . . they do not see that in this balance of annoyance and injustice . . . there is no advantage to any party; but there is a real loss to the whole of national commerce.
>
> (Turgot, Letter to L'Abbé Terray, cited
> in Groenewegen 1977: 183–4)

Underneath the practical reasons that were put forward in recognition of mutual gains from trade, the idea of a *system* of interdependence emerged. One of the images of society that captivated many in the eighteenth century was that of a machine or mechanism composed of interacting parts.[10] In this mechanical analogy, society was understood as tending toward a state of equilibrium, resulting from the mutual interaction between the self-reliant parts whose operation is governed by laws of nature. The resulting equilibrium or harmony in society as the outcome of the social mechanism was often presented as the work of providence.[11] As such, the economic universe was seen as a network of economic reciprocity in which providence had arranged differences in factor endowments between nations so that nations may provide in one another's needs. As Jacob Vanderlint (1734) pointed out: "All Nations of the World, therefore, should be regarded as one Body of Tradesmen, exercising their various Occupations for the Mutual Benefit and Advantage of each other" (cited in Wiles 1974: 64). The ties that bind people together in their economic activities constitute a system of interdependence, a providential or natural order that establishes a finely balanced equilibrium, allowing the economy to thrive. Based on such views, critical voices grew against government's intervening in this system of reciprocal relations of exchange to manipulate the distribution of gains and losses in favour of private parties. The resulting "strange Medley of Error", as North had it in his *Discourses upon Trade* (1691: Preface), hurt the public good by its detrimental effects upon trade and wealth. The perception of trade and commerce as a positive-sum game in which people depend upon one another to secure their gains challenged the role of public authority to curb greed in order to keep the system stable. Whereas government intervention had previously been deemed necessary to ensure that economic activity was not at the expense of state and society, government interference now came to be held responsible for obstructing the mutuality of advantage.

These ideas come together in the thoughts of the French magistrate Boisguilbert[12] (1646–1714). Fascinated by this natural balance, Boisguilbert argued that this balance could be upset by government interference or/and attempts (often backed by government) to profit at each other's expense. Sustaining this natural order and its benign effects requires that everyone shares in the benefits.

> nature, or Providence, alone can observe this justice . . . and this is how she does it. She established in the first place an equal necessity to sell and to buy in all sorts of trade, so that the desire for profit is the spirit of all markets, as much in the seller as in the buyer; and it is by the use of this equilibrium or balance, that one and the other are both equally forced to listen to reason and to submit to it.
>
> (Boisguilbert [Dissertation 1707] in Spengler et al. 1966: 992, as translated and cited in Routh 1977: 60)

Boisguilbert argued that the providential order creates the conditions for equilibrium, while this equilibrium in turn provides the necessary framework of restraints to advance prosperity and harmony. In his exposition of the Frenchman's views, Faccarello (1999) described how Boisguilbert takes society as characterised by the incessant movement of the parts of which it is composed. The interaction between individuals engaged in reciprocal relationships brings about a dynamic equilibrium producing harmony and prosperity. Communication and coordination of activities of individuals as the parts in the dynamic operation of the machine, Boisguilbert insisted, however "naturally defective" in themselves, shape up together "a very perfect whole" (cited in Faccarello 1999: 93) provided that the following three conditions are met. First, reciprocity (by way of the price system) is essential in establishing such equilibrium. Given mutual dependence, everyone has a shared interest in the proper functioning of others. Prices must therefore be 'proportionate' in the sense that both buyer and seller profit from relations of exchange.

If 'reciprocal utility' or 'shared profit' is the first requirement to equilibrium, the second requirement is that economic agents do not break the chain of exchanges. The trader who does, destroys the ground beneath his own feet, since not only . . . will he cause [his neighbour] to perish through ceasing to buy, but he will cause even his own personal loss, by making it impossible for his neighbour to return to his business to shop, which will cause his bankruptcy and close his shop.

(Boisguilbert [Dissertation 1707] in Hecht 1966: 986,
as translated and cited in Faccarello 1999: 96)

Individuals, classes and professions all depend upon one another, linked together in a chain of opulence in which "disconnection of a single one makes the whole useless" (Boisguilbert cited in Faccarello 1999: 93). Instead of acting accordingly,

> However, through a terrible corruption of the heart, there is no individual who does not try from morning until night and does not employ all his efforts to ruin this harmony, though he has only his happiness to expect from its maintenance.
>
> (Boisguilbert [Factum 1707] in Hecht 1966: 891,
> as translated and cited in Faccarello 1999: 98)

Given that the behaviour of economic agents is dictated by cupidity,[13] Boisguilbert emphasised the prevalence of competition as a third necessary requirement to the fulfilment of the conditions of equilibrium. Hence, Boisguilbert's call for free play from which privileges and regulations were to be removed to ensure that each may benefit from exchange, providing for incentive as well as meeting standards of justice. Competition is a law of the providential order to which individual interests submit and thereby are subordinated to the general interest. Given that this social mechanism is self-regulating, the political order was to take a step back, its primary function being the enforcement of the conditions for establishing equilibrium.

In the eighteenth century, these ideas were knitted together into a doctrine as they were reviewed, refined, criticised and elaborated in the work of French and British authors. The idea gained ground that it was the relations of interdependence that frame the natural economic order that impose restraints upon greed, making human cupidity potentially subservient to human welfare by competition, i.e., balancing passions against one another in three ways:

(1) At the level of the individual, greed is held in check by other motives in human nature. In the Newtonian Age, not only the universe but also "man's inner motives must be balanced and harmonious. To think otherwise negates nature" (Myers 1972: 174). Balanced against other motives (such as the need for attention, approval and esteem) and stripped of their sharp edges, greed and avarice are conducive to public welfare.

(2) Between competing individuals, each seeking to maximise his or her own gain, greed acts as a counterpoise to itself. The natural order is seen as a mechanical system with some internal regulatory mechanism through which

economic activities in society are coordinated towards harmony, as a physical law in the social world much like the law of gravitation in the natural world.

(3) Passions are also balanced at the level of social classes in society, complementing each other in a functional way such as the prodigality of landowners and the hunt for profit of merchants (Herlitz 1993). The division of labour not only between individuals but also between social classes serves the public welfare as they pursue their self-interest by capitalising on natural differences in skills, aptitudes and interests.

Although Boisguilbert relied on the self-enforcing power of competition to make private interests concur, he still emphasised how precarious a state of equilibrium was in the face of man's destructive passions which corrupt the heart. In the Enlightenment, philosophers came to hold a more firm belief, not in the least because of the rehabilitation of the passions with the assumption of man's natural sociability. As Diderot put it, "people impute to the passions all of men's pains, and forget that they are also the source of all his pleasures" (cited in Gay 1977: 188).

Such a more qualified view of the passions also applied to greed and avarice. The want for comforts and conveniences – things over and above the necessary – was applauded as an incentive to industry, promoting diligence and productivity, and as a driving force behind technical progress. In the process of dressing up greed as prudential self-interest, ideas shifted on the mean, the excess and the defect with respect to greed. Having been condemned for ages, the desire of gain became rather harmless to the material interests of society in a system of interdependent relations as free play imposed constraints so that exchanges would be of mutual benefit. As Dudley North noted:

> The Glutton works hard to purchase Delicacies, wherewith to gorge himself; the Gamester, for Money to venture at Play; the Miser, to hoard; and so others. Now in their pursuit of those Appetites, other Men less exorbitant, are benefitted; and tho' it may be thought few profit by the Miser, yet it will be found otherwise, if we consider, that besides the humour of every Generation, to dissipate what another had collected, there is benefit from the very Person of the covetous Man; for if he labours with his own hands, his Labour is very beneficial to them who imploy him; if he doth not work, but profit by the Work of others, then those he sets on work have benefit by their being employed.
>
> (Discourses upon Trade 1691: 27)

Tellingly, Adam Smith refashioned the desire of gain and passion of accumulation as the desire of bettering our condition, a passion which does not ignite the same sentiments of moral indignation as greed. Smith also denounced all attempts to equate frugality or saving with avarice. Savings may be loaned at interest or used for investment, adding to the nation's stock of capital. Thrift as frugality and the passion of accumulation were to be applauded and carefully distinguished from thrift as the opposite of extravagance. Boundaries were redrawn. Moderate luxury (in contrast to ostentatious waste) was approved as an incentive to industriousness and driving force to economic progress. Even if such passions were driven to excess (avarice or extravagance), it would ruin the individual rather than harm the material advance of society.

Conclusion

It never fails to amaze how the harsh and definite way in which greed, trade and merchants were condemned earlier was turned around and developed into a new model of society that brought Addison in *The Spectator* to argue that

> [t]here are not more useful Members in a Commonwealth than Merchants. They knit Mankind together in a mutual Intercourse of good Offices, distribute the Gifts of Nature, find Work for the Poor, add Wealth to the Rich, and Magnificence to the Great.
>
> (Addison, cited in Gay 1977: 49)

Greed had come a long way indeed. Up until the end of the middle ages, avarice or the love of money or gain was presented as 'the root of all evil' or the most despicable of vices. It was emphasised that in a setting of self-sufficiency, indulging the passion of greed necessarily harms others.

Views on greed started to change with the breakdown of the self-sufficient community when individual interest was no longer strictly tied to the interest of the community. In this second stage, the pay-offs of greed changed. At the same time, the goal of economic activity shifted from self-sufficiency to development and growth. The idea took hold that surplus could be used more productively through investment and accumulation than spent on charity. Somewhere in the resulting matrix of pay-offs there were combinations to be had in which greed could be useful. In such considerations on the social utility of greed, mercantile and national interests loomed large, given the presumed importance of foreign trade to create surplus, at the same time that such a surplus had to be secured at the expense of the relative share of wealth of other nations.

The third stage was set at the end of the seventeenth century, when new ideas developed about the means by which greed was to be made beneficial. The rise of the growth-oriented economy brought with it the gradual realisation that larger economic units like nations were just as dependent upon one another in terms of welfare as the members of a self-sufficient community had been. The idea arrived of a system of reciprocal relations of exchange, represented as a mechanical system regulated by providential laws from which all would benefit. And if this system was allowed free play, competition would ensure that everyone shares in the benefits. The result would be a well-ordered and prosperous society as the outcome of exchange transactions between individuals, in which greed works only when one reckons with and tries to accommodate the needs of others.

Our exposition to understand the transitions in society and thought by which the notion of the social utility of greed was built into a model of society underlines Schumpeter's comment that the

> slow disintegration of one of the oldest elements of popular economic thought [the idea that in every exchange one man's gain is another man's loss] is one of the most important points to remember concerning the history of analysis in the seventeenth century.
>
> (Schumpeter 1972[1954]: 360)

If anything (and rather uncharacteristically), Schumpeter still was too modest in his claim, as he might have included the eighteenth century. We have seen how crucial this idea was in the way greed developed from deadly sin to social benefit, rendering greed socially useful by competition within a frame of interdependence. The internal regulatory mechanism of competition within the economic order balances the acquisitive passions by bringing them into competition with one another, coordinates, achieves allocative efficiency, and directs greed into the service of public welfare. In *The Wealth of Nations*, Smith, Todd Lowry asserted (1987: 20), "embraced an equilibrium of avarice, with the 'invisible hand' of market competition counteracting the destructive tendencies of unrestrained greed by guiding self-interested individuals, almost against their wills, to work for the public good".

Hirschman (1977) argued that the very qualities of predictability and constancy, for which the concept of interest had been acclaimed, suggested the identification of interest with the love of money. Avarice, whether dressed up as interest or not, was seen to be universal, predictable and insatiable. Especially its quality as a calm and persistent passion qualified greed as capable of taming the wild passions such as ambition and lust, earning greed or interest a favourable reading, as evidenced by Dr Johnson's famous remark that "[t]here are few ways in which a man can be more innocently employed than in getting money" (Hirschman 1977: 58). In this chapter, I emphasised that the taming qualities attributed to the love of money were 'forced' upon this passion in its dependence on the capacity to accommodate the needs of others to work (establishing a positive-sum game) under the restraining influence of competition (sustaining the positive-sum game). These restraining forces were seen to condition greed and, in allowing all to benefit, to justify the use of a more neutral term, interest. The rise of consequentialism, or the doctrine that actions are to be judged by their consequences, was most helpful here in absolving the acquisitive passion by its beneficial results.

However, more is needed than a fortunate concurrence of discrete actions and circumstances that works out well. If such a process or mechanism is at work, it works thanks to the form and contents the process assumes under the influence of the constellation of incentives, institutions and moral rules. Philosophers recognised the importance of social and institutional conditioning, rule-following and virtue to secure the beneficial nature of competition or to bring about improvement and refinement through trade and commerce. If the acquisitive passion assumes a constructive role in commercial society, and commerce and money-making are acclaimed as innocent ways to bring society order, wealth and power, what about the moral viability of an interest-driven society? To what extent is commercial society a virtuous society, and to what extent does commercial society need to be a virtuous society to be successful? It was Bernard Mandeville who ignited the debate by provocatively claiming commercial society to be a zero-sum game between wealth and virtue.

Notes

1 This chapter is a slightly adapted version of 'The rise of greed in early economic thought: from deadly sin to social benefit' (2012), published in *The Journal of the History of Economic Thought*, vol. 34(4): 515–39, Cambridge University Press. Reproduced with permission.

2 This most-quoted line from Smith's *The Wealth of Nations* goes as follows: "It is not from the benevolence of the butcher, the brewer, or the baker, that we expect our dinner, but from their regard to their own interest" (1976b[1776] *WN* I.ii.2).

3 In the literature, the industrial revolution is usually described as a transition from extensive growth to intensive growth. Intensive growth is institutionalised, self-sustaining growth, and usually defined as involving rising average real income per capita. Nevertheless, whatever contrasts are drawn to distinguish pre-industrial from industrial society, and contrary to the earlier view, the industrial revolution "was really a process, smaller, far less British, infinitely less abrupt, part of a continuum, taking much more time to run" (Jones 1988: 26).

4 Mercantilism continues to keep historians of economic thought occupied, given that different perspectives have been developed on mercantilism as an economic doctrine, as a system of (national) policy, or as a combination of both, engendering debate on goals, key features, development, issues of demarcation, etc. See DeHaye 2008; Magnusson 1994, 1993; and Coleman 1969.

5 Wrigley (1988) has characterised the industrial revolution as a transition from an organic economy to an economy based on minerals and fossil fuels, using inanimate sources of energy that lifted the natural restraints on growth imposed by photosynthesis.

6 See Schumpeter (1972: 357–60) for various rationalisations of this idea, as well as other misconceptions that surrounded the notion that one nation's gain is another nation's loss.

7 Jansenism was a religious movement inspired by the views of the bishop of Ypres, Cornelis Jansen (1585–1638), who, in his posthumous *Augustinus* (1640), had worked out a severe version of St. Augustine's doctrine of grace and predestination. Jansenist teachings conflicted with the official doctrine of the Catholic Church, and its adherents, such as Pascal, Arnauld, Nicole and Domat, were often engaged in controversies. One influential theme developed within Jansenist philosophy is the notion that self-love (*amour-propre*), led by providence, unintentionally imitates the working of charity, given that human beings, in order to satisfy their self-love, have to accommodate themselves to the needs of others, contributing to their well-being. See Sedgwick (1977) for a general introduction on Jansenism. Also useful is Keohane (1980).

8 To be sure, mercantilists did realise that, in many ways, the same benefits one nation derived from foreign trade equally applied to other nations. It was, for instance,

pointed out that 'vent for surplus' between nations would give each greater plenty. In this sense the mutual advantage of trade was acknowledged (Irwin 1996, Chapter 2). However, from the 1690s onwards, the idea was pursued that some of these benefits followed only from the interdependence of the economic development of trading partners, culminating in Hume's famous essay *Of Jealousy of Trade* in the view that "as a British subject, I pray for the flourishing commerce of Germany, Spain, Italy, and even France itself" (1987[1777]: 331).

9 Irwin (1996, Chapter 3) emphasised that pleas for free trade at first originated in efforts to get rid of exclusionary regulations and controls imposed by government. This meaning of free trade was not seen to conflict with the need for government regulation of trade to secure the gains from trade to the nation as a whole. Only later did 'free trade' become identified with the absence of import barriers or export subsidies, with consequent views on the harmful effects of government interference. This line of reasoning developed from the 1690s onwards with the idea that imports were not so much a loss to allow for exports as a way to benefit from competitive advantages that naturally exist between nations.

10 Since early times, philosophers have made use of pictorial models, images or metaphors of society, in attempts to understand society. Two well-known models are the image of society as a mechanism, like a clockwork or machine, and the image of a living organism, like the human body. Both models were often used interchangeable. See Deutsch (1951).

11 On the changing function and contents of economic providentialism in the sixteenth-, seventeenth- and eighteenth-century thought, see Hengstmengel (2015).

12 Spengler (1984:73) considered Boisguilbert one of the first authors to conceive of the idea of economic order as a complex whole of interrelated parts or system of relations.

13 Compare, for instance: "There is no worker who does not try with all his strength to sell his goods for three times more than they are worth, and to get his neighbour's good at a third of what it cost to produce" (Boisguilbert [Factum 1707] in Hecht 1966: 891, as translated and cited in Faccarello 1999: 179(n.25)).

References

Aristotle (1968). The Nichomachian Ethics. In: *Aristotle in Twenty Three Volumes*, vol. XIX, Loeb Classical Library, translated by H. Rackham. London: Heinemann/ Cambridge: Harvard University Press.

Aspromourgos, T. (1996). *On the Origins of Classical Economics*. London/New York: Routledge.

Balot, R.K. (2001). *Greed and Injustice in Classical Athens*. Princeton, NJ: Princeton University Press.

Brassey, A. and Barber. S. (eds) (2009). *Greed*. Basingstoke/New York: Palgrave Macmillan.

Campbell, W.F. (1987). The old art of political economy. In: *Pre-Classical Economic Thought*, Todd Lowry, S. (ed.), Boston, MA/Dordrecht/Lancaster: Kluwer Academic Publishers, pp. 31–42.

Cicero (1975). *De Officiis*. In: *Cicero in Twenty-Eight Volumes*, vol. XXI, Loeb Classical Library, translated by W. Miller, London: Heinemann/Cambridge: Harvard University Press.

Coleman, D. (1969). *Revisions in Mercantilism*. London: Merthuen.

Crouzet, F. (2001). *A History of the European Economy, 1000–2000*. Charlottesville and London: University Press of Virginia.

Davenant, C. (1698). *Discourses on the Publick Revenues, and on the Trade of England*, London. https://archive.org/details/politicalandcom00davegoog (07–9-2017).

de Vries, J. and Woude, J, van der (1997). *The First Modern Economy: success, failure, and perseverance of the Dutch economy, 1500–1815*. Cambridge: Cambridge University Press.

Deutsch, K.W. (1951). Mechanism, organism, and society: some models in natural and social science. *Philosophy of Science*, vol. 18(3): 230–52.

Ekelund, R.B. and Tollison, R.D. (1981). *Mercantilism as a Rent-seeking Society: economic regulation in historical perspective*. College Station: Texas A&M University Press.

Faccarello, G. (1999). *The Foundations of Laissez-Faire: the economics of Pierre de Boisguilbert*. London and New York: Routledge.

Gay, P. (1977). *The Enlightenment: an interpretation/the science of freedom*. New York/London: W.W. Norton & Co.

Gordon, B. (1975). *Economic Analysis before Adam Smith: Hesiod to Lessius*. London/Basingstoke: The MacMillan Press Ltd.

Gray, A. (1959). *The Development of Economic Doctrine*. London: Longmans.

Groenewegen, P.D. (1977). *The Economics of A.R.J. Turgot*. Edited and translated by Groenewegen. The Hague: Martinus Nijhoff.

Gunn, J.A.W. (2010[1969]). *Politics and the Public Interest in the Seventeenth Century*. New York: Routledge.

Hazard, P. (1963[1935]). *The European Mind [1680–1715]*. Cleveland: The World Pub. Co.

Hecht, J. (ed.) (1966). *Pierre de Boisguilbert, ou la naissance de l'économie politique*. Paris: INED, vol. II: Oeuvres, manuscriptes et imprimées.

Heckscher, E.F. (1994[1935]). *Mercantilism*. Two volumes. London: Routledge.

Heilbroner R.L. and Milberg, W. (2009). *The Making of Economic Society*. 12th edition. New Jersey: Pearson Prentice Hall.

Hengstmengel, J. (2015). *Divine Economy: the role of providence in early-modern economic thought before Adam Smith*. Rotterdam: Erasmus Universiteit Rotterdam.

Herlitz, L. (1993). Conceptions of history and society in mercantilism, 1650–1730. In: *Mercantilist Economics*, Magnusson, L. (ed.), Boston, MA/Dordrecht: Kluwer Academic Publishers, pp. 87–124.

Hirschman, A.O. (1977). *The Passions and the Interests: political arguments for capitalism before its triumph*. Princeton, NJ: Princeton University Press.

Hont, I. (2010). *Jealousy of Trade*. Cambridge/London: The Belknap Press.

Hume, D. (1987[1777]). *Essays, Moral, Political, and Literary* (revised edition), E.F. Miller (ed.), Indianapolis, IN: Liberty Press.

Irwin, D.A. (1996). *Against the Tide: an intellectual history of free trade*. Princeton, NJ: Princeton University Press.

James, E.D. (1972). *Pierre Nicole: Jansenist and Humanist*. The Hague: Martinus Nijhoff.

Jones, E.L. (1988). *Growth Recurring; Economic Change in World History*. Oxford: Clarendon Press.

Karayiannis A.D. and Dodd, S.D. (1998). The Greek Christian Fathers. In: *Ancient and Medieval Economic Ideas and Concepts of Social Justice*, Todd Lowry, S. and Gordon, B. (eds), Leiden/New York/Koln: Brill, pp. 163–208.

Keohane, N.O. (1974). Nonconformist absolutism in Louis XIV's France: Pierre Nicole and Denis Veiras. *Journal of the History of Ideas*, vol. 35(4): 579–96.

Keohane, N.O. (1980). *Philosophy and the State in France: the Renaissance to the Enlightenment*. Princeton, NJ: Princeton University Press.

LaHaye, L. (2008). Mercantilism. In: *The New Palgrave Dictionary of Economics*, second edition, Durlauf, S.N. and Blume, L.E. (eds). Palgrave Macmillan. www.dictionaryofeconomics.com/article?id=pde2008_M000144. doi:10.1057/97802302 26203.1083.

Langholm, O. (1987). Scholastic economics. In: *Pre-Classical Economic Thought*, Todd Lowry, S. (ed.), Boston, MA/Dordrecht/Lancaster: Kluwer Academic Publishers, pp. 115–46.

Langholm, O. (1998). The Medieval schoolmen (1200–1400). In: *Ancient and Medieval Economic Ideas and Concepts of Social Justice*, Todd Lowry, S. and Gordon, B. (eds), Leiden/New York/Koln: Brill, pp. 439–501.

Letwin, W. (1963). *The Origins of Scientific Economics: English economic thought 1660–1776*. London/New York: Routledge.

Lewis, T.J. (1978). Acquisition and anxiety: Aristotle's case against the market. *Canadian Journal of Economics*, vol. 11(1): 69–90.

Little, L.K. (1978). *Religious Poverty and the Profit Economy in Medieval Europe*. New York: Cornell University Press.

Lovejoy, A.O. (1978[1936]). *The Great Chain of Being: a study of the history of an idea*. Cambridge/London: Harvard University Press.

Magnusson, L. (1987). The language of Mercantilism. In: *Pre-Classical Economic Thought*, Todd Lowry, S. (ed.), Boston, MA/Dordrecht/Lancaster: Kluwer Academic Publishers, pp. 174–84.

Magnusson, L. (1993). *Mercantilist Economics*. Boston, MA/Dordrecht: Kluwer Academic Publishers.

Magnusson, L. (1994). *Mercantilism: the shaping of an economic language*. London: Routledge.

Mandeville, B. (1988[1723]). *The Fable of the Bees or Private Vices, Publick Benefits*. Edited by F.B. Kaye in 2 volumes [1924]. Indianapolis, IN: Liberty Press.

Mason, P. (2009). *Meltdown: the end of the age of greed*. London/New York: Verso.

Meek, R.L. (1951). Physiocracy and classicism in Britain. *The Economic Journal*, vol. 61(241): 26–47.

Mokyr, J. (2006). Mercantilism, the Enlightenment, and the Industrial Revolution. In: *Eli Heckscher, International Trade, and Economic History*, Findlay, R. et al. (eds), Cambridge/London: The MIT Press, pp. 269–303.

Mokyr, J. (2007). The market for ideas and the origins of economic growth in eighteenth century Europe. *Tijdschrift voor Sociale en Economische Geschiedenis*, vol. 4(1): 3–38.

Muller, J.Z. (2002). *The Mind and the Market: capitalism in modern European thought*. New York: Alfred A. Knopf.

Mun, Thomas (1959[1664]). *England's Treasure by Forraign Trade, or, The Ballance of our Forraign Trade is The Rule of our Treasure*. Oxford: Basil Blackwell.

Myers, M.L. (1972). Philosophical anticipations of laissez-faire. *History of Political Economy*, vol. 4(1): 163–175.

Newhauser, R. (2000). *The Early History of Greed: the sin of avarice in early medieval thought and literature*. Cambridge: Cambridge University Press.

Nicole, Pierre (1696). *Moral Essays, Contain'd in Several Treatises on Many Important Duties*. 2 volumes. London: Bartley/Magnes. https://books.google.com/books?id=PmR 4znKlC1cC (09–05–2011)S.

North, Dudley (1691). *Discourses Upon Trade*. London: Tho Basset. https://ia601409.us.archive.org/4/items/sirdudleynortho00nortgoog/sirdudleynortho00nortgoog.pdf.

Pascal, Blaise (1962[1669]). *Pensées*. Paris: Editions du Seuil.

Perrotta, C. (1997). The preclassical theory of development: increased consumption raises productivity. *History of Political Economy*, vol. 29(2): 295–326.

Raab, F. (1964). *The English Face of Machiavelli: a changing interpretation, 1500–1700*. London: Routledge and Kegan Paul.

Routh, G. (1977). *The Origins of Economic Ideas*. New York: Vintage Books.

Rowlands, A. (1999). The conditions of life for the masses. In: *Early Modern Europe: an Oxford history*, Camera, E. (ed.), Oxford/New York: Oxford University Press, pp. 31–62.

Schumpeter, J.A. (1972[1954]). *History of Economic Analysis*. London: George Allen & Unwin.

Sedgwick, A. (1977). *Jansenism in the Seventeenth-Century France: voices from the wilderness*. Charlottesville: University Press of Virginia.

Smith, Adam (1976a[1759]). *The Theory of Moral Sentiments*. Macfie, A.L. and Raphael, D.D. (eds). Oxford: Clarendon Press.

Smith, Adam (1976b[1776]). *An Inquiry into the Causes and Nature of the Wealth of Nations*. Campbell, R.H. and Skinner, A.S. (eds). Oxford: Clarendon Press.

Spengler, J.J. (1984). Boisguilbert's economic views vis-à-vis those of contemporary réformateurs. *History of Political Economy*, vol. 16(1): 69–88.

Spiegel, H.W. (1971). *The Growth of Economic Thought*. New Jersey: Prentice-Hall.

Todd Lowry, S. (1987). The Greek heritage in economic thought. In: *Pre-Classical Economic Thought*, Todd Lowry, S. (ed.), Boston, MA/Dordrecht/Lancaster: Kluwer Academic Publishers, pp. 7–30.

Viner, J. (1978). Religious thought and economic society: four chapters of an unfinished work. *History of Political Economy* 10(1) spring.

Wiles, R.C. (1974). Mercantilism and the idea of progress. *Eighteenth-Century Studies* 8(1): 56–74.

Wiles, R.C. (1987). The development of mercantilist thought. In: *Pre-Classical Economic Thought*, Todd Lowry, S. (ed.), Boston, MA/Dordrecht/Lancaster: Kluwer Academic Publishers, pp. 147–73.

Wilson, C. (1984). *England's Apprenticeship 1603–1763*. Second edition. London and New York: Longman.

Wood, D. (2002). *Medieval Economic Thought*. Cambridge: Cambridge University Press.

Worland, S.T. (1987). Scholastic economics. In: *Pre-Classical Economic Thought*, Todd Lowry, S. (ed.), Boston, MA/Dordrecht/Lancaster: Kluwer Academic Publishers, pp. 136–46.

Wrigley, E.A. (1988). *Continuity, Chance and Change. The character of the industrial revolution in England*. Cambridge: Cambridge University Press.

Zaratiegui, J.M. (1999). The imperialism of economics over ethics. *Journal of Markets & Morality*, vol. 2(2) fall: 208–19.

3 The Mandevillean triangle

The powerful mix of pride and greed

Hirschman's *The Passions and the Interests* (1977) gives the impression that greed or the love of money, remodelled in the eighteenth century as interest, was the mediating and countervailing passion standing between the destructive passions and vulnerable virtue, turning passions into unintended vectors to the public good. Much the same claim is developed in Lovejoy's *Reflections on Human Nature* (1961) with respect to pride, vanity or *amour-propre*. Pride or vanity – the need for approbation, self-esteem, and the desire of distinction and superiority – in its various guises was seen as the defining passion in human nature and as such as a key passion in human motivation and behaviour. While Dr Johnson proclaimed that "[s]carce any man is abstracted for one moment from his vanity", Voltaire observed likewise that "[i]t is pride above all that has been the principal instrument with which the fair edifice of society has been built" (cited in Lovejoy 1961: 137 and 180). Pride, previously the deadliest of sins, was reappraised as "implanted in man by his Creator as a substitute for the Reason and Virtue which he does not possess" (*ibid.*: 157). Identified as "the sole subjective prompting of good conduct", the motive of pride was hauled as "the next best thing to actual virtue" (*ibid.*: 157 and 156; Verburg 2015).

This rise of the idea of the social utility of vanity and greed was tied in with the emergence of commercial society, i.e. a network of exchange relations knit together by relations of functional interdependence inherent to specialisation and the division of labour. The growth of a large and impersonal society, in which human actions become interwoven with effects far beyond the comprehension and intentions of individuals, dissects the connection between (individual) behaviour and its motives on the one hand and its consequences at the level of society on the other. Selfishly motivated actions may both harm and promote the public interest, may produce both good and/or evil. As Mandeville put it:

> It is in Morality as it is in Nature, there is nothing so perfectly Good in Creatures that it cannot be hurtful to any one of the Society, nor any thing so entirely Evil, but it may prove beneficial to some part or other of the Creation: So that things are only Good and Evil in reference to something else, and according to the Light and Position they are placed in.
>
> (Mandeville 1988[1723] I: 367)[1]

This distinctive feature of commercial society implies that the destructive consequences of man's passions cannot be attributed to man's selfishness alone. The selfish hypothesis – the view that all behaviour is motivated by selfish considerations – is not enough to build a theory of (commercial) society. Consequently, the emphasis in the debate gradually shifted from the question of the extent of man's selfishness or sociability to the proportionality between motives and outcomes and the conditions under which man's passions induce coordination and cooperation. How could a bunch of self-motivated individuals transform into a society of mutually supportive agents?

It is no coincidence that a growing body of literature has emerged in which a game-theoretic interpretation is given of seventeenth and eighteenth centuries thinkers, like Thomas Hobbes, Bernard Mandeville, David Hume and Adam Smith.[2] How to get from a negative or zero-sum society to a positive-sum society by overcoming problems of trust and free-riding? Dealing with such issues, this literature provides early descriptions of (non)cooperative games, coordination and prisoner's dilemma problems. Divergences between individual and collective rationality particularly inspired a fascination with society's mechanisms to channel human actions into socially beneficial directions.[3]

The suggestion that follows from the literature is that greed, striking a positive balance with pride, came to be considered as the cornerstone of explanations of social cooperation. Although absolutely unlikely candidates for inducing individuals to adopt the cooperative strategy, vanity and greed got the job. This chapter brings into focus the range of views on the significance of vanity and greed to social cooperation. For this purpose, the stage will be set by introducing the debate on order and cooperation and positioning the perspective taken in this chapter. The section that follows presents Mandeville's basic model of the social utility of vanity and greed that became the customary target in the eighteenth-century debate. Next the views of Hume and Rousseau are discussed, who offered opposing responses to Mandeville's challenge as to what it would take for vanity and greed to produce social cooperation.

The debate in perspective

In economics, the eighteenth-century debate on commercial society among moral philosophers and theologians is usually presented in terms of self-interest rather than greed, identifying its key problem as how to make self-interest serve the public welfare rather than how to arrive at a positive-sum society. The crystallisation of self-interest as the most basic drive in human nature and as the founding principle of economics is taken for granted and the inquiry into its relationship with the public good a logical, next step. The economic solution to the latter issue, featuring the division of labour and the doctrine of the free, competitive market, put political economy as a scientific discipline in business. This somewhat narrow interpretation of the growth of economic ideas leaves unanswered how greed was moulded into self-interest, or how ideas on the social implications of self-interest took shape.

The former question was taken up in Albert Hirschman's *The Passions and the Interests* (1977), and more recently in Pierre Force's *Self-Interest before Adam Smith* (2003), while Milton Myers' *The Soul of Modern Economic Man* (1983) provided an answer to the latter question.

The stage of Hirschman's narrative is set by the demolition of the aristocratic, heroic ideal and its core values of (personal) honour and glory, and the emergence of the bourgeois ethic in the seventeenth and eighteenth centuries build around values such as work, thrift, enterprise and abstinence. Against this backdrop he retraced the process of ideological transformation through which greed was acclaimed as a calm and persistent passion, capable of taming the destructive passions and redefined as interest. In assigning love of money a self-reliant role as tamer of passions, however, Hirschman neglected the role of pride and vanity in greed's rise to prominence for its appeasing and socialising qualities. This intimate link between man's love of money and vanity was highlighted from the start by Force (2003). Force worked his way through the various views of self-love, acknowledging that more motives play a role in conceptions of self-interest (whereby they may come to differ substantially between different eighteenth-century writers). Force's prime focus was on the intellectual debate through which self-love was transformed into interest and appointed as the first principle in economics. He was less concerned with the question of how man's unruly passions were to be restrained and made to serve the public welfare. The latter issue was taken up by Myers (1983), describing how, after Hobbes's indictment of self-interest as destructive and requiring the omnipresent authority of the state to be controlled, British moral philosophers and theologians responded by showing how self-interest was seen to serve the public welfare. Myers showed how, between Thomas Hobbes's political and Adam Smith's economic solution, the principles of design, gravity and division of labour were invoked to explain the social efficacy of self-interest. As his narrative unfolds, one is struck by the near self-evidence with which writers posited that a natural harmony existed between the self-interest of individuals and the public good as between parts and the whole, passing over problems of trust and free-riding which are essential elements of the debate on commercial society.

This chapter aims to fill some of these voids by focusing on the interaction between vanity and greed in commercial society and their contribution in making individuals cooperate with one another. Most contributors to the debate acknowledged that passions often called the tune and interfered with the rational pursuit of self-interest. Emphatically Thomas Hobbes had pushed fear of death and punishment to the fore as requirements for the preservation of order, fully aware that social cooperation and the compliance with the rules of society will not last if founded solely on an appeal to rational interest and self-interest. Consequently, rule-following and cooperation need to be firmly rooted in human passions. How did vanity and greed assume a central position in the debate on human nature, society and motives to adopt the cooperative strategy so as to produce a positive-sum society?

In pursuing such a perspective, the inquiry into the conditions of a positive-sum society may be seen as the quest for the conditions that specify the social utility of vanity and greed. The scope and content of such conditions depend on the underlying view of human nature or the measure of man's sociability. The view that man is fundamentally driven by selfish inclinations will inspire different perceptions of deficiencies and remedies to establish and maintain order than the view that man is naturally gifted with benevolence towards his brethren. Conditions also depend on the emphasis placed on the unintended consequences of human actions as having unfortunate or beneficial outcomes. It is from such assessments that views are built on the scope of the framework of restraints and regulations necessary to induce rule-following and cooperation to prevent society to turn into a zero/negative-sum game. On such considerations the debate, in its various guises, "increasingly lost the character of a binary moral choice between opposites. It became a debate about the golden mean, about how to define and strike a balance between opposed tendencies" (Winch 1996: 84).

Indeed, as the debate continued, most philosophers – despite differences of opinion and controversies – came to share a few basic ideas from which they constructed their own particular views.

One such shared conception concerned a view of man that allowed room for both the self-centred and the social orientations in human nature, emphasising man's unsociable sociability in Kant's felicitous phrase. In his *Idea for a Universal History with a Cosmopolitan Purpose*, Kant explained this antagonism as man's "tendency to come together in society, coupled, however, with a continual resistance which constantly threatens to break this society up" (Kant 1997[1784]: 44).

Second, it was argued that two opposing currents operate in society, generating its dynamics while implying the precarious nature of a positive-sum society. Without opposition and discord that arouse human passions there would be no development of talents and tastes, knowledge and industry. "Nature should thus be thanked for fostering social incompatibility, enviously competitive vanity, and insatiable desires for possession or even power" (*ibid*.: 45). It was increasingly acknowledged that conflict and discord were not to be banished from society and that passions should not be suppressed but cultivated through institutions. Given that man by nature is driven to society, inducing man to keep within non-destructive bounds, conflict is cultivating. Although man may not be naturally fit for modern commercial society, triggered by opposition man's passions may be – need to be – moulded, shaped and (re)directed to this effect. This is the notion of playing passion against passion to preserve the social energy of the passions while restraining them for the good of all. It is about balancing opposing forces such that benefits result through institutional arrangement that cultivate and restrain the underlying antagonism.

As such ideas took shape, the outlines of another idea became apparent. If man's passions and desires are properly directed and balanced through institutions that specify the conditions for balance, pride and greed were not only part of the problem but also part of the solution for making a commercial society work. One of the most defiant authors to create a view of society from these materials and construct the basic model was Bernard Mandeville.[4]

Mandeville, the basic model and its challenges

Following in his father's footsteps, Mandeville (1670–1733) studied philosophy and medicine at the University of Leiden and started to practice medicine.[5] Caught up in political strife of the Dutch Republic (Dekker 1992), he emigrated to England and established a medical practice in London. Taking up writing (poems, columns and a medical treatise), he developed one of his poems (*The Grumbling Hive: or, Knaves Turned Honest* 1705) into the *Fable of the Bees* (1714). His writings stirred up controversy (whereupon he was identified as Man-devil) when he published an enlarged edition in 1723. Mandeville added a second volume to the *Fable of the Bees* in 1727 and an unofficial third volume (*An Enquiry into the Origin of Honour*) in 1732. Delighted to show the paradoxes of modern commercial society, Mandeville fully exploited the antagonism involved in the description of human nature in terms of man's unsociable sociability. Unfolding his vision of society as the scene of contending forces, Mandeville set up the basic model, describing the development of society as resulting from the dynamic interaction between man's self-centred passions and the institutional setting.[6]

In his analysis of man's sociality and social order, Mandeville's starting-point is the belief that human actions ultimately spring from self-love. The whole design of life of every individual, he claimed, is to make the Self happy (II: 178). To this purpose, nature has implanted two instincts in man, namely self-love and self-liking. Self-love prompts man to attend to his preservation, and is supported by self-liking, an instinct "by which every Individual values itself above its real Worth" (II: 130). The growth of civilisation, according to Mandeville, tells the story of how man gradually transformed from an unsocial brute into

> a Disciplin'd Creature, that can find his own Ends in Labouring for others, and where under one Head or other Form of Government each Member is render'd Subservient to the Whole, and all of them by cunning Management are made to Act as one.
>
> (I: 347)

Mandeville pictures a step-by-step formation of society. First, people associate beyond the family to protect themselves from savage beasts. Second, association, based on qualities such as strength, agility and courage, is likely to trigger conflicts over power and superiority as men challenge each other's relative worth. Thus association also comes to serve the goal of defence against "the Danger Men are in from one another" (II: 66). The third step is taken with the emergence of the arts of speech and writing, as it allows people to write down rules and laws. Government develops as an independent arbiter, called into existence to uphold the rule of law. With conditions of peace and security of property sufficiently guaranteed, passions are roused and desires enlarged. As numbers increase, interactions increase; people aim to better their condition; knowledge is acquired; passions of pride, envy, avarice and emulation are roused, activating men's desires, promoting inventions, trades and the growth of arts and sciences in their efforts to gratify these desires. The more complex and diversified the tasks in society become, the more men become dependent upon one another to get what they want. Adapting to changing circumstances, men develop a fitness for society. None of these developments are intended or foreseen. Man is driven towards society from necessity, and once together he is confronted with others likewise inclined to overvalue their relative worth. The result is enmity and conflict. Society is and always remains a "jarring Discord of Contraries", as Mandeville put it (1999[1709]: 105). It is the establishment of the rule of law by government, the formation of society as a body politic, which allowed man to live together in peace. Forced by necessity to work together, man learns, with ups and downs, to use his (inherently destructive) drives and passions constructively and to cooperate to satisfy his (selfish) desires, in the process rendering society "opulent, knowing and polite" (I: 184).

In the first volume of the *Fable of the Bees* (1723), Mandeville describes the growth of civilisation as being the result of dexterous management by politicians and other wise men. Noting how everyone was charmed with praise and aversive to shame, they concluded that "Flattery must be the most powerful Argument that could be used to Human Creatures" (I: 42–3). Extolling the excellency of his nature, man is manipulated into seeking praise and avoiding disapproval to keep up the favourable self-image he has been taught to uphold. Through this "bewitching Engine" (I: 43), man is made dependent on these signs of approval and disapproval. Rules of conduct develop as the unintended outcome of rewarding through pride those actions which promote the good of others and punishing through shame actions that fail in this respect. In the second volume of the *Fable of the Bees* (1727), Mandeville acknowledged that it has been the spontaneous and gradual development of an institutional framework of norms and rules, rather than the cunning politician, through which man's passionate drives are redirected towards cooperation and cohesion (II: 142). Conforming his behaviour to these rules of society to accommodate the need for approval and esteem, man gradually learns to camouflage his self-love with the 'social virtues' that make social interaction run smoothly.

Despite such outward expressions of politeness and sociability, however, society remains "a collection of frauds, fakes, fops, and fortune-seekers" (Verburg 2015: 681), driven by ambition, greed and emulation, producing discord and conflict. If given half a chance, people will not pass up the opportunity to take advantage at the expense of others. In a large, commercial society, based on specialisation and exchange, it is ludicrous to suppose that "the means of thriving and whatever conduces to the Welfare and real Happiness of private Families must have the same Effect upon the whole Society" (I: 354–5). Such disparity is also evident in morality: "there is nothing so perfectly Good in Creatures that it cannot be hurtful to any one of the Society, nor any thing so entirely Evil, but it may prove beneficial to some part or other of the Creation" (I: 367). The claim that to Mandeville "[c]ommercial society is a zero-sum game" (Moss 1987: 170) and the assertion of unintended but beneficial social consequences of the efforts of individuals to advance their interests are both inadequate: society is the scene of two contending currents, one towards cooperation and cohesion, the other towards conflict and dissension. Their antagonism gives society its dynamics, allowing society to adapt to changing circumstances in balancing passions, rules and benefits, and that is what has happened in commercial society.

Increasingly being dependent on others in the gratification of his (social) desires, often disappointed and angered in being denied what he takes to be his due, man learns to adopt a more cooperative and peaceful method to confirm and strengthen his self-esteem. Experiencing that display of pride is offensive and unlikely to win the admiration and esteem of others, man comes to grasp that his desires are much better served by disguising his pride. Man not only learns to masquerade their pride in flatteries, good manners and humility but also learn to change natural for artificial symptoms of pride in

> Fine Cloaths, and other Ornaments about them, the Cleanliness observed about their Persons, the Submission that is required of Servants, costly Equipages, Furniture, Buildings, Titles of Honour, and every thing that Men can acquire to make themselves esteem'd by others, without discovering any of the Symptoms that are forbid.
>
> (II: 126)

Amassing material marks and tokens of esteem and distinction 'solves' the conflict between the urge to express one's pride and the desire for approbation. Wealth and property allow man to put his inflated sense of self on display in a socially acceptable manner and to illuminate his relative worth by basking in the evocative light of his possessions. In commercial society, given relations of interdependence and its disproportionality between intentions and outcomes, moreover, it is much more difficult to get acclaim for beneficial results: wealth says it all at a glance. Vanity and greed thus strike a positive balance. Mandeville sketched a society made up of individuals whose prime concern is to have their favourable self-image reflected in the signs of approval from others in their attention and admiration that the ostentatious display of goods commands (Hundert 2003). In a large, impersonal and differentiated society, "handsome Apparel is a main Point, fine Feathers make fine Birds", and all seek to be esteemed "not as what they are, but what they appear to be" (I: 127 and 128). The resulting drive for luxury within an expansionary model of desires promotes trade and industry, the arts and sciences and creates employment, income, wealth and power. "Commercial society flourishes upon the propulsive drive of man's desires, whereto the miser happily gains by providing the means to the spendthrift, the spendthrift's vanity lines the miser's purse and the 'sordid love of money' of both oils the machine" (Verburg 2015: 680).

In commercial society, man's pride is accommodated by claiming and showing off one's social worth through the acquisition and display of material possessions. The passions involved in these pursuits – vanity, pride jealousy, greed and so on – are the social energies that drive the economy. In the midst of all efforts by individuals to outdo one another, however, they need each other to gratify their material desires and their need for esteem at the same time. Accommodating their pride and the love of gain requires individuals to accept constraints upon their behaviour to preserve this framework of interdependence by becoming "a Disciplin'd Creature, that can find his own Ends in Labouring for others" (I: 347). Hence the importance of institutions, like markets, laws, property and the division of labour that shape relations of interdependence, signalling that everyone has an interest in sticking to the rules of the game.

Within this framework of incentives and restraints, competition becomes a vehicle for creating benefits out of the selfishly motivated actions of individuals, neutralising or eliminating the destructive effects of man's passions or self-seeking energies by playing passion against passion. That is the way to understand commercial society: it is the mutual emulation and friction between human passions that creates order and sociability. Building sociability and cooperation in order to satisfy themselves, vanity and greed tend to play an integrative rather than a destructive role in society. Mandeville thus emphasised that the growth of civilisation, man's sociability and morality are rooted in man's vainglorious desires and love of gain.

Mandeville's views, as Hume later put it, "gave a General Allarm to the Friends of Morality" (Mossner 1960: 231). The 1723 edition of the *Fable of the Bees* received a hostile reception, provoking many to snatch up their feather pen (Stafford 1997). He was seen to reduce benevolence to considerations of private gain and, adding insult to injury, to argue that this was all the better because, however unintended, society benefits most from individual efforts to gratify self-seeking desires. On such charges Mandeville was accused of recommending vice and ridiculing virtue.

And yet there is a more subtle discourse underneath the angry dismissals and refutations of Mandeville's satirical image of commercial society, which can be traced to the work of philosophers like Hume, Rousseau, Smith and Kant. In this discourse, authors built on Mandeville's basic model, adding their own emphases and looking for answers to the questions that his view had raised. In neutral terms, the basic model posits the intimate relationship between vanity and greed and their social utility in commercial society in six steps:

(1) The necessity of society to remedy man's infirmities brings man to associate.
(2) Association induces conflicts as people compete for esteem, admiration and distinction, and resources become scarce.
(3) Despite pre-political consensus and commercial sociability, a convention is needed that, inspired by considerations of private advantage, induces

individuals to comply with a set of rules concerning the preservation of 'lives, liberties and estates', in Locke's words.

(4) The resulting peace and security of property enable social and economic development and progress, allowing the materialisation of the advantages of society through which natural wants extend themselves in an ever-increasing spiral of desires.

(5) In commercial society, wealth and property are considered means to achieve social distinction and esteem, highlighting the acquisitive passion to satisfy man's ambition.

(6) Given the changing context of man's growing interdependence in commercial society, the role of man's passions within this expansionist model of desire changes, as does the way the passions are evaluated from a moral point of view.

It was the way Mandeville coloured the model rather than the model itself that inspired feverish rebukes. Especially the (Hobbesian) assumption of man's thoroughly selfish nature was held to be untenable. This assumption lurks behind the colourful images of man and society that Mandeville presents his readers. Human behaviour everywhere is tainted by hypocrisy, concealment, insincerity, discord and vice if one cares to look behind society's facade. With his sketches of the multiplicity of human endeavours at strategy and deceit, Mandeville emphasised the unintended consequences of vanity and greed. The same desire for esteem and admiration that induces the individual to outdo others and to claim a larger share of mankind's admiration makes him susceptible to the opinions and sentiments of others and likely to comply with the rules of society. The same efforts to exploit private advantages, including the breaking of rules (defection), is part of the process by which rules and regulations are adapted to reinforce norms of trust and reciprocity (Bianchi 1993). The same passion of pride, worked up by the seductive flatteries of the skilful politician, is the root of moral behaviour. The same greed that fuels man's desire for wealth and property requires him to cooperate. Playing the idea of good (evil) springing out of evil (good) as "naturally as Chickens do from Eggs" (I: 91), Mandeville argued that society is and always will be the scene of contending forces. And if there is a tendency towards a positive-sum society, it is constantly challenged and under threat of being put in reverse. In summary,

> Throughout his work Mandeville emphasised the ongoing interaction between the motivational structure (the disruptive, self-serving, and innovative passions) and the institutional structure (rules and constraints) through which benefits are wrought from the passionate impulses of men. The alliance of vanity and greed works if both structures are balanced as to make, in Mandeville's idea of harmony, "Jarrings in the main agree" (I: 24). Although Mandeville's evolutionary perspective is usually interpreted as a trend towards a positive-sum society, this balance between passions and institutions is always precarious.
>
> (Verburg 2015: 685)

Given the zero-sum nature of the emulative drive for recognition and distinction, Mandeville allowed that there was an inherent tendency in men's passions towards excess. Institutional failure may also upset the balance. Rules and conventions create advantages by solving coordination problems but as long as most people comply there is a strong incentive to defect unilaterally. Despite transformations of the game, it never transforms into a coopera-tion game[7] and strategies and decisions of individual players may combine to put public benefits on the line. Such disturbances may well turn competi-tion destructive. Moreover, if the growth of civilised society has provided a balanced system of incentives and restraints that promotes the cooperative strategy by way of an evolving institutional framework, the system only func-tions insofar as individuals consider the cooperative strategy to be conducive to the gratification of their vain and selfish desires. If no such advantage is perceived, the same motive of private gain may bring individuals to resort to fraud, to cheat and harm others whereby the competitive struggle between individuals serving their own gain may exacerbate the tendency towards con-flict and dissension.

Mandeville was fully aware of the fragility or instability of social cooperation in commercial society based on a rational calculation of individual advantage derived from such cooperation: "no Man would keep a Contract longer than that Interest lasted, which made him submit to it" (II: 267–8). However, the assumption of man's selfish nature and Mandeville's austere definition of virtue[8] left him no room to assume the existence of disinterested reasons to rule-following. There is no intrinsic value attached to rules and cooperation. Man's sociability is skin deep; morality is counterfeited. Although institutional norms develop to arrive at a working order that encourages people to adopt the cooperative strategy, ultimately society and cooperation are sought for their contribution to individual ends. Such outcome, Mandeville insists, is not on offer for each and every individual, given that often one man's gain is anoth-er's loss in the face of conflicting interests and desires. Moreover, if society is organised in such a way that vices necessarily enter into the materialisation of benefits in society, and actions that produce public benefits are assigned the highest merit and praise, the structure of incentives in commercial society points away from true virtue. Modern commercial society thus has a corrupt-ing influence on (private) morality.

In the end Mandeville's provocative version of the basic model, while high-lighting the public benefits resulting from the alliance of vanity and greed in his selfish theory, is incapable of stabilising the cooperative strategy. If interests conflict, individuals may opt for strategies that protect their own interest at the expense of others, eroding norms of trust and reciprocity. The unintended con-sequences of vanity and greed then may produce far less favourable outcomes. David Hume (1711–76) took up the challenge, developing the argument that commercial society is neither fragile nor rooted in vice.

Hume: sociability and the socialisation of vanity and greed

In the seventeenth and eighteenth centuries, philosophers conceived pride or the need for approbation as the distinguishing feature of mankind. This desire for praise had different guises. Lovejoy (1961) distinguished (1) the basic need for approval, esteem, praise and sympathy; (2) the desire for self-esteem, i.e., the need to think well of oneself; and (3) the desire for superiority. Although often lumped together as the love of praise or pride, differences mattered. The desire for esteem requires individuals to attune their behaviour to whatever is generally esteemed by the very people whose esteem is sought and tends to generate compliance with norms and regulations. In the case of the desire for self-esteem and the desire for distinction, however, individuals may be induced to defy social conventions and rules. Although both currents are discernible in many appraisals, recognising the existence of forces pulling towards a positive-sum society as well as tendencies towards a zero-sum society, Lovejoy emphasised "the tendency of writers on the subject to dwell upon only one side of the shield" (1961: 138).

As a consequence, views diverged on the question of whether this characteristically human passion was to be appraised as a handicap or an advantage (Lovejoy 1961). Both positions were defended, often related to assessments of human nature. On the bright side, it was argued that pride, however sinful, was a useful substitute for virtue as it tended to serve the same purpose. Man's desire for praise causes him to attune his sentiments and behaviour to that of others. Moreover, pride was seen to bring about public benefits. Given such beneficial consequences, pride would strengthen mutual trust and compliance. On the other side, those who took a grim view emphasised that emulative approbation would set forth competition and discord, inspire jealousy and hypocrisy and lead to moral corruption as people try to exploit one another's desire for praise and esteem.

Mandeville's work recognised both positions but tended to focus on the manipulative current and, befitting his characterisation of human nature as selfish, emphasised pride as the desire for self-esteem and emulative distinction. This is what the distinction drawn by Mandeville between self-liking and pride is all about. Hume may be said to pass more easily between the different guises of pride to build his argument of their tendency towards cooperation.

Hume's argument of the positive interaction of vanity and greed is rooted in a different conception of human nature than Mandeville's selfish conception. He opposed the selfish hypothesis (Norton 1993), as well as the view that sociability is an acquired quality to accommodate man's self-seeking passions. Instead, Hume built his version of the basic model from a conception of human nature in which man's sociability is hardwired into his nature rather than the outcome of his efforts to get others to help him to gratify his selfish desires. He emphasised in all creatures a remarkable desire of company, which associates them together, without any advantages they can ever propose to reap from their union. This is still more conspicuous in man . . . who has the most ardent desire of society, and is fitted for it by the most advantages.

(T: 363)[9]

Man has a natural love of society, expressed in man's love of companionship and the desire of praise and esteem of his fellowmen, which cannot be reduced to a calculated valuation of the advantages he expects to derive from it. Man's social nature and needs drive him into society. Agreeing that most men have a tendency to overvalue rather than undervalue themselves (EPM: 264), Hume allowed that we seek the good opinion of others in order to fix and confirm our favourable opinion of ourselves (EPM: 303). This need for approbation motivates man to be susceptible to society's signals of approbation and disapprobation concerning his character, views and conduct.

Key to Hume's account of morality is the principle of sympathy.[10] Sympathy is a natural propensity in human nature through which we are able to communicate our sentiments and inclinations with one another. This propensity is basic to human life because our sense of self is developed in interaction with others (Postema 1988). Self-consciousness is rooted in social experience. Society and conversation with others provide individuals with a common point of view from which to correct the particularity and irregularity of their private experiences as to enable a stable, coherent sense of self. "Men always consider the sentiments of others in their judgments of themselves" (T: 303). Sympathetic communication allows man to view himself from the perspective of others and to adopt a common point of view. For Hume man's natural desire for sympathetic communication is the mechanism through which individuals come to adopt a moral point of view or public perspective to orient and evaluate their feelings and actions. As sympathy imbues us with a concern for society whereby each individual has an interest in society, we judge the quality of a person's character by its tendency to promote the interest of society. Sympathy "takes us so far out of ourselves, as to give us the same pleasure or uneasiness in the characters of others, as if they had a tendency to our own advantage or loss" (T: 579). In many ways man's need for approbation and esteem and virtue are close relatives.

Hume's conception of human nature not only ventures beyond the narrow assumption of man's selfish nature but also does away with the view that man's sociability is a learned response to get what he wants. For Hume the love of gain is to a large extent impassioned by society and a consequence of sociability: "[w]e can form no wish, which has not a reference to society" (T: 363). He relates the acquisitive passion in particular to vanity and pride, describing avarice as "a species of ambition . . . chiefly incited by the prospect of that regard, distinction, and consideration, which attend on riches" (Hume, cited in Miller 1980: 264). Hume underlines the intimate relationship between man's desire of esteem and greed: "Nothing has a greater tendency to give us an esteem for any person, than his power and riches; or a contempt, than his poverty and meanness" (T: 357). Elaborating on the causes of the esteem in which the possessor of riches is held, he emphasised the crucial role of sympathy, "the soul or animating principle" of all passions (T: 363). Hume argued that riches give pleasure to the possessor, and this pleasure, brought home to the beholder by the imagination and found agreeable, produces a sympathy with the pleasure and esteem of the possessor. The esteem of the beholder is an additional pleasure to the possessor, a reflection of the original pleasure (which again resonates in the beholder's pleasure). "This secondary satisfaction or vanity becomes one of the principal recommendations of riches, and is the chief reason, why we either desire them for ourselves, or esteem them in others" (T: 365).

The gratification of the need for sympathetic communication and correspondence of sentiments to underpin our favourable opinion of ourselves is one of the chief attractions of riches and power. As it makes no sense to use means in a way harmful to the aspired end, the love of society and sociability act as powerful restraints upon greed. As Miller summarised Hume's point of view:

> Such desire is rational only to the extent to which it is compatible with more basic human motives, such as the love of society. Beyond this limit, greed would not only be pointless but might be positively dangerous, in so far as it would incline us to breach the rules of property and satisfy our desires at other people's expense.
>
> (Miller 1980: 267)

Hume argued that human beings do not seek riches for the sake of riches alone but as a means to fulfil their social aspirations. For most of us this is simply a matter of satisfying the need for esteem and sympathy, to secure benefits for one's intimate circle and being able to maintain or improve one's place in the ranks of society. Man's acquisitive passions, in Hume's view, are a derivative of these aspirations and as such restrained by this desire for esteem and praise.

In these revisions of Mandeville's selfish theory, Hume is able to show how the cooperative strategy can be stabilised. (1) He explains first how considerations of private gain gave rise to a common understanding of a shared interest or convention in the establishment of rules that make society and cooperation possible. With time, these rules develop into a system of laws of justice that coordinates human actions. (2) Hume next explains how these self-interested motives to cooperate are moralised and as moral obligations reinforce norms of trust and reciprocity through sympathy associated with sentiments of moral (dis)approbation. As a consequence, Hume's version of the basic model strikes a lighter chord.

(1) Man's natural impulse towards society does not mean that Hume described the growth of society as a smooth trend towards a positive-sum society. It takes the rise of a situation in which the interests of individuals clash to the effect that it threatens to make everyone worse off. Indeed, Mandeville's

basic model clearly shines through in Hume's account of the rise of justice in book III of his *Treatise of Human Nature*.[11]

Hume argued that society, in providing additional force, ability and security, compensates for the niggardliness of nature in its disproportion between man's needs and the means to satisfy them. Man learns that society is advantageous within the family, the basic form of life and seedbed of the social affections. These social affections give rise to man's acquisitive passions. However, natural man's generosity is limited to his relations and acquaintances. We care first and foremost about ourselves and our own, and by natural inclination we are bound to be partial in our affections. This partiality fuels our acquisitive passions, when man's selfishness and confined generosity in the face of scarcity (T: 494) create a competitive struggle over goods, which threatens the existence of society (T: 487). Hume considered disputes over goods and property in the face of man's desire for gain as the source of the chief disturbances in society.

> This avidity . . . of acquiring goods and possessions for ourselves and our nearest friends, is insatiable, perpetual, universal, and directly destructive of society. There scarce is any one, who is not actuated by it; and there is no one, who has not reason to fear from it, when it acts without any restraint, and gives way to its first and most natural movements.
>
> (T: 491–2)

Man's desire for gain or greed may turn society into a negative-sum game. Hume gives the example of two corn farmers who need each other to bring in their harvest but because neither is prepared to help the other first, suspecting to wait in vain for the reciprocal service, both harvests are lost (T: 520). Both farmers gain or lose together. Given that this problem of coordination crops up each year, the farmers' interest may be satisfied if they are able to coordinate their behaviour. Hume argued that some artifice is required to overcome problems of trust and reciprocity and make mutually advantageous exchange possible.

In order to remedy the disturbances of society arising from man's acquisitiveness, the love of gain is to be regulated or restrained. However, such is the force of man's avidity, Hume posits, that "[t]here is no passion . . . capable of controlling the interested affection, but the very affection itself, by an alteration of its direction" (T: 492). The development of a positive-sum society depends on the extent to which the role of greed may be turned constructive.

Having acquired a taste for society[12] and having become aware of the conditionality of the benefits of society on the cooperation of others, men enter into an agreement or convention to solve this coordination problem. Instead of relying on sovereign power or conscious design by human agency, Hume describes the rise of such a convention as an evolving institutional pattern. Such patterns evolve from the realisation of interdependence ("actions of each of us have a reference to those of the other") and mutual benefit ("perform'd upon the supposition, that something is to be perform'd on the other part"), which develops "gradually, and acquires force by a slow progression, and by our repeated experience of the inconveniences of transgressing it" (T: 490). Such a convention establishes rules for the identification of property and the stability of possession. This tacit agreement is provisional in being founded upon the expectation of reciprocity: "where every single act is perform'd in expectation that others are to perform the like . . . and 'tis only upon the supposition, that others are to imitate my example, that I can be induc'd to" cooperate (T: 498). As Hume has it, this convention is to be conceived of as

> a general sense of common interest; which sense all the members of the society express to one another, and which induces them to regulate their conduct by certain rules. I observe, that it will be for my interest to leave another in the possession of his goods, *provided* he will act in the same manner with regard to me. He is sensible of a like interest in the regulation of his conduct. When this common sense of interest is mutually express'd, and is known to both, it produces a suitable resolution and behaviour.
>
> (T: 490)

This convention creates a new motive (T: 522) by providing a new pay-off structure that rewards trust and (altruistic) reciprocity. With cooperation secured and rules and conventions crystallised into a system of laws of justice that coordinates human actions, benefits abound. That is why Hume asserts that the love of gain is much better served by its restraint than by its liberty. Even though in society our wants and desires multiply, abilities to satisfy them are augmented more, making everyone better off. Hume's description of the development of society shows "his deployment of a favourite thesis of the eighteenth century, namely that men have natural wants which gradually extend in a self-sustaining spiral" (Skinner 1993: 232). On man's active disposition and drive to better his condition, trade and industry are promoted, the arts and sciences develop; knowledge increases and manners are polished. Commerce, industry and the arts develop together, Hume insisted, reinforcing one another and propelling society towards further social and economic progress (Wennerlind 2006). As Hume emphasised "Thus *industry, knowledge, and humanity*, are linked together by an indissoluble chain, and are found, from experience as well as reason, to be peculiar to the more polished, and, what are commonly denominated, the more luxurious ages" (E-RA: 271; italics in original).

The framework of rules and conventions directs the love of gain towards socially beneficial behaviour by way of a system of incentives and disincentives through which man can only benefit himself if his efforts at private advantage also are to the benefit of others. Like Mandeville, Hume deployed the strategy of countervailing passion. Tranquillising the acquisitive passion by playing it against itself, however, does more than cancel out the destructive side of man's avidity. The idea of conquering passion by opposing contrary passions is to produce moderation and to turn the love of gain into a calm passion that allows man to recognise the advantages of co-operation and to act from his long-term interest (Immerwahr 1992). The distinction between calm and violent passions is essential to Hume, because calm passions are capable of controlling the violent and weak passions. "Generally speaking, the violent passions have a more powerful influence on the will; tho' 'tis often found, that the calm ones, when corroborated by reflection, and seconded by resolution, are able to controul them in their most furious movements" (T: 437–8).

Describing love of gain and the drive to acquire wealth as a calm and strong passion, he enlisted greed to restrain the violent and weak passions to the benefit of society.

(2) Hume acknowledged the limitations of the self-interested motive to comply with social conventions and rules. Interest is not enough to stabilise the cooperative strategy. Going beyond Mandeville, Hume showed in his *Treatise of Human Nature* how, from a perception of a shared interest in concerted action, a moral obligation developed that strengthened compliance with the rules of society beyond the motive of self-interest.

Individuals are not always guided by reflection and resolution, and self-interest can bring them to violate the rules of society. He presented the case of the sensible knave, who "may think that an act of iniquity or infidelity will make a considerable addition to his fortune, without causing any considerable breach in the social union and confederacy" (EPM: 282). Hume's reply[13] to the knave to convince him that he has interested reasons to act with a view to public utility, ultimately runs down on short-sightedness and ignorance. As society develops and becomes more numerous, man's immediate interest in the observance of the rules by which society is preserved becomes more remote (T: 499). Nor do men readily perceive that disorder and confusion follow upon every breach of these rules. In commercial society, where human actions become interwoven with effects far beyond the comprehension and intentions of individuals, the intricate link between private actions and public outcomes is hidden from view. Failing to recognise the full consequences of his actions, the individual has a distorted view of his interest, leading him to think that he can benefit from norm violation if all others observe the norm.

On the supposition of man's selfish nature, this is as far as it gets and society, as Mandeville argued, remains a "jarring Discord of contraries" (1999[1709]: 105). Starting from a different view of human nature, however, Hume does have a second foundation besides self-interest on which to build and stabilise the cooperative strategy: man's basic need for sympathetic communication of sentiments and esteem. It is by sympathy alone that human beings are able to transcend their private interest and develop a perspective in which they are part of a larger whole. In this perspective, each individual is a stakeholder in society and has an interest as a member of the group separate from his private interest. Hume argued that once rules have been established, it is through the mechanism of sympathy that people come to annex the idea of virtue (vice) to actions that promote (harm) the public interest. As Hume concluded, "*Thus self-interest is the original motive to the* establishment *of justice: but a* sympathy

with public interest is the source of the moral approbation*, which attends that virtue*"
(T: 499–500; italics in original).

The motive of self-interest, insufficient to stabilise the cooperative strategy and geared towards a sub-optimal outcome, is supported by a moral obligation to observe the rules of the game. Associated with sentiments of moral (dis)approbation, man's sense of justice motivates conformity to the rules of the game and reinforces norms of trust and reciprocity (Gauthier 1992: 148).

Elaborating on Mandeville's basic model, Hume extensively addressed the problems of strategic distrust and free-riding in describing the historical development of society as a general trend towards a positive-sum society. He denied that rule-following is primarily a calculated behavioural response with a view to private advantage (at the expense of virtue) as it had been to Mandeville. Instead he claimed that man develops a sense of justice, ingrained by habit, whereby we are inclined to comply with the rules of justice as a general rule rather than judge the merit of compliance on a case-by-case basis. Morality and rule-following, being a function of the passions and giving rise to sentiments of pleasure and pain if actions are conducive or harmful to society, harbour an additional motive to act according to moral duty and compliance with the rules of society.

Then again, Hume knew that the rise of a moral obligation to justice does not imply that people will faithfully perform their obligations ever after, despite clear recognition of the necessity of justice to preserve society. "Yet, notwithstanding this strong and obvious necessity, such is the frailty or perverseness of our nature! it is impossible to keep men, faithfully and unerringly, in the paths of justice" (E-OG: 38). The most important reason Hume mentions why "a man finds his interests to be more promoted by fraud and rapine, than hurt by the breach which his injustice makes in the social union" (*ibid.*: 38) is man's natural and incurable preferment of present over distant interests. Hume is not prepared to put his faith in education or fanciful expectations about the perfectibility of human nature. Given the need "to palliate what they cannot cure" (*ibid.*: 38), government is needed to protect and promote the public interest, the advantages of living together in society, which men share in common in the pursuit of their individual interests. Instituting some system of checks and controls assuming people to be governed by their interest (Forbes 1975: 227), government is to change the setting of calculation such that rule-following is our immediate interest (T: 537).

At the same time Hume leaves no room for doubt that breaches of law with a view to private advantage are expressions of misapprehensions.[14] All of man's efforts are coloured by man's 'remarkable desire of company' and basic need for esteem and praise. Riches are desired for its promises of esteem and admiration in which the possessor is held. This is the gist of Hume's reply to the sensible knave, who may be said to have lost sight of the instrumentality of the love of gain.

> And in a view to *pleasure*, what comparison between the unbought satisfaction of conversation, society, study, even health and the common beauties

of nature, but above all the peaceful reflection on one's own conduct; what comparison, I say, between these and the feverish, empty amusements of luxury and expense?

(EPM: 283–4)

Set in the context of man's social aspirations, the acquisitive passions are restrained by this desire for esteem and praise. Even though such desires may venture beyond the pleasure of esteem and pass over into emulative distinction, Hume argued that such vanity is to be considered "a social passion, and a bond of union among men" (T: 491). In one of his essays Hume even went so far as to exclaim that

> vanity is so closely allied to virtue, and to love the fame of laudable actions approaches so near the love of laudable actions for their own sake, that . . . it is almost impossible to have the latter without some degree of the former.
>
> (E-DM: 86)

Within a framework of institutions and rules, man's pride and vanity are part of the forces of socialisation in society for Hume and help to explain how and why individuals attach intrinsic and moral value to rules and cooperation, as an additional motive to comply with norms of trust and conformity.

In similar vein Hume aims to dissuade his contemporaries in his economic essays from the view that tended

> to consider all trading states as . . . rivals, and to suppose that it is impossible for any of them to flourish, but at their expence. In opposition to this narrow and malignant opinion, I will venture to assert, that the encrease of riches and commerce in any one nation, instead of hurting, commonly promotes the riches and commerce of all its neighbours.
>
> (E-JT: 328)

Given the mutual benefits of trade, Hume insists, commerce, competition and the love of gain are vehicles for prosperity and improvements and reason enough to substitute the "spirit of jealous emulation" for "the prudent view of modern politics" (E-BP: 339). This applies to states as well as to individuals (E-JT: 329). It is important to understand that modern commercial society has fundamentally changed social, political, economic and cultural relations. Commercial relations developed once people came to recognise the benefits of agreements about property, markets and money, and the need for government to secure and protect the rules of society against violations. So people have found ways to allow the larger benefits of long-term self-interest, although more indirect in being tied up with the interests of others, to prevail over their narrowly defined self-interest set on instant gratification. Within such an institutional structure and constitutional form of society (Wennerlind 2006),

Hume took industry, commerce and the arts to be the driving forces of this process of improvement. Paying tribute to the merchant class (Schabas 2014), he sketched how industry, commerce and the arts interact in a virtuous circle (Boyd 2008). Developing in concert, they improve "[l]aws, order, police, discipline", stimulate "mildness and moderation", while "factions are . . . less inveterate, revolutions less tragical, authority less severe, and seditions less frequent" (E-RA: 273–4).

Initiated by the self-regarding impulses and expectations of private gain, but redirected in a process of socialisation and public instruction along growth of commerce, industry and the arts, greed is fitted for purpose for the mutual benefit of all. Upon these conditions, there is every reason to expect the growing preponderance of the constructive and integrative tendencies in society, making for growth, improvement and refinement.

Rousseau: 'public identities, private unhappiness'

If Mandeville appeared to accept the (moral) paradoxes of commercial society, Rousseau (1712–78) emphatically did not. He abhorred the unholy alliance of vanity and greed on which commercial society rested. Elaborating upon Mandeville's basic model, Rousseau's image of commercial society is a pessimistic mirror image of Hume's optimistic account. His was the dissenting voice of the nonbeliever to the Enlightenment project and its promises of progress and happiness. Instead, Rousseau (Charvet 1972, 1974; Shklar 1985; Cranston 1986) presented the ascent of man as a tragedy in which the very process of socialisation, that Hume had marked to account for the positive social function of vanity and greed, corrupted man's nature and turned his attempts at improvement into a state of slavery, misery and vice.

It all started quite idyllic. Rejecting the selfish hypothesis, Rousseau argued that man is good by nature, acting in accordance with his natural impulsions without harming anyone. "I see him satisfying his hunger under an oak, quenching his thirst at the first stream, finding his bed at the foot of the same tree that furnished his meal; and therewith his needs are satisfied" (SD: 105).[15] Stripped of all references to society, man in the state of nature is a self-sufficient and solitary, free, innocent and compassionate being. Driven by physical needs and without instinctive drive to society, he acts on two principles: the principle of self-preservation or *amour de soi* and the principle of pity, a natural compassion with the suffering. In Rousseau's view, it is with society that pride or the yearning for distinction enters the stage and increasingly spoils man's nature. Modelled after the second volume of Mandeville's *Fable of the Bees* (1727), Rousseau described the development of man from his original state to civil society in his *Discourse on the Origin and Foundations of Inequality Among Men*.

Social ties developed very gradually. Man left the state of nature as families were established, fixed settlements came in use and 'property of a sort' was introduced. Rousseau describes nascent society – halfway between "the stupidity of brutes and the fatal enlightenment of civil man" (SD: 150) – as the best of times. As numbers increased and natural abundance gave way to scar-city, a next step was taken when associations were formed to combine strength and secure subsistence. With society, man became sociable and "[e]ach one began to look at the others and to want to be looked at himself, and public esteem had a value" (SD: 149). Increasingly, people compared themselves to others to be able to pride themselves in being superior to others and to be esteemed by them. *Amour de soi*, a natural sentiment directed towards oneself, is turned into *amour-propre* or pride, which is "only a relative sentiment, artificial and born in society, which inclines each individual to have a greater esteem for himself than for anyone else, inspires in men all the harm they do to one another" (SD: 222).

In the social state, man's sense of self is a social construction built from the opinions of others. The other becomes the measure of man's needs, of how he sees himself and his well-being, driving him to seek the aspired recognition, admiration and honours in the opinion of his fellows. He needs to solicit their esteem and admiration to feel good about himself, losing his natural liberty and identity in the process. Social comparison and dependence, both in sat-isfying material needs and in forming man's identity, create competition and inequality. As social relationships extended with the increase of numbers and the invention of new methods of providing for subsistence in conditions of scarcity, private property was introduced, extending inequalities along artificial lines. The existence of property, division of labour and inequality, multiplying needs and inflaming passions led to conflict, digressing into a war between each and all in pre-political society.

Rousseau agreed with Hobbes and Locke that political or civil society was established by a social contract to end this state of war. In order to remedy the disturbances arising from the destructive passions, men entered into an agree-ment to establish the rule of law upheld by government, which all agree to obey. He rejected, however, the notion that (political) society was founded upon a rational calculation of advantages, identifying social cooperation as the best strategy to achieve private ends. Surely all benefitted from establishing peace by uniting forces by covenant, but some managed to benefit more than others, effectively legitimising conditions of inequality and injustice. Rousseau took the historical contract as a bold move on the part of the rich to transform the (rules of the) game, at the expense of the poor, to protect their superior position of power and status (SD: 158–60). Whereas Hume described the convention that settled the stability of possession as the foundation of society, which set in motion a development towards a positive-sum society, Rousseau took the social contract as an arrangement that legitimised a zero-sum society, given that "[t]he rich can be rich only *because* the poor are poor" (Winch 1996: 72). The social contract, omitting to establish conditions of reciprocity and justice, failed to create the conditions from which a moral obligation could emerge to be committed to its ensuing laws and regulations. For Rousseau no moral motive that backed up the self-interested motive strengthening trust and cooperation.

With such views Rousseau took Mandeville's argument about the fragility of commercial society one step further. Failing to benefit from the arrangement, the poor had no reason to adopt a cooperative attitude but had little choice, given the conditions of dependence, shaped by private property and division of labour, to secure provision. Neither did Rousseau think much of the idea of the unintended but beneficial consequences of man's attempts at improvement. There is no reason to believe that man, in pursuing opportunities to better his condition, unintentionally stumbles upon institutional arrangements, which direct self-interested behaviour to serve the public good. "If I am answered that society is so constituted that each man gains by serving the others, I shall reply that this would be very well, if he did not gain still more by harming them" (SD: 194–5). However masqueraded, the game of gain is quite grim and Rousseau is not prepared to define the sensible knave[16] as the exceptional case. It is not simply a matter of individual interest improperly understood, or a case of failing socialisation. These are patterns woven into the very fabric of commercial society:

> Let human society be as highly admired as one wants; it is nonetheless true that it necessarily brings men to hate each other in proportion to the conflict of their interests, to render each other apparent services and in fact do every imaginable harm to one another. What is to be thought of intercourse in which the reason of each individual dictates to him maxims directly contrary to those that public reason preaches to the body of society, and in which each man finds his profit in the misfortune of others? . . . Thus do we find our advantage in the detriment of our fellow-men, and someone's loss almost always creates another's prosperity.
>
> (SD: 193–4)

Man's desire of gain undermines social cooperation, reinforces strategic distrust and free-riding, making society ever more fragile. Indeed, the (historical) social contract not only coagulated artificial inequalities but also did nothing to avert the corruption of the human passions: "the usurpations of the rich, the bricandage of the poor, the unbridled passions of all, stifling natural pity and the as yet weak voice of justice, made man avaricious, ambitious, and evil" (SD: 157). Here Rousseau unfolds the full force of the alliance of pride and greed. Like Mandeville, he argued that man's efforts to satisfy his *amour-propre* increasingly concentrated in economic activity as the battle for superiority is fought in the realm of wealth. Men in commercial society avail of "a hitherto unimagined armoury of goods whose display functions as the primary vehicle for the construction of the self that has the opinion of others as an indelible part of its content" (Hundert 2003: 35). The desire for accumulating goods that satisfy the need for recognition and reputation stirs up greed, by which accumulation only spurs desire. Man's lust for money is triggered, given that money is a "token of inequality" (Rousseau 1986[1953]: 304), establishing a common measure by which claims of superiority can be assessed. Consequently, *amour-propre*, "the source of all wickedness", is further excited and failing the restraining influence of pity, "inspires in men all the harm they do to one another" (SD: 222). In this way, "[l]uxury, impossible to prevent among men greedy for their own commodities and the esteem of others, soon completes the evil that societies began" (SD: 199).

The production of luxury goods assumes relations of interdependence and cooperation at the same time that the chief source of satisfaction of articles of luxury is that "others are deprived of them" (SD: 175). It all turns on vainglorious pride that drives man to claim or pretend to be able to claim superiority. This continuous concern for the opinions of others requires people to carefully monitor fashions and fancies as these define the ways most likely to be successful in managing the other's signs of esteem, given that "nothing appears good or desirable to individuals which the public has not judged to be such" (Rousseau, cited in Shaver 1989: 276). To Rousseau the mutual dependence required for gratifying desires that society prescribes implied economic enslavement rather than a predisposition to cooperation and sociability.

Efforts to uphold and improve identity in the eye of others create and direct the escalating needs of the consumer which drive the progress of commercial society. Progress in wealth, the arts and sciences in turn creates further opportunities to produce goods for purposes of display and the management of one's image through the imagination. Rousseau granted Mandeville that sociability and the drive for luxurious living develop together and that morality in commercial society is rooted in vanity and man's concern for his public identity.

Rousseau disagreed, however, with the Mandevillean paradox of commercial society that private vices could be said to generate public benefits. The real paradox is that commercial society represented a world ruled by appearance and 'make believe' to seek distinction. Successful in ever more sophisticated means and ways of creating things, it made man ever more miserable as the gap with his original and compassionate nature widened: public identities, private unhappiness. As Rousseau observed: "To be and to seem to be became two altogether different things; and from this distinction came conspicuous ostentation, deceptive cunning, and all the vices that follow from them" (SD: 155–6). Driven by vanity and greed, man seeks false riches in goods that are valued by their potential to impress others. Man is enslaved by the pursuit of his desires and driven to behaviour that harms others, although unable to find his happiness in such exploitive efforts. This ever-increasing spiral of desires and passions, aiming at the satisfaction of man's pride and vanity by drawing upon oneself the admiration and esteem of others, tends towards a zero-sum game, is inherently self-destructive and spreads moral corruption.

Do not confuse sociability and virtue, Rousseau agreed with Mandeville. It is from necessity that man becomes sociable: "It is man's weakness which makes him sociable. It is our common miseries which turn our hearts to humanity" (1979: 221). Within society, however, pity – man's compassion with his fellowmen – has been corrupted. Pity, a natural virtue in which all the social virtues are rooted, is increasingly smothered in society in the vainglorious desires to show off one's own superiority in outward appearances. People no longer identify with those who suffer; they are denatured and have lost the natural virtue and happiness of the state of nature.

While Hume expressed hopeful endorsement about the cause of virtue, refinement of the arts and sciences, and luxury, Rousseau regarded these developments with dismay. And instead of a process in which man's destructive passions are controlled and led into beneficial channels, passions turn more and more destructive in commercial society. Mandeville had been content to show the positive social function of the passions within an expansionist model of desires, promoting knowledge, industry and wealth. Agreeing with the basics of Mandeville's analysis of commercial society, Rousseau emphasised the destructive side of man's passions, given their inherent trend towards excess and conflict: "whosoever has nothing desires little; and whosoever commands nothing of anyone has little ambition. But superfluity arouses covetousness; the more one has, the more one wants. He who has much comes to want everything" (Rousseau, cited in Pignol 2010: 212).

With such views, Rousseau built his case of the moral corruption that accompanied commercial society. Driven to emulate for admiration and esteem in the public eye and given that such rewards are only to be had by participating in a framework of incentives and disincentives that serve inequality and injustice, moral depravity spread. While Hume had come to deny Mandeville's growing divide between wealth and virtue, Rousseau endorsed the view of the corruption of morality in modern society.

Hume had argued that institutional arrangements in society establish a setting of opportunities and restraints through which man's destructive passions are channelled towards cooperation and mutual benefit. If commercial society is characterised by the disentanglement of private motives and behaviour and its consequences, at the same time sympathy and the socialising influence of society through culture and refinement reaffirm the compatibility of private and common opinions, sentiments and interests. Rousseau countered that such views failed to understand that it is society that has deformed man. Instead of improvements in the way passions and needs are balanced and restrained for the benefit of all, balance had increasingly been lost. Passing from the state of nature into society, man's self-love had become oriented towards the other, activating his *amour-propre*. In nascent society, a certain balance prevailed as *amour-propre* was "restrained by natural pity from harming anyone" (SD: 150). In political society, this balance had been lost as this state of reason "engenders vanity . . . and turns man back upon himself" (SD: 132). Man living outside of himself had become self-regarding in his zeal to create a favourable public identity. The great paradox was that man in the state of nature, living "within himself", was compassionate with others, while civilised man, living "outside of himself" (SD: 179), was bound to harm others. So much for the benefits of culture and refinement.

How to remedy a state of things in which "all men are forced to flatter and destroy one another, and where they are born enemies by duty and swindlers by interest" (SD: 194)? The basic problem consists in man's concern for his particular identity and value relative to others, defining his interests as opposite to those of others and society as a zero-sum game. Rousseau's solution is to reconcile nature and society by the identification of each man's particular identity and interest with one common identity and interest. Such identification requires (1) moral education, creating a moral order which allows (2) the establishment of political principles that should govern society.

In *Emile, or, on Education* (1979[1762]) Rousseau explained his views on education to upgrade natural man and prepare him for life in society. Rousseau described how he tutors his protégé by controlling his acquaintance with society to prevent Emile from falling victim to comparison, corrupted dependence and emulation. When *amour-propre* stirs, Rousseau utilised pity to develop identification with the weak, to impress upon Emile the need to extend *amour-propre* over others, so that the preference we have for ourselves is extended to include others. In other words, "that each individual believes himself no longer one but part of the unity and no longer feels except within the whole" (1979: 40).

Extending *amour-propre* also implies universalising one's interest to arrive at a common interest of all men, whereby "[t]he advancement of the good of one is the advancement of the good of all. No one can gain at another's expense" (Charvet 1974: 87). This requires a setting of mutual dependence in which each has a stake in the common good instead of corrupting dependence, which lures man from his true happiness and riches, as it sets him in rivalry with others and enslaves him to his desires which makes him miserable. In *The Social Contract* (1762), Rousseau described a social contract which leaves behind such ties of submission, subjugation and inequality. In such a genuine contract, men trade their independence for freedom. It is a good deal because by surrendering their natural rights, individuals gain civil liberty and rights, providing security and moral legitimacy which natural liberty lacks. Men place themselves and their property under the rule of the body politic. As they themselves make up the body politic, each man transfers his power to himself and his fellows. Given that if he obeys the law he obeys himself, man is both ruler and ruled. As each subsumes his particular will under the general will, Rousseau's image of civil society under the conditions of the genuine contract resembles Hume's. Rousseau likewise pointed out that perhaps prudence may have been the initial motive to accept the contract, but that the resulting social intercourse will create a genuine concern for the well-being of others as men learn to think and act like a part of a greater whole. A crucial difference between the two authors is that Rousseau expected such charges to be brought about by the interventions of the wise lawgiver who educates men to be free and obedient.

Moreover, Rousseau's remedy for the destructive dynamics of commercial society is to re-establish the interdependence of private virtue and the public good[17] within a personal network of social relationships; to break down the spiral of desires to take the wind out of greed's sails and to tie private interests strictly to the common good. Instead of a setting that makes greed productive, Rousseau aimed at a setting that makes greed counterproductive. Only a small and self-sufficient society, in combination with simplicity of lifestyle, equality in position and wealth, and the absence of luxury (Pignol 2010), allows the provision of basic needs to be guaranteed without being subjected to the corrupting influence of the virus of desire. His remedy mirrors his deeply felt conviction that society and its institutions promote an ideal, a life and a self of man that breed moral corruption. In *Emile* and *The Social Contract*, Rousseau tried to show what was needed to turn commercial society into a positive-sum society.

Mirror images of commercial society

Pride, the most powerful motive in human behaviour, manifests itself in men's inclination to overestimate their own worth, as a consequence of which "men are continually in competition for Honour and Dignity", as Hobbes put it (1985[1651]: 225). In commercial society, such admiration and distinction was sought by way of riches. We seek riches to gratify our inflated sense of self in getting the admiration and esteem of others. With the focus on wealth and property as the way to command the admiration of others, greed entered into an alliance with vanity. In the seventeenth and eighteenth centuries, the idea of the social utility of vanity and greed was explored, highlighting their unintended contribution to extract cooperation and compliance from uncooperative individuals. How did vanity and greed assume a central position in the debate on human nature, society and motives to adopt the cooperative strategy as to produce a positive-sum society?

In the model he constructed, Mandeville argued the growth of cooperation as man, confronted with the destructive consequences of his passions, learns to restrain and redirect his self-interested impulses by the establishment and maintenance of rules and institutions. In this development of society, he emphasised the positive social function of pride and greed. "The true Object of Pride or Vain-glory", Mandeville asserted, "is the Opinion of others; and the most superlative Wish, which a Man possess'd, and entirely fill'd with it can make, is, that he may be well thought of, applauded, and admired by the whole World" (Fable II: 64). The resulting drive for distinction in material marks and tokens of esteem and admiration is accommodated by greed, and together they are powerful instruments in producing public benefits. Building sociability and cooperation in order to satisfy themselves, vanity and greed tended to play an integrative role in society. Nevertheless, given the self-centred passions that drive the search for esteem and distinction in wealth and property, commercial society strikes a precarious balance between vanity and greed, based on a rational calculation of advantages. Society is a product of cohesive and dissociative forces and the direction into which society moves depends on the way passions interact with institutions. Mandeville left the question of how to stabilise the cooperative strategy.

Taking up the question, Hume described the growth of cooperation and trust as the unintended social outcome of a process of fermentation of individual passions and actions, triggering changes in habits, rules and manners and promoting the arts, sciences and wealth. Schneider (1967: xxxvii) spoke of Hume's "ways of indirection". It is wishful thinking to build the public welfare on natural benevolence. Attempts to infuse "a passion for the public good" by moral education would also prove ill-fated and even counterproductive. Rather, "it is requisite to govern men by other passions, and animate them with a spirit of avarice and industry, art and luxury" (E-Co: 262–3). Public welfare is far better served by rousing men's self-motivated passions. That is where vanity and greed come in. Man's desire for distinction and desire for gain trigger activity, and in trying to deal with the consequences of individual actions, man stumbles upon arrangements that secure a progressive trend in processes of social cooperation and cohesion. What does it take for vanity and greed to produce social cooperation and turn the aggregate effect of the animating passions beneficial to society? Hume described a gradual transformation of the game and the progressive rise of a positive-sum society as man's animating passions being conditioned by man's love of society and propensity of sympathy, the rules of justice, moral obligation and the correcting hand of government. Cooperation is a tentative process in which man gradually learns the benefits of society and, in order to secure these benefits, to comply with rules of law and to acknowledge their moral status. Hume marvelled at the process of refinement in tastes, manners and morals, through which vanity and the love of gain are educated and socialised and whereby man comes to recognise that "[t]he interest of society appears . . . to be in some degree the interest of each individual" (EPM: 223). Hume argued against Mandeville, in that social cooperation is strengthened with the socialisation of vanity and greed: commercial society is neither fragile nor rooted in vice. As the unintended consequence of a process of refinement and socialisation, vanity and greed strike a durable balance to the good of society.

Rousseau rode high on Mandeville's other current. These contrary assessments of (commercial) society originated in critical differences between Hume and Rousseau concerning (1) human nature; (2) the role of society in the creation of a true sense of self; and, following from the first two differences; (3) the beneficial or harmful nature of the unintended social outcome of individual actions; and (4) the role of intentional design. Rousseau stressed the increasingly preponderant role of man's "consuming ambition, the fervor to raise one's relative fortune less out of true need than in order to place oneself above others, inspires in all men a base inclination to harm each other" (SD: 156). Greed is vanity's necessary companion, crucial to the advance of wealth, sought for purposes of display and motivated by the desire for recognition as a (deceitful) way to a construction of self that is held favourably in the opinions of others. Culture and refinement develop in order to accommodate the passions and desires that society breed. With growth of knowledge and the development of the arts and sciences, a "uniform and false veil of politeness" (FD: 38) develops. Idleness and vanity create a drive for luxury which acclaims wealth at the expense of the exercise of virtue: "what will become of virtue when one must get rich at any price?" (FD: 51). The commercial system founded upon mutual dependence through the division of labour is based on behaviour motivated by "the hidden desire to profit at the expense of others" (SD: 156). "[T]his ardor to be talked about" would not only drive society towards "making all men competitors, rivals, or rather enemies" (SD: 175), with rivalry proving itself to be a malevolent mechanism. As moral reasoning in modern life bends to the goals of ambition, avarice and power in the name of a false happiness, ambition also corrupted morality.

Rousseau underlined the destructive consequences of man's yearning for distinction and *amour-propre*, describing a process through which society slides down to a negative/zero-sum society. The harmful tendencies inherent to vanity and greed would only reinforce one another. He argued that the unintended and unanticipated consequences of human action rather worked for the bad of all. The process of socialisation resulting from the interaction of men driven by their passions and desires was to be seen as a process of corruption as dependence drove desires and passions towards excess. Modern culture is dominated by pride and the only way to extinguish the fatal consequences of pride is to eradicate the distinction between the particular and the common self. Cooperation and trust can only be secured if men adopt the common interest as their particular interest, which requires a setting in which, contrary to Hume's theory of indirection, the direct relationship between private virtue/actions and the public good is restored by the identification of the one with the other. Rousseau emphasised the need for moral instruction and a new social contract, relying on intentional design to transform the game into a cooperation game by extinguishing the passions of pride, greed, envy and ambition.

Both Hume and Rousseau, representing the positive and negative leg of the triangle, worked their way through Mandeville's paradoxes. Both agreed that self-interest and competition, within relations of dependence shaped through division of labour, property and markets, were insufficient to sustain cooperation. Hume relied on industry, commerce and the arts to bring about a process of socialisation and refinement, creating the conditions for economic, political and moral improvement. Rousseau constructed his assessment from the same elements as Hume had, but described a tendency towards conflict and corruption. Both emphasised the emergence of social virtues and processes of socialisation and institution-building to capture the nature of relations of interdependence, self-interest and competition in commercial society and their effects upon conditions of mutual benefit. It resulted in a sharp contrast between Hume's vision of a world of mutual benefits and Rousseau's zero-sum world. In 1755, Adam Smith joined the debate with his review of Rousseau's second discourse on inequality in *The Edinburgh Review*.

Notes

1 As most references to Mandeville's work are taken from *The Fable of the Bees*, references are given as I (volume 1) and II (volume 2), followed by the relevant page(s). Quotations from Mandeville's other writings are specified as such in the text.

2 See for such interpretations on Hobbes among others: Gauthier 1969; Moss 1991; Kavka 1986; Hampton 1986 and Taylor 1987; on Mandeville: Bianchi 1993; Hume's early contributions to game theory are discussed in Gauthier 1979; Charron 1980; Binmore 1996, Sugden 2004 and Kline 2012; while Smith is targeted in Tullock 1985; Ortmann and Meardon 1996; Sally 2000 and 2001; Smith 2010 and Paganelli 2011.

3 To be sure, the use of the game-theoretic terminology to describe the views of eighteenth-century writers is more than a typical case of reading present-day economics into past ideas. The idea that the striving for economic gain was a zero-sum game was characteristic of economic thinking well up into the eighteenth century. One of the major intellectual challenges involved the question of how a society of self-regarding individuals progressed from a non-cooperative, competitive game into a positive-sum, i.e., a cooperative enterprise for the mutual gain of the participants. Cooperation implies more than a coordination problem of attuning perfectly parallel interests. Participants have a common interest in preserving the conditions that allow mutual advantages to come about, but may have conflicting interests in allocating contributions and rewards. By way of arrangements of incentives and restraints, a society develops mechanisms to structure such choices. In the eighteenth century, emphasis in economic thinking shifted from regulation to competitive markets to organise the economy as a cooperative enterprise. In this debate, views differed on human nature, the potency of reason and design, the need for explicit agreement (contract) versus the evolutionary development of implicit agreement, and the role of government in bringing about a concurrence of interests. Given such differences, interpretations diverged of the nature, the emergence and stability of equilibrium, guarantying a positive-sum society in which everyone shares in the benefits jointly produced. Moreover, cooperation and competition do not necessarily conflict. If such a conflict is assumed (see the utopian authors in Chapter 6), cooperation is argued to involve the preponderance of the common interest over private interests to the effect that competition is ruled out.

4 Hobbes looms large behind Mandeville, equally reviled and equally emphasising the elements of greed, vainglory and competition to build his model (Pacchi 1987; Slomp 2000). Consequently, Hobbes's views have frequently been used as point of reference, contrasting the socio-economic solution to the problem of order of the Scottish philosophers with the political solution of Hobbes. However, Hobbes's model is not the same as the basic model from which political economy sprang, here identified with Mandeville, and discussed and elaborated by Hume, Rousseau and Smith. This model is concerned with the nature, consequences and meaning of commercial society rather than the problem of order. It does not present reason and passions as opposites, uses an evolutionary perspective on the rise of sociability and morality (instead of an ahistorical, contractual point of view), and allows a view of society in terms of emergent properties. See Hurtado 2004; Tolonen 2013; Schabas 2005, 2015).

5 On the intellectual background of Mandeville's thought, see Horne 1978; Kaye 1988; Goldsmith 1985; Hundert 1994, 2003; Cook 1999 and Verburg 2016.

6 This section draws on Verburg 2015, to which the reader is referred for a more extensive exposition of Mandeville's views on the social utility of pride and greed.

7 In cooperative games, once an equilibrium solution is reached, no one has any incentive to violate it, given that players win or lose together. If interests diverge and conflict, however, norms are not self-enforcing and may encourage free-rider behaviour.

8 According to Mandeville, virtue is a matter of self-denial. Virtuous action is disinterested and rational and as such, contrary to the impulses of human nature (I: 49). Given that humankind can only act out of self-love, with reason merely being an instrument played upon by the passions, Mandeville made virtue an unattainable ideal. Consequently, any action which promotes the good of society must be ascribed to a base impulse, which led Mandeville to claim that private vices are public benefits.

9 In references to Hume's work T is used for *A Treatise of Human Nature* (1739–40), EPM for the *Enquiry Concerning Human Understanding and Concerning the Principles of Morals* (1751), and E for *Essays, Moral, Political, and Literary* (1758). The following abbreviations are used for individual essays: JT for *Of Jealousy of Trade* (1760); BP for *Of Balance of Power*; RA for *Of Refinement in the Arts* (1752); DM for *Of the Dignity or Meanness of Human Nature* (1741); Co for *Of Commerce* (1752) and OG for *Of the Origin of Government* (1777).

10 When the *Treatise of Human Nature* proved disappointingly unsuccessful, Hume cast his argument anew in the *Enquiries*. In this revised account of the origin of moral distinctions, Hume emphasised 'the circumstance of usefulness' in the *Enquiries*, giving far less importance to the principle of sympathy.

11 See Tolonen (2013) on the relationship of Mandeville's *Fable of the Bees* and Hume's *Treatise on Human Nature*.

12 Hume argued that the practice of restraining interest to coordinate behaviour learned in the micro-society into which human beings are born, is extended to the level of society (T: 486, 489, 492–3, E: 192; Postema 1988: 117).

13 For a detailed analysis of Hume's answers to the sensible knave, see Costa 1984; Postema 1988; Gauthier 1992 and Kline 2012.

14 Given the sympathetic foundation of the rules of justice and the instrumentality of the love of gain to man's social aspirations and desire for esteem and praise, Hume is at a loss for words of persuasion if these motives fail to convince, as in the case of the sensible knave. In this vein Kline concluded that "the sensible knave, in the presence of conventions, is abnormal. His passions are not usual-they are literally outside the norm" (2012: 170).

15 In references to Rousseau's work, FD stands for First Discourse (*Discourse on the Sciences and Arts* 1751), and SD for the Second Discourse *(Discourse on the Origin and Foundation of Inequality* 1755).

16 In *Emile* (1762), Rousseau argued: "The wicked man gets advantage from the just man's probity and his own injustice. He is delighted that everyone, with the exception of himself, be just" (1979: 235(n)).

17 In the dedication of his *Second Discourse* to the Republic of Geneva, Rousseau wrote that he wished himself a state where all have only one and the same interest and in which "all the individuals knowing one another, neither the obscure maneuvers of vice nor the modesty of virtue could be hidden from the notice and judgment of the public" (SD: 79).

References

Bianchi, M. (1993). How to learn sociality: true and false solutions to Mandeville's problem. *History of Political Economy*, vol. 25(2): 209–40.

Binmore, K. (1996). Right or seemly? *Analyse & Kritik*, vol. 18(1): 67–80.

Boyd, R. (2008). Manners and morals: David Hume on Civility, Commerce, and the Social Construction of Difference. In: *David Hume's Political Economy*, Wennerlind, C. and Schabas, M. (eds), London/New York: Routledge, pp. 65–85.

Charron, W.C. (1980). Convention, games of strategy, and Hume's philosophy of law and government. *American Philosophical Quarterly*, vol. 17(4): 327–34.

Charvet, J. (1972). Individual identity and social consciousness in Rousseau's philosophy. In: *Hobbes and Rousseau*, Cranston, M. and Peters, R.S. (eds), New York: Anchor Books, pp. 462–83.

Charvet, J. (1974). *The Social Problem in the Philosophy of Rousseau*. London/New York: Cambridge University Press.

Cook, H. (1999). Bernard Mandeville and the therapy of 'the clever politician'. *Journal of the History of Ideas*, vol. 60(1): 101–24.

Costa, M.J. (1984). Why be just? Hume's response in the Inquiry. *Southern Journal of Philosophy*, vol. 22(4): 469–79.

Cranston, M. (1986). *Philosophers and Pamphleteers; Political Theorists of the Enlightenment*. Oxford/New York: Oxford University Press.

Dekker, R. (1992). Private vices, public virtues revisited: the Dutch background of Bernard Mandeville. *History of European Ideas*, vol. 14(4): 481–98.

Forbes, D. (1975). *Hume's Philosophical Politics*. Cambridge: Cambridge University Press.

Force, Pierre (2003). *Self-Interest before Adam Smith: a genealogy of economic science*. Cambridge: Cambridge University Press.

Gauthier, D. (1969). *The Logic of Leviathan: the moral and political theory of Thomas Hobbes*. Oxford: Clarendon Press.

Gauthier, D. (1979). David Hume, Contractarian. *The Philosophical Review*, vol. 88(1): 3–38.

Gauthier, D. (1992). Artificial virtues and the sensible knave. *Hume Studies*, vol. 18(2): 401–27.

Goldsmith, M.M. (1985). *Private Vices, Public Benefits: Mandeville's social and political thought*. Cambridge: Cambridge University Press.

Hampton, J. (1986). *Hobbes and the Social Contract Tradition*. Cambridge/New York: Cambridge University Press.

Hirschman, Albert O. (1977). *The Passions and the Interests: political arguments for capitalism before its triumph*. Princeton, NJ: Princeton University Press.

Hobbes, Thomas (1985[1651]). *Leviathan*. Harmondsworth: Penguin Classics.

Horne, T.A. (1978). *The Social Thought of Bernard Mandeville: virtue and commerce in early eighteenth-century England*. New York: Columbia University Press.

Hume, David (1981[1739–40]). *A Treatise of Human Nature*. Second edition, edited by L.A. Selby-Bigge. Oxford: Clarendon Press.

Hume, David (1985[1751]). *Enquiries concerning Human Understanding and concerning the Principles of Morals*. Third edition, edited by L. A. Selby-Bigge. Oxford: Clarendon Press.

Hume, David (1987[1758]). *Essays, Moral, Political, and Literary*. Revised edition, edited by E.F. Miller. Indianapolis, IN: Liberty Press.

Hundert, E.G. (1994). *The Enlightenment's Fable: Bernard Mandeville and the discovery of society*. Cambridge: Cambridge University Press.

Hundert, E.G. (2003). Mandeville, Rousseau and the political economy of fantasy. In: *Luxury in the Eighteenth Century: debates, desires and delectable goods*, Berg, M. and Eger, E. (ed.), Basingstoke: Palgrave.

Hurtado Prieta, J. (2004). Bernard Mandeville's heir: Adam Smith or Jean-Jacques Rousseau on the possibility of economic analysis. *The European Journal of the History of Economic Thought*, vol. 11(1): 1–32.

Immerwahr, J. (1992). Hume on tranquillizing the passions. *Hume Studies*, vol. 18(2): 293–314.

Kant, Immanuel (1997[1784]). Idea for a universal history with a cosmopolitan purpose. In: *Political Writings*, Reiss, H. (ed.), translated by H.B. Nisbet. Second, enlarged edition. Cambridge/New York: Cambridge University Press.

Kaye, F.B. (1924). *Introduction to Mandeville's fable, The Fable of the Bees or Private Vices, Publick Benefits*. Edited by F.B. Kaye, 2 volumes. Indianapolis, IN: Liberty Classics.

Kaye, F.B. (1988 [1924]). *Introduction to Mandeville's* Fable of the Bees. Indianapolis, IN: Liberty Classics.

Kavka, K.S. (1986). *Hobbesian Moral and Political Theory*. Princeton, NJ: Princeton University Press.

Kline, William (2012). Hume's theory of business ethics revisited. *Journal of Business Ethics*, vol. 105(2): 163–74.

Lovejoy, A.O. (1961). *Reflections on Human Nature*. Baltimore, MD: The John Hopkins Press.

Mandeville, B. (1988 [1723]). *The Fable of the Bees or Private Vices, Publick Benefits*. Edited by F.B. Kaye, 2 volumes. Indianapolis, IN: Liberty Classics.

Mandeville, B. (1999[1709]). *By a Society of Ladies; essays in the female tatler*. Edited by M.M. Goldsmith. Bristol/Sterling: Thoemmes Press.

Miller, D. (1980). Hume and possessive individualism. *History of Political Thought*, vol. 1(2): 261–78.

Moss, L.S. (1987). The subjectivist mercantilism of Bernard Mandeville. *International Journal of Social Economics*, vol. 14(6): 167–85.

Moss, L.S. (1991). Thomas Hobbes's influence on David Hume: the emergence of a public choice tradition. *History of Political Economy*, vol. 23(4): 587–612.

Mossner, E.C. (1960). Of the Principle of Moral Estimation: a discourse between David Hume, Robert Clark and Adam Smith; an unpublished ms by Adam Ferguson. *Journal of the History of Ideas*, vol. 21(2): 222–32.

Myers, M.L. (1983). *The Soul of Modern Economic Man; Ideas of Self-Interest: Thomas Hobbes to Adam Smith*. Chicago, IL/London: University of Chicago Press.

Norton, D.F. (1993). Hume, human nature and the foundations of morality. In: *The Cambridge Companion to Hume*, Norton, D.F. (ed.), Cambridge: Cambridge University Press, pp. 148–81.

Ortmann, A. and Meardon, S. (1996). Self-command in Adam Smith's theory of moral sentiments. A game-theoretic reinterpretation. *Rationality and Society*, vol. 8(1): 57–80.

Pacchi, Arrigo (1987). Hobbes and the passions. *Topoi: An International Review of Philosophy*, vol. 6(2): 111–19.

Paganelli, M.P. (2011). The same face of the two Smiths: Adam Smith and Vernon Smith. *Journal of Economic Behavior and Organization*, vol. 78(3): 246–55.

Pignol, Claire (2010). Money, exchange and division of labour in Rousseau's economic philosophy. *The European Journal of the History of Economic Thought*, vol. 17(2): 199–228.

Postema, G.J. (1988). Hume's reply to the sensible knave. *History of Philosophy Quarterly*, vol. 5(1): 23–40.

Rousseau, J.J. (1964[1751 and 1755]). *The First and Second Discourses*. Edited by R.D. Masters. New York: St Martin's Press.

Rousseau, J.J. (1968[1762]). *The Social Contract*. Translated and introduced by Maurice Cranston. Harmondsworth: Penguin Classics.

Rousseau, J.J. (1979[1762]). *Emile: or On Education.* Introduction, translation and notes by Allan Bloom. USA: Basic Books.

Rousseau, J.J. (1986[1953]. Constitutional Project for Corsica. In: *Political Writings,* Watkins (ed. and trans.), Wisconsin: University of Wisconsin Press.

Sally, D. (2000). A general theory of sympathy, mind-reading, and social interaction with an application to the prisoners' dilemma. *Social Science Information,* vol. 39(4): 567–634.

Sally, D. (2001). On sympathy and games. *Journal of Economic Behavior and Organization,* vol. 44(1): 1–30.

Schabas, M. (2005). *The Natural Origins of Economics.* Chicago, IL/London: University of Chicago Press.

Schabas, M. (2014). "Let your science be human": David Hume and the honourable merchant. *European Journal of the History of Economic Thought,* vol. 21(6): 977–90.

Schabas, M. (2015). Bees and silkworms: Mandeville, Hume, and the framing of political economy. *Journal of the History of Economic Thought,* vol. 37(1): 1–15.

Schneider, L. (1967). *The Scottish Moralists; On Human Nature and Society.* Chicago, IL/London: Phoenix Books/University of Chicago Press.

Shaver, R.W. (1989). Rousseau and recognition. *Social Theory and Practice,* vol. 15(3): 261–83.

Shklar, J.N. (1985). *Men & Citizens; A Study of Rousseau's social theory.* Cambridge: Cambridge University Press.

Skinner, A. (1993). David Hume: principles of political economy. *The Cambridge Companion to Hume.* Edited by D.F. Norton. Cambridge: Cambridge University Press, pp. 222–54.

Slomp, G. (2000). *Thomas Hobbes and the Political Philosophy of Glory.* New York: St. Martin's Press.

Smith, V.L. (2010). What would Adam Smith think? *Journal of Economic Behavior and Organization,* vol. 73(1): 83–6.

Stafford, J.M. (1997). *Private Vices, Publick Benefits? The contemporary reception of Bernard Mandeville.* Solihull: Ismeron.

Sugden, R. (2004). *The Economics of Rights, Co-operation and Welfare.* Hampshire: Palgrave Macmillan.

Taylor, M. (1987). *The Possibility of Cooperation.* Cambridge: Cambridge University Press.

Tolonen, M. (2013). *Mandeville and Hume: anatomists of civil society.* Oxford: Voltaire Foundation, University of Oxford.

Tullock, G. (1985). Adam Smith and the prisoners' dilemma, *Quarterly Journal of Economics,* vol. 100 (supplement): 1073–81.

Verburg, R. (2016). The Dutch background of Bernard Mandeville's thought: escaping the procrustean bed of neo-Augustinianism. *Erasmus Journal for Philosophy and Economics,* vol. 9(1): 32–61.

Verburg, R. (2015). The need for greed: Mandeville's provocative vision of commercial society. *The European Journal of the History of Economic Thought,* vol. 22(4): 662–91.

Wennerlind, C. (2006). David Hume as a political economist. In: *A History of Scottish Economic Thought,* Dow, A. and Dow, S. (eds), London/New York: Routledge.

Winch, D. (1996). *Riches and Poverty: an intellectual history of political economy in Britain 1750–1834.* Cambridge: Cambridge University Press.Lit eseque verore volupta con conem fugitibusam, audis eveleseque coresedit quassim oluptat faces ea prerum

4 Adam Smith's struggle with Rousseau's critique of commercial society

Balancing out favourably?

The eighteenth century saw the ascent of a positive-sum narrative over dissenting opinions that voiced the concern that the increased wealth of commercial society came at a price. Driven by the desire for distinction and recognition duly combined with greed, it was argued, a society geared towards wealth and luxury breeds rivalry and tends to corrupt morals. Increasingly, however, a more hopeful future was envisioned. Man's passionate drives and interests, harnessed by institutional guidance, would bring forth cooperation, highlighting commerce as a mediating channel producing material as well as immaterial progress. Commerce – taken in a broad sense as the interaction and exchange of culture, knowledge, manners, goods and services – would bring people together and allow them to learn from each other and cooperate to mutual benefit. Such benign effects of trade and commerce upon prosperity and civilisation would bring about the cultivation of morals rather than their corruption. Montesquieu famously wrote "that everywhere there are gentle mores, there is commerce and that everywhere there is commerce, there are gentle mores" (Montesquieu 1989[1748] Book 20, Chapter 1: 338).

These narratives, while nicely capturing the development of the eighteenth-century debate on commercial society, emerged from explorations into the conditions of a positive-sum society. Philosophers discussed underlying patterns of interactions of passions and actions of men and how these patterns initiated an institutional structure to direct behaviour for the common good. Assessments varied with the nature of key assumptions about human nature, society and social control. An image of commercial society unfolded as a network of inter-relations between men, founded upon exchange, mutual dependence and competition. Some sketched commercial society as a framework of economic enslavement and corruption, with competition as a malignant mechanism for deceiving and harming others. Most endorsed the idea of society as a framework of cooperation and cohesion, in one way of another, with competition as a benign mechanism that promoted growth and prosperity. Consequential conclusions were drawn about the extent to which commercial society was a positive-sum society from which everyone benefits.

Usually, and with due reference to the invisible hand, Adam Smith is taken as an exponent of the positive-sum narrative (Zak 2008; Paganelli 2010). Others subscribe to a more pessimistic interpretation of Smith's diagnosis of commercial society, pointing at the concerns he expressed about its disadvantages and undesirable tendencies (Brown 1994; Winch 1997; Alvey 1998, 2003), which led some to argue a proto-Marxian interpretation of Smith stressing the self-destructive tendencies in capitalism (Heilbroner 1973; Pack 1991). Avoiding any chance of a one-sided interpretation, a third group argues that Smith carefully weighted the advantages and disadvantages of the commercial age and, if not ambivalent, on balance argued in favour of capitalism (West 1971; Ignatieff 1990; Rosenberg 1990; Hill 2006; Rasmussen 2008). Lastly, there is the historicised view (Raphael 1975; Dickey 1986; Evensky 1989) which holds that Smith became more pessimistic towards the end of his life, as evidenced by the substantial revisions to *The Theory of Moral Sentiments* that Smith made in the sixth edition he published shortly before his death in 1790.[1]

This chapter sides with the claim that the balance between both tendencies in the development of commercial society shifted for Smith, or that the leap of faith regarding human progress became somewhat bigger (Evensky 2011). Indeed, Smith's reflections show an awareness of the existence of contrary forces operating in society. Numerous authors have pointed out that Smith spoke with two voices (Heilbroner 1982; Evensky 1987), and even though nobody seriously considers the principles exposed in the TMS and the WN to be incompatible anymore, the Adam Smith problem of the contents of and relationship between the two voices is very much alive and kicking (Montes 2003). Whatever its precise nature, Smith's two voices reflect the century's preoccupation with the dualist character of commercial society that Mandeville had exploited so provocatively earlier. Many took Mandeville's view on the nuts and bolts of the benefits of commercial society in the *Fable of the Bees* as point of reference in debating the fears and hopes of commercial society. His views went against the grain, claiming the advance of society's wealth and human vices were a package deal, provoking many to challenge his paradoxical image of commercial society.

Fully aware of the dualism of man and society, Smith's work is in many ways an attempt at assessing commercial society, building his own account in the face of the views of two of the most illustrious philosophers of the age, Rousseau and Hume, each claiming the growing dominance of one of Mandeville's opposing trends in society. How did Smith meet the challenge of assessing commercial society? How did Smith perceive the development of human sociability and moral sentiments in the context of a setting of mutual dependence and cooperation? Considering Smith's work in the context of the debate between Mandeville, Rousseau and Hume on the merits of commercial society,[2] this chapter argues that Smith continued to struggle with Rousseau's criticisms of commercial society and became less positive than Hume had been.

Smith's general frame of thought

Smith's account is built on the view of man's passions as the driving forces of his actions. These passions are tied to physical and social needs that individuals try to satisfy in a way that improves their condition. In these attempts to improve, "man has almost constant occasion for the help of his brethren" (WN I.ii.2), not only regarding the provision of the material necessities of life, but also with respect to his social and moral needs. Smith argued that man has a natural love of society that cannot be reduced to a calculated valuation of the advantages he expects to derive from it. Man's social nature and needs drive him into society. Only in the mirror of society is man able to shape his character and faculties and give meaning to his drive to improve. At the same time Smith, following Hume's description of man's unsociable sociability, emphasised the limitations of man's rationality as well as the fact that man's benevolence diminishes with social distance (Nieli 1986; Otteson 2002). From the recognition of common and interdependent needs as well as recurrent causes of conflict, a framework of norms and institutions develops, aiming to direct the passions into socially beneficial directions (Evensky 2005).

Key to understanding the social dynamics is the notion of the unintended and unanticipated consequences of human action, built from the indirect method by which nature attends to its ends. Rather than trusting upon man's reason, Smith argued that nature has endowed man with an appetite not just for the ends but also for the means to attain these ends, prompting us "to apply those means for their own sakes, and without any consideration of their tendency to those beneficent ends which the great Director of nature intended to produce by them" (TMS II.i.5.10). The instincts of hunger, the love of pleasure etc. are given to us to attend to our self-preservation. In the same manner, man is endowed with a desire for esteem and admiration and a natural desire for distinction (TMS IV.1.8). Smith called this latter class of passions "the irascible part of the soul; ambition, animosity, the love of honour, and the dread of shame, the desire of victory, superiority, and revenge" (TMS VII.ii.1.4). He considered these passions a necessary part of human nature as they lead us "to defend us against injuries, to assert our rank and dignity in the world, to make us aim at what is noble and honourable, and to make us distinguish those who act in the same manner" (TMS VII.ii.1.5).

Smith argued that in advanced societies man's physical needs are easily met and that man's social needs – the need for esteem, distinction, reputation and superiority – increasingly call the tune. With the growth of society, man's desires multiply not only as a consequence of improved standards of decency but also because the advance of wealth increases the demand for the vain "desire of the conveniencies and ornaments of building, dress, equipage, and household furniture" which "seem to be altogether endless" (WN I.xi.c.7).

Smith's account emphasised the desire for social recognition and approval as the most important drive in human nature (Hill 2012) and duly noted the need to keep the passion of pride within the bounds of propriety. Initially it did not have a hint of the destructive consequences of man's yearning for distinction Rousseau painted. It is only in the sixth edition of the TMS that Smith grew somewhat more sympathetic to the Rousseauan point of view, whereby his views on vanity got their bite. To corroborate this view, we first need to establish their initial disagreement and find out next why Smith came to feel his counterclaims were not fully persuasive.

Smith agreed with Rousseau's emphasis on the increasingly preponderant role of man's insatiable ambition.[3] Greed is vanity's companion in the desire for wealth, sought for purposes of display and motivated by the desire for recognition as a way to a construction of self that is held favourably in the opinions of others.

Views started to diverge as soon as Rousseau built these ideas into the history of the growth of man's slavery and unhappiness as social pressure on man mounts to live outside himself to satisfy his desires. The growth of society implied a process of denaturation as man's self is increasingly defined by his public image. Alienated from his natural self and set in a context in which his public self is man's prime asset for gratifying his desires, cheating and deceiving is in the very nature of commercial society. As Rousseau described the way man is torn in commercial society: "To be and to seem to be became two altogether different things; and from this distinction came conspicuous ostentation, deceptive cunning, and all the vices that follow from them" (SD: 155–6).

Moreover, man's original characteristic through which he relates to others – pity or compassion with the suffering – is pushed aside, given that gratification of the desire for distinction is mutually exclusive, "making all men competitors, rivals, or rather enemies" (SD: 175). Culture and refinement develop in order to accommodate the passions and desires that society breed, reducing everything to appearances. With the growth of knowledge and the development of the arts and sciences, a "uniform and false veil of politeness" (FD: 38) develops. Idleness and vanity create a drive for luxury, which acclaims wealth at the expense of the exercise of virtue: "what will become of virtue when one must get rich at any price?" (FD: 51).

Smith agreed with many of the motivational forces Rousseau identified but, starting out in line with Hume's position, he denied their increasingly destructive role. His first answer to Rousseau is found in *The Theory of Moral Sentiments* and the *Early Draft of Part of the Wealth of Nations*. In the TMS he elaborated on Hume's account of sympathy, showing how man's want for mutual sympathy checks the improper expression of man's self-love. Rather than man being increasingly forced to indulge his self-love in order to live up to the demands of his artificial self, constructed through the views of others as Rousseau would have it, man is capable of transcending his self-love precisely because of the input of the views of others. Whereas for Rousseau the mirror of society fixed man up with a set of incentives and behaviours that interact towards misery and unhappiness, Smith, following Hume, took that same mirror as the root of happiness and morality. That is what he set out to explain in the TMS, showing how man's moral sentiments developed from reflection upon the sentiments and conduct of individuals.

In the *Early Draft*, Smith extended his argument of the benefits of mutuality to trade and commerce. Arguing that the division of labour had triggered the interested passion to foster cooperation and prosperity, he countered Rousseau's claim about the degeneration of commercial society into a zero-sum game.

In later work, Smith was to extend, revise and qualify his position. Entering the debate on commercial society with his letter to the editors of the *Edinburgh Review* (1755) in which he discussed Rousseau's *Second Discourse*, both elements that made up Smith's answer to Rousseau were already present: the mirror of society and the nature of mutuality. The same issues, however, made him revise the TMS at the end of his life to the effect that it "was virtually a new book" (Raphael 1975: 85).[4] Smith grew more sympathetic to Rousseau's critique of commercial society, although he never shared Rousseau's condemnation. This changing stance on commercial society explains the variety of views on the characterisation of the relationship between Rousseau's and Smith's views. Some interpret Rousseau's and Smith's views as contrasting (West 1971; Ignatieff 1990; Hurtado 2004; Hill 2006). Others are inclined to describe Smith's attitude toward Rousseau as ambivalent (Horne 1981; Alvey 1998). Increasingly it has been argued that Smith was sympathetic to Rousseau's views (Force 2003; Hanley 2008; Rasmussen 2008, 2013), even if he did give commercial society his vote of confidence.[5] Despite such revisions, Hont (2015) has argued that we still underestimate the extent to which Smith and Rousseau held similar aims and views. All of these different interpretations of Smith's attitude to Rousseau's views have their element of truth once it is realised that Smith came to entertain more doubts about commercial society, as witnessed by the evolution of his thought between the ED and TMS 1, TMS 2 and the WN and TMS 6, each of which is considered in the following sections.

Adam Smith's first response in *The Theory of Moral Sentiments* and the *Early Draft of the Wealth of Nations*

In his letter to the editors of the *Edinburgh Review*, Smith proposed to extend coverage by also reviewing books published beyond Scotland. He especially recommended contributions to French moral philosophy for inclusion and spent some pages on Rousseau's *Discourse on Inequality*. He positioned Rousseau's views vis-à-vis Mandeville and Hobbes, offered a few observations and presented three translations of passages from the book. The selection was not only to show the reader Rousseau's eloquence (the stated reason), it also served to show how challenging views from innovative authors might enliven the *Review*. Clearly Smith recognised the contribution of 'Mr. Rousseau of Geneva', ranking him on a par with English philosophers like Hobbes, Locke, Mandeville, Shaftesbury, Butler, Clark, as well as his own teacher Hutcheson. The first passage posited the evil consequences of the division of labour (introducing property, inequality and dependence). Trading independ-ence and happiness for dependence and enslavement to his desires, Rousseau argued in the other two excerpts that living in society makes man develop his potential in a direction that makes him unhappy. He underlined the destruc-tive consequences of man's yearning for distinction and *amour-propre* at the expense of virtue, describing a process through which society slides down to a negative/zero-sum society. These claims cried out for commentary and that is what Smith did.[6]

Smith's point of departure in setting forth his theory of sympathy and approval was man's desire for understanding and agreement. "The great pleas-ure of conversation and society . . . arises from a certain correspondence of sentiments and opinions, from a certain harmony of minds, which like so many musical instruments, coincide and keep time with one another" (TMS VII.iv.28). In order to gratify the desire for mutual understanding and agree-ment, people take an active interest in others and are continuously in search of mutual sympathy.

> As the person who is principally interested in any event is pleased with our sympathy, and hurt by the want of it, so we, too, seem to be pleased when we are able to sympathize with him, and to be hurt when we are unable to do so.
>
> (TMS I.i.2.6)

This principle of human nature is the foundation of moral judgements.

In explaining the origin of man's moral sentiments, Smith extended the scope of Hume's concept of sympathy.[7] Hume had taken sympathy as a principle of communication of feelings and opinions, operating through the imagination, transmitting a reflection of an original passion in the agent through impres-sions. Rather than some passive reflection, Smith allowed the possibility that the spectator sympathises, even though he does not share the same feelings with the agent. Moreover, he emphasised that sympathy arises from the situ-ation by which it is excited and involves an active effort on the part of the spectator. In his answer to Rousseau, Smith soaked off sympathy from the principal agent, developing sympathy from a passive registration into an active construction of mutuality between agent and spectator.

Smith argued that the judgement of propriety of action is the result of a process of comparative evaluation of sentiments in which the spectator and the agent experience a correspondence of sentiments or mutual sympathy. Whenever we, as spectators, witness the passionate response of someone to the cause or circumstances which gave rise to the original passion of the agent, we attempt by way of our imagination, to conceive "what we ourselves should feel in the like situation" (TMS I.i.1.2). This occasions the rise of the sympathetic feelings of the spectator,[8] which are then compared to the original passion of the person principally concerned. If these sentiments coincide, we approve of the agent's reactions as proper to the situation (Otteson 2002).

Even if such a harmony of sentiment signifies approbation and esteem and as such essential input to building a positive self-image, Smith emphasised that the want of sympathy cannot be reduced to self-interested considerations (TMS I.i.2.1). Smith seemed to consider the pleasure of sympathy as multifaceted, including the natural desire for mutual sympathy and the attraction of the aesthetic quality and beauty involved in harmony. Whatever its motivational springs, for the pleasure of sympathy, both agent and spectator are prepared to make an effort in order to arrive at such a harmony of sentiments.

The agent is aware that the spectator judges the propriety of his action by reflecting upon the fitness of the original passion from which the action proceeds in relation to the cause. He is also aware that he is differently affected by this cause, so the desire for agreement induces the agent to lower "his passion to that pitch, in which the spectators are capable of going along with him" (TMS I.i.4.7) by viewing his own conduct as he imagines an impartial and informed spectator would do. This 'flattening of the original passion', as Smith calls it, requires a certain degree of self-command.

Equally eager to establish sympathetic concord and experience the pleasure of mutual sympathy, the spectator has to imagine himself in the situation of the agent principally concerned and, upon sensing the passions involved, to determine if and to what extent he can go along with the agent's response. If the agent needs to control and tone down his passions to allow sympathetic concord, exercising the respectable virtues, the spectator is called upon to exercise the amiable virtues of humanity. The less the agent is acquainted with the spectator, the higher the degree of self-command (agent) and the degree of sensibility (spectator) to achieve mutual sympathy. Moreover, the extent to which the spectator is willing to go along varies from passion to passion. The degree to which selfish passions, for instance, may be expressed and the extent to which the spectator can go along with them is lower than in the case of the expression of social passions.

Having explained how we, as spectators, judge the sentiments and conduct of others by stating the conditions under which we sympathise, Smith then argued that the same principles apply in the way we judge our own sentiments and conduct. Experiencing that our judgements concerning the propriety of our own conduct differ from the judgements of others, we learn to consider our passions and conduct "how these must appear to them, by considering how they would appear to us if in their situation. We suppose ourselves the spectators of our own behaviour" (TMS III.1.5). How would our sentiments and conduct look to others if they were well-informed about our motivating affections in relation to our conduct and the situation which gave rise to these passions? To capture Smith's insistence on the importance of situational factors in the structure of moral evaluations, Haakonssen (1981) speaks in this context of 'situational propriety'.

Motivated by their desire for social approval, men seek a common point of reference in passing moral judgements on human conduct. In this ongoing search, as certain patterns of behaviour are promoted and other patterns discouraged by way of expressions of approbation and disapprobation, moral rules are shaped that direct men to adjust their conduct to the changing conditions of life. Motivated by the desire to be the object of praise and to avoid blame while observing what is approved or disapproved of and noting what inspires praise and gratitude or blame and resentment in society, man comes to direct his actions by certain general rules which he considers to be useful means by which to gratify this desire. Thanks to our respect for those general rules of conduct inflicted upon the mind by habitual reflection, our natural impulse of self-love is corrected and we are induced "to act . . . with some sort of impartiality between ourselves and others" (TMS III.3.7) and adopt a cooperative attitude. Following Hume, Smith held that man's desire for approbation and esteem drives him to adopt rules of conduct that secure him the good opinion of others. Pride and vanity only tend to increase man's susceptibility to society's signals of approbation and disapprobation and as such are instrumental in controlling man's self-interested passions. Smith described the emergence and maintenance of basic social institutions that foster cooperation from processes of social exchange between individuals with a sanction mechanism, effected by sentiments of approval and disapproval to control behaviour (Elsner 1989).

In consequence of the way Smith described the process of attaining mutual sympathy in terms of an exchange of sentiments in the TMS, commentators have pointed out similarities with Smith's account of exchange processes in the WN (Otteson 2002). Smith envisioned the same mutuality of benefit in the economic sphere as in the search for sympathetic communication between agent and spectator. Here we meet with Smith's second line of argument with which he took up position against Rousseau. The argument is to be found in its rudimentary form in the *Early Draft* of the WN and presents the claim that trade and commerce are mutually beneficial.

Denying that within a framework of mutual dependence efforts at individual gain promote the good of others, although unintentionally, Rousseau thought differently. The commercial system, founded upon mutual dependence through the division of labour, is based on behaviour motivated by "the hidden desire to profit at the expense of others" (SD: 156). Rousseau felt that commercial society was characterised by conditions of inequality established by social contract. It legitimised a situation by law in which the rich appropriated all the advantages of society without much scruples about leaving the poor empty-handed. Driven by vanity and greed, moreover, social relationships are increasingly reduced to relationships of exchange in which private interest and competition predominate, while man's insatiable ambition "inspires in all men a base inclination to harm each other" (SD: 156).

In his *Early Draft*, Smith countered that there is no reason to be depreciatory about exchange relationships (LJ(ED): 571). Noting how degrading it had been for people relying on charity to have to solicit for the favour of their superiors, Smith preferred exchange relationships in which people are free to better their condition as they see fit in transactions that make everyone better off. Parties have something to offer each other and the relationship is not prone to develop into one of submission. Feudal society and its model of charity had not been all that charitable and laudable, and despite its faults commercial society is much to be preferred.

Moreover, far from deteriorating into a zero-sum game, trade and commerce were mutually beneficial. The notion of mutual benefit was central to Smith's response to Rousseau. In the *Early Draft*, Smith emphasised that the common labourer, despite conditions of oppressive inequality, is much better off than the rich in primitive societies. Despite all who take their share from the produce of the labourer, the advance made possible by the division of labour is large enough to enable the common labourer a standard of living that beats the comforts of an African king. Illustrative of this difference between Rousseau and Smith is their description of man's intent in his dealings with his fellow men. Rousseau wrote (in Smith's translation in his *Letter to the Edinburgh Review* 14; SD: 156): "He is obliged therefore to endeavour to interest them in his situation, and to make them find, either in reality or in appearance, their advantage in labouring for his". Note the different orientation in Smith's phrasing:

> He will be much more likely to prevail if he can interest their self love in his favour, and show them that it is for their own advantage to do for him what he requires of them. Whoever offers to another a bargain of any kind proposes to do this. 'Give me that which I want and you shall have this which you want', is the plain meaning of every such offer.
>
> (LJ(ED): 571)

Given his premise of a zero-sum game, this strategy at persuasion is not open to Rousseau. Modern man did not have much choice but to yield to the pressure of society and pursue a life of deceptive appearances once emulative passions are awakened in social relationships. Smith denied any such inevitability and was at pains to describe how the mirror of society brought men to stay within the bounds of propriety. For Rousseau, all the attendant evils of property and inequality follow from the fact that a system based on division of labour and mutual dependence is to be characterised as a zero-sum game. Consequently he denounced the model of personal interest, mutual dependence and reciprocal needs that would "oblige each of them to bring about the happiness of others in order to achieve his own", as it would lead to a "state of affairs where each, while pretending to work for the fortune and the reputation of others, seeks but to augment his own above theirs and at their expense" (Rousseau, *Narcisse* 2011[1752]).

Assuming that man has a natural love of society, Smith denied that human relationships in commercial society are necessarily deceptive and instrumental. And even if specialisation and market exchange point towards increased functional relationships based on interest, self-interest necessarily implies mutuality, involving as it does the contemplation of the other's interest relative to one's own. Human nature shows a multi-coloured palette of human emotions and motivations and cannot be reduced to a few simple operating principles. Self-interest is part of a larger variety of motives, and behaviour is the result of interacting passions, each with its own distinctive orientation, strength and persistence. That is why one-dimensional qualifications about the moral quality of human motives such as benevolence or self-love are misplaced. Reminiscent of Mandeville's argument that virtue and vice are relative notions, Smith argued that man's passions and affections, being a package deal, seldom qualify as unambiguous from a moral point of view. In the abstract, the moral quality of passions and interests is never unequivocal and Smith emphasised that the worth of all passions, including the selfish and unsocial passions, "cannot be determined simply from a description of the passions themselves but only from an account of their appropriateness to specific occasions" (Mehta 2006: 248). The moral quality of actions depends on how passions and interests in particular circumstances balance out, hence Smith's insistence on the situational determinacy of sympathy. Moral evaluations involve a process of feeling out mutuality which cannot be seen in isolation of the context in which action takes place.

Strengthening the argument: the second edition of *The Theory of Moral Sentiments* and *The Wealth of Nations*

Rather than seeing each other as rivals, people actively seek companionship and the approval and esteem of others. For this purpose they are willing to restrain their natural impulse of self-love, and are prepared to attune their views, sentiments and interests to one another. Smith emphasised the importance of the context, or social setting, in which exchange takes place to arrive at a correspondence of sentiments and mutuality. But precisely the situational determinacy of mutuality raises questions.

First, if we learn to pass judgement on the propriety of conduct of others as well as our own by observing and experiencing expressions of approval and disapproval of society, our self-evaluations may be said to simply reflect public opinion. The objection that he had reduced moral judgement to (the whims of) public opinion (Hundert 1994) was raised against Smith by Sir Gilbert Elliot and occasioned a revision in the second edition of the TMS.

Smith's second line of argument is equally vulnerable to the intervening impact of contextual influences. Smith acknowledged that the institutional setting in establishing perverse incentives (Rosenberg 1960) may impair the realisation of mutual gains from trade.

Such considerations induced Smith to strengthen his argument by developing the concept of the impartial spectator in the second edition of the TMS (Raphael 1975: 91) and by spelling out in the WN the conditions for general enrichment and the institutional structures through which, despite divergent interests, all orders benefit. With these upgrades, Smith further developed the conditions of mutuality.

The independence of conscience: the notion of the impartial spectator

If morality is explained in terms of the generalisations of feelings of what is proper conduct in a situation upon which people come to agree, how may conscience go against public opinion? Sir Gilbert Elliot objected that upon Smith's account morality was no more than the reflection of prevailing social attitudes. This would bring Smith close to Rousseau's (and Mandeville's) view that "moral reasoning itself was a species of fashion and, like changing habits of dress, a dependent feature of the universal search for esteem" (Hundert 2003: 32). Smith's answer was designed to show how conscience can be independent of public opinion. He first argued than man is principally accountable to God. But reckoning with the weakness of human nature, Smith argues, "the author of nature has made man the immediate judge of mankind" (Corr. 40: 53).[9] Gifted with an original desire to please and aversion to offend and anxious to be esteemed by others, man first forms an idea of the rules by which he is judged from expressions of social approval and disapproval before conscience develops. Learning from experience that we always rub someone up the wrong way and thus that "universal approbation is altogether unattainable . . . [w]e soon learn to sett up in our own minds a judge between ourselves and those we live with" (Corr. 40: 54). This judge is imagined as unrelated and disinterested: "neither father, nor Brother, nor friend, either to them or to us; but is merely a man in general, an impartial Spectator who considers our conduct with the same indifference with which we regard that of other people" (Corr. 40: 54). Led by his desire for agreement and understanding to seek approval, man appeals to the impartial spectator whose moral judgement is an 'ideal' to both agents and spectators in indicating the 'proper' degree of self-command (agent) and degree of sensibility (spectator). As such, the imagined judgement of the impartial spectator represents a point of reference which we may use to criticise or pre-empt the judgements of others about our sentiments and conduct. This enables man to seek a moral independence, which goes beyond social opinion and the mere desire for the approval of others.

Smith took the rulings of this impartial spectator as superior, even though he has been shown the ropes by the judgements of man. If we feel wronged by our fellow men, we take refuge with "a Superior tribunal established in their own minds" and "if the man within condemns us, the loudest acclamations of mankind appear but as noise of ignorance and folly" (Corr. 40: 53/55). It is only by having recourse to such an impartial perspective from which to look at and judge the behaviour of others and our own that we learn "[t]he real littleness of ourselves" (Corr. 40: 56), overcoming the delusions of self-love and are capable of understanding the injustice in pursuing our own interest at the expense of others.

It is the man within to which Smith points to deny the subjugating role of public opinion and the search for approval and esteem. Smith saw no merit in Rousseau's argument that public opinion, prone to deceive and be deceived by appearances depriving people of freedom, may thwart men's sentiments and directs passions towards evil ends (O'Neal 1986: 456). The man within provides a certain independence, which prevents that when the world injures people, "they are incapable of doing themselves Justice and are in consequence necessarily the Slaves of the world" (Corr. 40: 55).

Far from vanity or *amour-propre* running wild, we flatten the manifestations of our self-love for the sake of establishing a correspondence of sympathetic feelings with others within the limits set by sentiments of propriety. And instead of knowing "how to live only in the opinion of others" (SD: 179), there is an inner voice that points out to us the need for proper perspective.

> We must view them [some other's interests], neither from our own place, nor yet from his, neither with our own eyes nor yet with his, but from the place and with the eyes of a third person, who has no particular connection with either and who judges with impartiality between us.
>
> (Corr. 40: 56)

So Smith argued the need to take up a middle position in order to properly compare and establish the conditions for reciprocity and mutuality by correcting any inflated sense of self. As we moderate and subdue our expression of vanity and pride in order to obtain the sympathetic reaction of others, Smith denied that commercial society showed a growing gap between vanity and (true) virtue. At the same time he emphasised the individual's prerogative to appeal to a tribunal to arrive at true mutuality and reciprocity, unhindered by outward dependence due to social pressure or power. The same thrust imbued *The Wealth of Nations*.

Contextuality and the trend towards mutual benefit

In the TMS Smith presented man as a compound of passions and traits, ranging from selfish to social passions, fitted to environmental circumstances in order to pursue his good (as he sees it). Different circumstances conjure up a different configuration of relevant passions and desires and, as a consequence, opportunities for and constraints upon the manifestations of man's passions, behavioural patterns, manners and morals develop in response to changing conditions of life (TMS V.2.13). Turning to man's economic relations in the WN, Smith brings man's natural disposition to better his condition into the limelight as the driving motive of his actions, rather than generosity or benevolence. Just as well, because man in commercial society is fully dependent on "the cooperation and assistance of great multitudes" (WN I.ii.2) and only beggars choose to rely on benevolence in such circumstances (Coase 1976). Analysing how man's drives and passions interact and work out within an evolving historical setting of institutions, laws, regulations etc., Smith elaborated on how results of human actions often diverge from the intentions of the agents. Following Mandeville and Hume, Smith sketched the evolution of society as the unanticipated consequence of social action.

Far from assuming benign consequences or a trend towards a positive-sum society, Smith was very much aware that the way passions and institutions interact may have constructive as well as destructive tendencies. The often unanticipated and unintended consequences of human actions may be beneficial and/or harmful to either the individual (or group of individuals) and/or society at large. Muller's description of the WN as "an encyclopedia of the effects of unintended consequences in human affairs" (1995: 85) is quite appropriate, while Mehta handsomely captured the implication of Smith's view when he wrote: "The paradox is that the very motive, self-interest, that allows that system to produce the beneficial consequences it does, constantly threatens to undermine it" (Mehta 2006: 257). And so the WN tells the story of the instrumentality of self-interest in the advance of liberty and the growth of order and wealth, as well as how that same self-interest is the foundation on which oppressive institutions were erected which effectively impeded progress. The manifestation of the desire to better our condition depends on conditions and arrangements of society, and at the extremes may be smothered (as in the case of slavery) or be given free reign (and invite mean rapacity). Consequently, one of the aims on which the WN was designed was to inquire into the institutional mechanisms "which will eliminate zero-sum (or even negative-sum) games" (Rosenberg 1960: 560) by creating an incentive structure in which "self-interest can only be effective through *mutuality, reciprocity* and *cooperation*" (Danner 1976: 324; italics in original).

In the WN, Smith showed the opportunities for 'mutuality, reciprocity and cooperation', offering a number of reasons for the potential gains from trade. He pointed out not only the Pareto-improving qualities of mutual exchange, but also discussed the benefits from developing patterns of production which accommodate differences in resource bases and the advantages in economies of scale involved in the division of labour, human capital formation and international specialisation (Rothschild and Sen 2006: 358). Making much of the advantages of the division of labour, competition and the essential role of capital accumulation to the formation of surplus and investment (Aspromourgos 2009), Smith argued that growth of opulence depends on two interrelated factors: labour productivity and the ratio of productive labour to unproductive labour. Expanding labour productivity through the division of labour and innovation increases surplus and allows capital accumulation. This can be used to substitute productive for unproductive labour. As the economy expands, Smith argued, rents, profits and wages increase (although profit rates decline with growing competition), while prices of necessities fall. Wealth and population increasing together, the market expands further, advancing the division of labour and the rise of labour productivity, creating a virtuous circle of growth. Guided by an appropriate setting of laws and institutions, the commercial system, run on the private desires and drives of individuals, would produce results that could never be expected from expressions of benevolence and generosity.

If only commercial society was allowed to work like that. Page after page in the WN, Smith showed his concern about imbalances of economic power created by the mercantile system with its close alliance of commercial interests and government, its regulations of trade by interested officials, guilds and corporations and its laws that prohibited the free movement of capital and labour. The mercantile system is severely castigated for its design framed by class interests, appropriating the benefits of cooperation through rent-seeking at the expense of society and impeding progress. For reasons of advantage, mercantile interests impose upon government to regulate and restrict the free operation of the market. Such regulations and restrictions hamper economic growth and hence the extent to which the growth of opulence benefits all ranks in society. However ineradicable, man's drive to better his condition may be thwarted or impeded by ill-producing, malfunctioning or wayward institutions. As such, the WN is a catalogue of instances in which institutional restraints operating on incentives influence the way benefits are distributed among the various classes and interests. Smith knew better than to expect too much from his plea to break down the system of privileges and restraints and replace it with a system of natural liberty and justice: "Not only the prejudices of the publick, but what is much more unconquerable, the private interests of many individuals, irresistibly oppose it" (WN IV.ii.43). Again the interfering influence of the (institutional) context seems to undercut Smith's response to Rousseau, and here Smith strengthens his argument by pointing out how the structural changes arriving with commercial society had redefined incentives and rewards conducive to mutuality.

In the WN, Smith advanced his argument by showing how in the evolution of society efforts to satisfy desires motivated by vanity and greed – instead of goading one another towards destruction – put into motion a process, which subordinated these two easily inflammable passions to the much more calm and dispassionate desire of bettering our condition. Smith is at his best when he relates how the allodial lords and the clergy unintentionally furthered the cause of human happiness by their fascination for "trinkets and baubles, fitter to be the play-things of children than the serious pursuits of men" (WN III.iv.15). This fascination awakened as soon as products became available for which they could exchange their large revenues, previously spent on the maintenance of a large number of (unproductive) dependents by way of "the most profuse hospitality" and "the most extensive charity" (WN V.i.g.22) that upheld their power and authority. Having found a way to spend their wealth on themselves, "for the gratification of the most childish, the meanest and the most sordid of all vanities, they gradually bartered their whole power and authority" (WN III.iv.10). Seduced by their vain desires, the rich set in motion a profound change in patterns of consumer expenditures, which was to revolutionise society. Most importantly, it brought 'order and good government' or a stable constitutional and institutional structure of society and security of expectations (Rosenberg 1968). Smith's account is not just a wonderful illustration of Mandeville's dictum 'private vices, publick benefits' but allows him to strengthen his case in two ways.

First, the transformation of society from an allodial feudal system into commercial society presents a key argument in defending commercial society to

Rousseau.[10] Rather than lamenting the loss of hospitality and charity by the rich, Smith emphasised that in their spending on trivial gadgets, the rich proprietors provided work and maintenance for their former retainers without the latter being stuck in a state of dependence and idleness. Unleashing the desire of bettering condition, they provided encouragement to industry and the arts, promoting growth of wealth with its accompanying opportunities for improvements in the material condition of labour. Smith's favourable assessment of commercial society was firmly grounded in its ability to provide adequately for the poor (as against pre-commercial societies which may have been more equal but were also miserably poor) (Himmelfarb 1984; Ignatieff 1990; Rasmussen 2008). Thus 'the most childish vanity' of the great proprietors and the merchants and artificers and the "pedlar principle of turning a penny wherever a penny was to be got" (WN III.iv.17) proved a powerful mix as their marriage unintentionally procured benefits in terms of liberty, industry and wealth. As such, commercial society substituted growth and innovation for self-sufficiency and backwardness, traded independence and industry for dependence and idleness, and replaced sloth and indolence for efficiency and diligence. Nowhere perfect, but it constituted a significant improvement over feudal society.

Second, Smith argued that commercial society had created a new environment which redefined the pay-off structure of man's vanity and greed so as to contribute to material and moral improvement in society. This new pay-off structure, revising the conditions for success, brought Smith to distance himself not only from Mandeville's claims about the necessity of luxury spending to growth and prosperity, but also from Rousseau, by arguing that this new setting restrained instead of inflamed man's vanity.

The view of the beneficial consequences of luxury spending gained acceptance in the eighteenth century since its bold assertion by Barbon (Finkelstein 2000) and Mandeville (Hont 2006). With growing poise it had been argued that extravagance produces desirable effects in terms of employment and income in maintaining a high level of effective demand, while frugality is "an idle dreaming Virtue that employs no Hands, and therefore very useless in a trading Country" (Mandeville *Fable* I: 105). Increasing aggregate demand for economic goods to supply the limitless wants that originated in pride, vanity, envy and emulation was a source of employment and income to the poor. The expenditures on luxury to show one's vain pride, moreover, would promote trade and industry in an ever-rising spiral of growth and make society affluent and powerful.

Smith agreed that the luxurious expenditures of the rich to gratify their vanity offered opportunities and encouragement to industry, triggering into action the desire to better their condition of independent labourers and artisans. The same drives act as spurs to manage estates with efficiency to increase surplus. Pointing out the structural changes in the economy and society that commercial society entailed, however, Smith diverged sharply from Mandeville on the causes of growth of wealth (Winch 1996: 66ff). Change not only shifted power away from the landowning classes and feudal institutions towards capitalist institutions; it also implied changes in consumer patterns, production and distribution, changing conditions for growth. These developments, Smith argued, implied changes in the level and composition of output and aggregate demand, signifying the growing taste for (durable) goods as opposed to services (Rosenberg 1968). Hence Smith's insistence on the drive for profit and the accumulation of capital as the basic cause of growth as he came to conceptualise profit "as an income uniquely associated with the use of capital in the employment of wage-labour" (Meek 1954: 139). He posited the rise of a class of capitalists or those who lived by profit that started to call the tune in commercial society. Against this background, Smith hammered at the distinction between capital and revenue, claiming that their proportion determined the proportion between industry and idleness or between productive and unproductive labour (WN II.iii.13), key factor to growth. Smith argued that the causes and conditions of generating wealth define the conditions of success in terms of frugality rather than prodigality and extravagance. As Smith remarked:

> An augmentation of fortune is the means by which the greater part of men propose and wish to better their condition. It is the means the most vulgar and the most obvious; and the most likely way of augmenting their fortune, is to save and accumulate some part of what they acquire, either regularly and annually, or upon some extraordinary occasions. Though the principle of expence, therefore, prevails in almost all men upon some occasions, and in some men upon almost all occasions, yet in the greater part of men, taking the whole course of their life at an average, the principle of frugality seems not only to predominate, but to predominate very greatly.
>
> (WN II.iii.28)

It is frugality and its consequent accumulation of capital and investment which increases the productive powers and hence the nation's stock of wealth (WN II.iii). Capital accumulation is the key factor in the growth of the wealth of a nation, given that both the productivity of labour and the proportion between productive and unproductive labour ultimately depend on capital accumulation. Capital increases by parsimony and we are prompted to save and augment our fortune by the desire of bettering our condition. In sharp contrast to Mandeville's eulogy, Smith argued that prodigality merely feeds "the idle with the bread of industrious, tends not only to beggar himself, but to impoverish his country" (WN II.iii.20). Therefore "every prodigal appears to be a publick enemy, and every frugal man a publick benefactor" (WN II.iii.25). Even though the virus of vanity spreads across society as soon as desires venture beyond basic needs, Smith argued against Rousseau that changing conditions of growth and prosperity in commercial society limited the scope for extravagance and vain expenditures in the range of behavioural patterns conducive to success. To Smith self-interested behaviour is moulded by the environmental characteristics of commercial society (Hollander 1977: 141). The mercantile system, for instance, is said to have generated habits of "order, oeconomy, and attention" (WN III.iv.3), encouraged parsimony and took success or failure to depend on people's "opinion of his fortune, probity and prudence" (WN I.x.b.20). And if the environmental characteristics of society change, so do the character and attitudes of people.

> In mercantile and manufacturing towns, where the inferior ranks of people are chiefly maintained by the employment of capital, they are in general industrious, sober, and thriving; as in many English, and in most Dutch towns. In those towns . . . in which the inferior ranks of people are chiefly maintained by the spending of revenue, they are in general idle, dissolute, and poor.
>
> (WN II.iii.12)

Reminiscent of Hume's account of how the acquisitive passion is tamed by setting it against itself, Smith developed a historical account of how vanity and greed, roused by the growth of economic surplus, put in motion a process of change that imposed restraints upon the manifestations of ambition, vanity and greed. With the growth of the capitalist sector, the requirements for success changed, demanding a different set of qualities to augment one's fortune in order to gain the admiration of mankind. In the case of demand-driven growth – aggregate demand and particularly expenditures on luxury as the critical factor in determining for prosperity – a conflict would have existed between standards of propriety and the extravagance or immoderation implied in luxury spending. Growth based on capital accumulation however calls for frugality and moderation, and whether inspired by the desire to augment one's fortune or by wanting to act with propriety to obtain sympathy, it allowed Smith to argue that fortune and virtue tend to converge happily. Aiming at both fortune and virtue required thrift, discipline, orderliness, honesty and industry, a set of qualities that Smith captured in the virtue of prudence. Commercial society not only allows growth of opulence but also encourages the development of propriety and virtue. Given conditions of mutual dependence, people in commercial society need to satisfy their material as well as their immaterial needs and desires through the medium of exchange. Want satisfaction through negotiation and persuasion, whether in terms of goods, sentiments or approbation, requires agents to enter into and adapt to one another's passions, views and interests. Given that we tend to exaggerate the importance of our own interest and depreciate that of others, Smith argued, it is "reason, principle, conscience, the inhabitant of the breast, the man within, the great judge and arbiter of our conduct" who informs us "that we are but one of the multitude, in no respect better than any other in it" and is "capable of counteracting the strongest impulses of self-love" (TMS III.3.4). Supported by the approval of the impartial spectator, man learns to adopt a common point of view that transcends his selfish passions and to exercise the respectable and amiable virtues, self-command and humanity, increasingly recognising his own interest in that of others. Cultivating social and economic virtues by the interaction and exchange of views, ideas, passions, sentiments and goods and services, commerce 'refines', 'polishes', 'improves' and 'softens' humans and their relationships and, whether of a social or economic nature, ideally is "a bond of union and friendship" (WN IV.iii.c.9).

The two roads of the sixth edition of *The Theory of Moral Sentiments*

Any bold assertion of Smith's adherence to the *doux commerce* thesis, however, sits uncomfortably with some of Smith's additions to the TMS when he came to publish a sixth edition at the end of his life.[11] In these additions, Smith once again felt the need to emphasise the independence of conscience and elaborate further on the conditions of mutual benefit. Moreover, he also explicitly discussed the possibility of the corruption of man's moral sentiments, a leading idea in all accounts critical of commercial modernity. Without having to qualify Smith as a "good disciple of Rousseau", as Force wrote (1997: 63), clearly he sympathised with Rousseau's concerns and took undesirable effects of commercialism into account in assessing commercial society. As Rasmussen pointed out, Smith defended commercial society not so much on ideological grounds but on the basis of a cost-benefit analysis of commercial society vis-à-vis other ages, to conclude that commercial society offered "the best chance for the most people to lead a decent life" (2008: 13).[12] Even though Rasmussen correctly asserted that Smith felt that Rousseau's critiques of commercial society were "not finally convincing" (*ibid.*: 91), the additions to TMS 6 make clear that Smith did not consider his answers to be fully persuasive either. Smith was increasingly aware that the same principles and mechanisms he utilised to answer Rousseau might very well defy his very purpose. Specifying the conditions for 'mutuality, reciprocity and cooperation' implies that if these conditions are not met, society may develop in other directions.

In the WN, Smith had argued in favour of establishing a system of natural liberty and justice to make greed as self-interest conducive to progress in a way that allows everyone to share in the benefits, albeit not equally. Smith works up the same idea in TMS 6, when he emphasised the importance of the independence of conscience in moral judgements, free from considerations of interest or reward. To strengthen the independence of man's conscience from public opinion,[13] Smith explicitly distinguishes between the love of praise and the love of praiseworthiness. By nature man not only desires to be praised, he reasoned, but also to know himself to be the worthy object of praise, irrespective of whether he is in fact praised. Likewise, man not only dreads becoming the object of blame, but also the knowledge that he deserves to be blamed, even if no one actually accuses him of a lack of propriety in his conduct. In both cases, it is the moral judgement of the impartial spectator, the judge within or conscience upon which man relies in getting what he (really) deserves (pleasure arising from approval and praise, or pain in the case of disapproval and blame) in the absence of reactions from his fellow-men or when induced to go against public opinion. This love of praiseworthiness and dread of blameworthiness is as much a necessary condition to man's fitness for society as the "original desire to please, and an original aversion to offend his brethren" (TMS III.2.6).

Smith uses the distinction to strengthen the jurisdiction of conscience, the man within, vis-à-vis the tribunal of man. He maintains that the jurisdictions of the two tribunals (conscience and the man without), although akin and resembling, are founded upon different and distinct principles (TMS III.2.32). Linking the jurisdiction of the man without to the desire of actual praise and the aversion to blame, the jurisdiction of the man within is argued to be founded upon the love of praiseworthiness and aversion to blameworthiness (TMS III.2.32). In Smith's view, man develops conscience from the tribunal of man in the same manner as people are shown the ropes in a process of maturation. Through a process of socialisation and internalising, man develops a perspective, soaked off from public judgements, whereby praise is only pleasurable if deserved. The approbation of others merely confirms, and is only pleasurable to the extent that it corresponds with, our own self-approbation. In other words, man needs to link his self-worth to the extent to which he acts with propriety. This is important because otherwise he is only prompted "to the affectation of virtue, and to the concealment of vice" (TMS III.2.7) and, being driven by the desire for praise, to abandon higher standards of virtue and perfection. Contenting oneself with some average standard of proper conduct undermines the respectable and amiable virtues, undermines self-command and humanity, and thereby threatens to undermine cooperation. That is what happens when vanity as a driving motive takes over. In the case of vanity, people desire to be praised without being praiseworthy: "it was the mark of vanity to be flattered by the praise of society and to ignore the truer judgement of conscience" (Raphael 1975: 92).

It is on this distinction[14] that Smith levelled his rebuke at Mandeville, arguing that Mandeville had failed to discriminate between the desire for praise and the desire for praiseworthiness. Smith distinguished between the love of virtue ("the desire of doing what is honourable and noble"), the love of true glory ("the desire of acquiring esteem by what is really estimable") and vanity (desire of praise for qualities which are not or hardly praiseworthy) (TMS VII. II.4.8). He pointed out that Mandeville (mis)used the affinity between vanity and the love of true glory (and the love of virtue) in its reference to the opinions of others, to impose the claim upon his readers that all behaviour is infected by the desire for praise and hence to be regarded as vicious (thus arriving at his paradox) (TMS III.2.27 and VII.II.7–12). Winch has remarked that "when Smith was dealing openly and covertly with Mandeville in *The Theory of Moral Sentiments*, he was also answering some of Rousseau's arguments" (1996: 60).[15] And indeed, Smith utilised the same distinction with which he took Mandeville to task to deny that appearance is everything. In successive editions of the TMS, Smith developed the idea of the love of praiseworthiness as a distinctive moral motive. Rather than "the semblance of all the virtues without the possession of any" (FD: 36), Smith emphasises in Lovejoy's words, "[i]t is the desire to be and not merely the desire to appear" (1961: 264).

At the same time, Smith had always recognised that the passions of vanity, avarice, and ambition ruled behaviour in commercial society. In TMS 1, Smith left no-one in doubt about the moving forces in the bustle of life:

> For to what purpose is all the toil and bustle of this world? what is the end of avarice and ambition, of the pursuit of wealth, of power, and prehemi-nence? . . . From whence . . . arises that emulation which runs through all the different ranks of men, and what are the advantages which we propose by that great purpose of human life which we call bettering our condition? To be observed, to be attended to, to be taken notice of with sympathy, complacency, and approbation, are all the advantages which we can pro-pose to derive from it. It is the vanity, not the ease, or the pleasure, which interests us.
>
> (TMS I.iii.2.1)

Like Mandeville, Hume and Rousseau, Smith observed that the folly of vanity and its struggle for distinction and status takes the shape of a relentless pursuit of material objects in commercial society. This "most ardent desire" (TMS I.iii.2.1) is universal and insatiable, and discernible in the desire for place or social status:

> [p]lace, that great object which divides the wives of aldermen, is the end of half the labours of human life; and is the cause of all the tumult and bustle, all the rapine and injustice, which avarice and ambition have introduced into this world.
>
> (TMS I.iii.2.8)

In explaining why wealth commands admiration, Smith paid tribute to Hume for advancing the idea that our pleasure derives from the fitness of an object to serve its intended purpose. He made the further claim that what interest us is "not so much this conveniency, as that arrangement of things which promotes it" (TMS IV.1.4). Smith depreciated the real satisfactions that may be derived from power and riches, describing them as "enormous and operose machines contrived to produce a few trifling conveniences" (TMS IV.1.8). The real appeal of wealth and greatness suggested to our imagination, rather than its utility, is the beauty and fitness of the arrange-ment in being adapted to its purpose of satisfying human desires (Diatkine 2010). We imagine this admiration felt for such fitness of these objects of wealth to reflect upon its owner. Entering more easily into sentiments of joy than sorrow, man has a natural disposition to sympathise with the rich and powerful (TMS I.iii.2.1). People readily image the pleasures which would befall them in like material circumstances, and as a consequence, the pleasures of wealth and greatness "strike the imagination as something grand and beautiful and noble" (TMS IV.1.9).

This natural disposition to sympathise more readily with joy than with sorrow and hence man's natural inclination to admire the rich and powerful does have its uses. The distinction of ranks and the order of society depend on it. It is this disposition by which Smith explains man's compliance with the rules of society[16] rather than any expectation of benefit or because the rich deceived the poor into an arrangement that legitimises inequality and oppression. Earlier work also showed that Smith knew too well that there is no guarantee that (the interaction of) passions, institutions and principles have beneficial outcomes (Rothschild 2002). But this time it is different.

The newly added text of TMS 6 shows that Smith was very much aware that everyday life does not exactly conform to the ideal. Smith acknowledged that there is often a thin line between the desire of praise and the desire to be praiseworthy. And while the agent himself is often unable to say which part originates in the one and which in the other, this is even more difficult for the spectator, who often judges by his own imagination (TMS III.2.26). Moreover, he argued that "in every well-informed mind this second desire *seems* to be the strongest of the two" (TMS III.2.7; italics added). Smith furthermore allowed that the more we are uncertain about the accuracy of our own judgements, the more we tend to care about the sentiments and opinions of others (TMS III.2.16, 24). On all these qualifications, Smith's firm assertion about the primacy of man's love of praiseworthiness dissolves, and man's vanity and love of praise light up again, pointing at Smith's awareness that the same passions, principles or mechanisms may work out in opposite directions.

Man's imagination is pivotal. Smith made much of man's imagination in developing his own notion of sympathy and that of the impartial spectator. With the independence of conscience, he increasingly emphasised the role of the imagination.[17] It is in the imagination that we change positions with the agent/spectator and feel out the amount of self-command and humanity necessary to adapt sentiments to that pitch that allows sympathetic accord. It is the imagination through which we learn the amiable and respectable virtues. It is an essential asset to the proper functioning of the impartial spectator and man's love of praiseworthiness. However, imagination may also trick us into excessive self-estimation or vanity. Linking vanity to the "illusion of the imagination" (TMS III.2.5), Smith argued the importance to people of keeping this illusion intact. Unconvinced of his own superiority, the groundless pretentions man displays make him eagerly solicit for the esteem and admiration of others. "He flatters in order to be flattered" (VI.iii.36), aiming to keep up appearances.

From the additions to TMS 6, it is apparent that Smith takes man's basic need for approval and sympathy to the next level of a yearning for distinction and admiration. Man's desire for approbation, previously highlighted as being instrumental in shaping moral behaviour, now seems less effective to restrain the self-regarding passions. TMS 6 is different in building such critical reflections into a potential pattern towards corruption.

Our disposition to admire the rich and neglect the poor, however, may also have adverse effects and run our moral sentiments off course. The same mechanism of sympathy that makes us susceptible to society's signals of approbation and disapprobation, teaching us to act morally, works up wealth and greatness as a shortcut to earning the esteem and admiration of others. As a consequence, "people tend to be seduced, by the very mechanism that ought to lead them to virtue, into seeking wealth instead" (Fleischacker 2004: 115). Seduced by the dazzling splendour of wealth and greatness, man directs his attention, sympathy and esteem to the rich irrespective of whether any real merit is due, dreaming of similar acclaim. As such people are provided with two models on which to fashion their conduct and character:

> To deserve, to acquire, and to enjoy the respect and admiration of mankind, are the great objects of ambition and emulation. Two different roads are presented to us, equally leading to the attainment of this so much desired object; the one, by the study of wisdom and the practice of virtue; the other, by the acquisition of wealth and greatness. Two different characters are presented to our emulation; the one, of proud ambition and ostentatious avidity; the other, of humble modesty and equitable justice.
>
> (TMS I.iii.3.2)

Although wisdom and virtue should command respect and admiration, the great majority of people award their respect to the rich and powerful. The admirers of wisdom and virtue are but "a small party" (TMS I.iii.3.2). Eager to distinguish themselves, people relentlessly pursue the acquisition of goods of frivolous utility in striving to satisfy the nonmaterial desire for status by imitating and emulating the rich and obtain similar admiration. Nevertheless, Smith claimed, "In the middling and inferior stations of life, the road to virtue and that to fortune, to such fortune, at least, as men in such stations can reasonably expect to acquire, are, happily in most cases, very nearly the same" (TMS I.iii.3.5).

In true Mandevillean vein, Smith argued here that most people only tend to act virtuously because it serves their purpose. The relief with which the reader takes in the claim of this happy confluence masks how precarious such a balance may be. He put forward at least two causes whereby this balance can easily be upset: the corruption of man's moral sentiments and inequality.

In TMS 6 Smith returned to the theme of class morality (WN V.i.g.10), arguing that the higher classes, supported by their wealth, tend to exhibit a loose standard of morals, which by its appeal to the imagination tends to be imitated, infecting society with inappropriate drives and aspirations. Such attitudes and standards are no relics from a feudal past. In the WN Smith had warned against the harmful effects of a high rate of profit, emphasising that it would destroy parsimony. As Smith drily remarked: "A man of a large revenue, whatever may be his profession, thinks he ought to live like other men of large revenues; and to spend a great part of his time in festivity, in vanity, and in dissipation" (WN V.i.g.42).

Supported by protectionist regulations that restrain competition and keep profits high, capitalists may earn their fortunes at leisure and feel inclined to indulge themselves in ostentation and dissipation (Birch 1998).

> When profits are high, that sober virtue seems to be superfluous, and expensive luxury to suit better the affluence of his situation. But the owners of the great mercantile capitals are necessarily the leaders and conductors of the whole industry of every nation, and their example has a much greater influence upon the manners of the whole industrious part of it than that of any other order of men
>
> (WN IV.vii.c.61)

With the superior stations of life as their point of reference, the rich and powerful lead the fashion. Society is infused by a code of morals that promotes vanity, emulation and ambition,[18] inspiring people to imitate the rich and aspiring to the same glamour, fashioning themselves to the rich.

> Their dress is the fashionable dress; the language of their conversation, the fashionable style; their air and deportment, the fashionable behaviour. Even their vices and follies are fashionable; and the greater part of men are proud to imitate and resemble them in the very qualities which dishonour and degrade them. Vain men . . . desire to be praised for what they themselves do not think praise-worthy, and are ashamed of unfashionable virtues which they sometimes practise in secret, and for which they have secretly some degree of real veneration.
>
> (TMS I.iii.3.7)

Smith speaks of a corruption of moral sentiments, lowering moral standards or even abandoning the road to virtue, as people consider that their future exaltation will extenuate the means used to arrive at the aspired position. Instead of wealth trickling down to all ranks of society, creating opportunities for immaterial progress, the follies and vices of mankind dissipate in society, driving a wedge between the road to virtue and the road to fortune.

The same threat exists as a consequence of the oppressive inequality in commercial society (Verburg 2000). Everyone seeks the approbation and admiration of mankind. In principle this desire can be gratified through the splendour wealth affords and by the exercise of wisdom and virtue. In commercial society, man seeks the rewards of sympathy and admiration through the acquisition of wealth and property, crowding out virtue as a means to gain the admiration of mankind. At the same time, inequality in commercial society is oppressive:

> Wherever there is great property, there is great inequality. For one very rich man, there must be at least five hundred poor, and the affluence of the few supposes the indigence of the many. The affluence of the

rich excites the indignation of the poor, who are often both driven by want, and prompted by envy, to invade his possessions. It is only under the shelter of the civil magistrate that the owner of that valuable property . . . can sleep a single night in security. He is at all times surrounded by unknown enemies.

(WN V.i.b.2)

If people are only inclined to travel along the road to virtue as long as it is in the same direction as fortune, and if wealth, instead of extending itself through the ranks of society, accumulates in 'the monied interest' due to preferential arrangements and monopolistic advantages, what reason is there to continue along the road to virtue, especially if virtue does not attract the attention it deserved. It is as if Rousseau is talking and sighs "what will become of virtue when one must get rich at any price?" (FD: 51). The mirror of society may reflect images and values that undermine the conditions of mutuality that uphold a positive-sum society, while the drive for distinction may create a zero-sum game fuelled by envy and jealousy. Smith was more prepared than Hume to contemplate such tendencies, accepting that it depends on how forces balance out, which way the nature of the system of relations of interdependence develops.

Interestingly, Smith returned in TMS 6 to the themes of competition and national animosity he had discussed in the WN. In the WN, Smith had contrasted two contexts of competition. For ages commerce and warfare had gone hand in hand. The mercantile age was no different. The demise of the feudal system had made the rise of absolute monarchy possible in which wealth, knowledge and military power centralised as means to compete with other states for wealth and honour in a zero-sum game. Smith vehemently attacked the political economy and practices of such jealous rivalry, based on an unholy combination of class interests and military power, as a mechanism of obstruction. Given that nations advance together and not at the expense of one another,[19] competition is a mechanism of cooperation, although the moving parts of the mechanism are largely ignorant of the greater purpose they serve. In a natural system of liberty and justice, competition pits passions and interests against one another in a way that increases the welfare of all. Although motivated by considerations of gain, success favours virtuous qualities like prudence and honesty, whereby attempts to outdo one another turn into a competition of industry, innovation, and excellence. In TMS 6, Smith extended the idea of the beneficial effects of the balancing and soothing of the desire for gain and the desire for distinction to the international arena (Hont 2015).

Smith added new passages on contexts of competition, contrasting rivalry larded with national animosity and hostility on the one hand, and emulation, excellence and universal benevolence on the other. He deplored the jealousy and envy following from a misdirected love of one's own nation and national animosity. In conflicts between nations, the impartial spectator is afar off and the laws of justice often violated, while such violations are met with applause from fellow-citizens rather than that they bring dishonour (TMS III.3.42). He argued that for France and England

> to envy the internal happiness and prosperity of the other, the cultivation of its lands, the advancement of its manufactures, the increase of its commerce, the security and number of its ports and harbours, its proficiency in all the liberal arts and sciences, is surely beneath the dignity of two such great nations. These are all real improvements of the world we live in. Mankind are benefited, human nature is ennobled by them. In such improvements each nation ought, not only to endeavour itself to excel, but from the love of mankind, to promote, instead of obstructing the excellence of his neighbours. These are all proper objects of national emulation, not of national prejudice or envy.
>
> (TMS VI.ii.2.3)

Smith proposed a system of national emulation founded upon the love of mankind. The mercantile system, mixing the drive for national gain with jealousy and envy, produces animosity, violation of rights and war. It should be replaced by a system of national emulation, seeking economic benefit by competing for excellence, which finds national pride and honour in exploring opportunities for mutual advantage in growth. Taking the happiness of the whole of mankind as our point of reference in judging gain and honour allows nations to transcend 'national self-interest'. With these additions, Smith clearly showed the extent to which the nature of competition – benign or malevolent – depends on the institutional environment in which it is embedded. Consequently, any definite claim about directions in the growth of commercial society may be presumptuous in the absence of fully persuasive, unequivocal answers.

Growing doubts

In commercial society, everyone is aware that "the respect of our equals, our credit and rank in the society we live in, depend very much upon the degree in which we possess, or are supposed to possess those advantages [of external fortune]" (TMS VI.i.3). Understandably ambition and greed are often mentioned in the same breath, but, as Hume had argued, that does not imply that commercial society is fatally flawed. Approvingly Smith referred to the Stoic view that "the vices and follies of mankind" are equally "a necessary part of the plan of the universe as their wisdom or their virtue" and "made to tend equally to the prosperity and perfection of the great system of nature" (TMS I.ii.3.4). Deception, fraud and falsehood, greed and ambition all have their place. In commercial society these vices and follies are set in a context in which people need to cooperate in order to satisfy their wants. As a consequence, the need for distinction, reputation and approbation is instrumental in providing incentives to industry, in establishing the order and ranks of society, inducing people to adapt their views, interests and sentiments to those of others and to develop and keep up rules of morality. Surely they will try to get as much out of a deal as possible, but everyone has an interest in preserving order, ranks and benefits, while having a personal interest in the exercise of the commercial virtues to preserve reputation. This way wealth and virtue can support one another.

But then again, they may not. It may work the other way around. The same principles and mechanisms that link up the road to wealth and the road to virtue may drive them apart. The want for sympathy and imagination which are essential as instruments of virtue may bring man to abandon the road to virtue. The imagination may be seduced by illusions drawn from the glittering attraction of wealth as the most effective way to gain the admiration of mankind. Driven by vanity, seeking praise in favour of praiseworthiness, man comes to gratify his want for sympathy by way of wealth. Too often competition is a mechanism of obstruction. In TMS 6 Smith expressed his concerns about how a corruption of man's moral sentiments may result if society rewards vanity and greed by way of admiration and approbation and fails to offer virtue the same courtesy. It is not only that the loose morality of the rich may infect the whole of society, undermining the commercial virtues, the lower classes may be denied the possibility to earn approbation, and to have a positive self-image by way of their industry and prudence. Enlarged into a desire for distinction and superiority, man's want of sympathy and approbation can also have its undesirable consequences.

"Two different roads are presented to us", Smith wrote, "equally leading to the attainment of this so much desired object" (TMS I.iii.3.2): wealth and virtue. Mandeville had presented these roads as leading in opposite directions. Hume had made the case that they would increasingly converge, while Rousseau had emphasised how man's nature was being corrupted in commercial society at the expense of true virtue, riches and happiness. According to Smith, it depends. It depends on processes of socialisation and internalisation, supported by appropriate institutions. It depends on the extent to which people feel free to follow their conscience rather than being eager only for praise. It depends on the extent to which mutual dependence goes hand in hand with liberty. It depends on the extent to which competition is allowed to operate as a mechanism of cooperation and conditions of mutuality are met. Developing his own assessment of commercial society, Smith argued that it is not a forgone conclusion that commerce and manners and morals are positively correlated but neither is there any necessity that in commercial society the growth of wealth is at the expense of virtue. Given changing circumstances and the interplay of passions and institutions, assessments of commercial society are always tentative.

Notes

1 In this chapter, I will follow convention by referring to the *Theory of Moral Sentiments* as TMS, WN for *The Wealth of Nations*, LJ for the *Lectures on Jurisprudence* and ED for the *Early Draft of Part of the Wealth of Nations*. If relevant to the argument, I will add a number to the TMS to denote the edition. So TMS 6 refers to the sixth edition of the *Theory of Moral Sentiments*.

2 Although the secondary literature on each of these authors is staggering, literature which analyses the relationships between them is much more scarce but growing. A good start is offered by Colletti 1972; Hundert 1994; Force 2003; Hurtado 2004; Rasmussen 2008, 2013; Hont 2015; and Sagar 2016.

3 Rousseau wrote than man's ambition led him "to raise one's relative fortune less out of true need than in order to place oneself above others" (SD: 156). Smith is equally insistent about the universal desire "to obtain a good name, to rise above those about and render himself some way their superiors" (LJ(A) i.24).

4 During Smith's lifetime, six editions of *The Theory of Moral Sentiments* were published. The first edition saw the light in 1759, the sixth edition in 1790 a few weeks before Smith died (Ross 1995, especially Chapter 23). All editions had minor corrections and rearrangements, editions two and six contained substantial revisions. In the second edition (1761), Smith added a footnote to I.iii.1.9, replying to Hume's criticism, and III.ii, in which Smith developed the notion of the impartial spectator. The sixth edition contained more new materials, including I.iii.3 (on the corruption of moral sentiments), III.2–3 (further developing the theory of the impartial spectator and conscience as well as the virtue of self-command) and part VI (on ethical theory, including the virtues of prudence, benevolence and self-command and a part on the passions of pride and vanity). Having mentioned here only the most important revisions, more details can be found in the introduction to *the Glasgow Edition of TMS* by Macfie and Raphael (1976), as well as in Raphael (1975).

5 Robertson (2005) even argues that Smith was won over to Rousseau's point of view. As with Mandeville, generally speaking, the emphasis in interpretations of Smith's relationship to Rousseau seems to have shifted from critical to sympathetic in the past decades. Some scholars have pointed at the changing economic, cultural and political climate that might explain why Smith's views tilted (Dickey 1987; Garbo 2016).

6 Sagar (2016) has argued that the idea of Smith responding to Rousseau's critique of commercial society is too generous an interpretation of Rousseau's influence on Smith. Everyone will agree that Smith's 'encounter' with Rousseau is to be set in the larger context of the debate on commercial society. Nevertheless, confronted with two opposing assessments of commercial society in which the debate seemed to culminate, Smith's 'responses' to Rousseau are a convenient shorthand way for discussing Smith's assessment (even though others often raised the same issues).

7 See Raphael (1975); Haakonssen (1981); and Broadie (2006) on differences between Hume and Smith in their account of sympathy.

8 Smith did not always distinguish clearly between the various meanings of sympathy. Sympathy may refer to (1) the feelings summoned by the imaginary change of situation by the spectator; (2) the judgement of correspondence and hence approbation of the sentiments as expressed by the agent principally concerned; and (3) the various stages involved in the whole mechanism of sympathy.

9 This notation is an abbreviation for the Correspondence of Adam Smith. The letter to Mr Gilbert Elliot is listed as number 40, and contains Smith's draft version of his amendments for TMS 2 in answer to Elliot's objection.

10 Rasmussen supplied a book length analysis of the similarities and differences between Rousseau and Smith. The key question he aims to answer is why Smith, sympathetic to Rousseau's concerns, took it upon him to defend commercial society, while fully aware of its potential drawbacks (2008: 8). Rasmussen identifies three different critiques (the 'divisions of laborers' critique, undermining the intellectual, social and martial virtues, the 'empire of opinion' critique, arguing that in the commercial age everything is appearance at the expense of man's true nature, and the 'pursuit of unhappiness' critique, stating the futility of the pursuit of wealth and recognition to man's happiness. According to Rasmussen, Smith claimed that despite its faults, commercial society is a definite improvement over the poverty, insecurity and dependence that dominated almost all pre-commercial ages (2008: 9). Hont's *Politics in Commercial Society; Jean-Jacques Rousseau and Adam Smith* followed in 2015.

11 The most important newly written parts of the sixth edition of the *Theory of Moral Sentiments* (1790) are I.iii.3, III.2, parts of III.3 and part VI.

12 In *Adam Smith and the Stock of Moral Capital* (1990), Nathan Rosenberg developed a comparable argument.

13 Hanley (2008) likens Smith's insistence on the importance of the independence of conscience to Rousseau's search for self-sufficiency, arguing that both authors underscored the need for moral education to transform vanity into virtue.

14 Hanley takes this distinction as Smith's solution to Rousseau's critique that commercial society inspired a fury for distinction which corrupts man and society. With this solution, Hanley claims, Smith felt he had answered Rousseau's objections he initially shared, allowing him to take a middle position in assessing commercial modernity. Considering Smith's remark on the chances of his system of natural liberty ("as absurd as to expect that an Oceana or Utopia should ever be established in it [Great Britain]" (WN IV.ii.43) to be applicable here, Hanley's qualification of Smith's distinction as a solution seems to overstate the case.

15 Nevertheless, Rousseau and Mandeville would have disagreed on the *doux commerce* thesis. This has much to do with their different conception of the state of nature (Jack 1978). As Smith observed in his letter to the *Edinburgh Review*: "Dr. Mandeville represents the primitive state of mankind as the most wretched and miserable that can be imagined: Mr Rousseau, on the contrary, paints it as the happiest and most suitable to his nature" (Letter to the Edinburgh Review 1980[1755]). Indeed, Mandeville had his own variant of the notion of polishing civilisation, although he denied that the hybrid (or counterfeited) morality that resulted qualified as virtuous. Instead he argued that man's sociability and cooperative attitude were built on considerations of private advantage, and as such are testimony to man's hypocrisy as "the requisite mask for hiding avaricious economic vanity from the moralizing gaze of one's fellows" (Hundert 1994: 179). Rousseau shared much of the moral diagnosis of commercial society by "the most excessive detractor of human virtues" as he called Mandeville (SD: 130), and agreed to "the semblance of all the virtues without the possession of any" (FD: 36). Unlike Mandeville, Rousseau abhorred the consequences for the cause of virtue and happiness, arguing that the growth of civilisation and its relentless pursuit of wealth to satisfy needs of pride breed moral deception and illusions of happiness.

16 "Our obsequiousness to our superiors more frequently arises from our admiration for the advantages of their situation, than from any private expectations of benefit from their good-will" (TMS I.iii.2.3).

17 Although Smith's position on the formation of man's moral sentiments remained unchanged through the various editions of the TMS, as Raphael concluded, "[i]n the first edition he stressed the effect of men's social situation more than the work of the imagination; in the second and the sixth editions he reversed the emphasis" (1975: 94).

18 Reflecting on the principles of self-estimation and self-command, Smith draws a distinction between "the idea of complete propriety and perfection" and the standard of some "common degree of excellence which is usually attained" (TMS I.i.5.9/10). The wise and virtuous tend to judge from the ideal standard, while the rich and powerful, supported by their wealth, have to maintain only an ordinary degree of propriety to acquire respect and admiration. Most people focus in self-evaluation on the second and average standard, and consequently are prone to excessive self-estimation. The desire to imitate and emulate the rich only stimulates this inclination.

19 Smith is careful to avoid any unqualified claims. See Schumacher (2016) for Smith's position on the 'rich country-poor country' debate.

References

Alvey, J.E. (1998). Adam Smith's three strikes against commercial society. *International Journal of Social Economics*, vol. 25(9): 1425–41.

Alvey, J.E. (2003). Adam Smith's view of history; consistent or paradoxical. *History of the Human Sciences*, vol. 16(2): 1–25.

Aspromourgos, T. (2009). *The Science of Wealth: Adam Smith and the framing of political economy*. London/New York: Routledge.

Birch, T.D. (1998). An analysis of Adam Smith's theory of charity and the problems of the poor. *Eastern Economic Journal*, vol. 24(1): 25–41.

Broadie, A. (2006). Sympathy and the impartial spectator. In: *The Cambridge Companion to Adam Smith*, Haakonssen, K. (ed.), Cambridge/New York: Cambridge University Press.

Brown, V. (1994). *Adam Smith's Discourse*. London: Routledge.

Coase, R.W. (1976). Adam Smith's view of man. *Journal of Law and Economics*, vol. 19(3): 529–46.

Colletti, L. (1972). *From Rousseau to Lenin: studies in ideology and society*. London: NLB.

Danner, P.L. (1976). Sympathy and exchangeable value: keys to Adam Smith's social philosophy. *Review of Social Economy*, vol. 34(3): 317–31.

Diatkine, D. (2010). Vanity and the love of system in Theory of Moral Sentiments. *European Journal of the History of Economic Thought*, vol. 17(3): 383–404.

Dickey, L. (1986). Historicizing the 'Adam Smith problem': conceptual, historiographical, and textual issues. *Journal of Modern History*, vol. 58(3): 579–609.

Elsner, W. (1989). Adam Smith's model of the origins and emergence of institutions: the modern findings of the classical approach. *Journal of Economic Issues*, vol. 23(1): 189–213.

Evensky, J. (1987). The two voices of Adam Smith: moral philosopher and social critic. *History of Political Economy*, vol. 19(3): 447–68.

Evensky, J. (1989). The evolution of Adam Smith's view on political economy. *History of Political Economy*, vol. 21(1): 123–45.

Evensky, J. (2005). *Adam Smith's Moral Philosophy*. Cambridge: Cambridge University Press.

Evensky, J. (2011). Adam Smith's essentials: on trust, faith, and free markets. *Journal of the History of Economic Thought*, vol. 33(2): 249–67.

Finkelstein, A. (2000). Nicolas Barbon and the quality of infinity. *History of Political Economy*, vol. 32(1): 83–102.

Fleischacker, S. (2004). *On Adam Smith's Wealth of Nations: A Philosophical Companion.* Princeton, NJ, and Oxford: Princeton University Press.

Force, P. (1997). Self-love, identification, and the origin of political economy. *Yale French Studies*, vol. 92: 46–64.

Force, P. (2003). *Self-Interest before Adam Smith: a genealogy of economic science.* Cambridge: Cambridge University Press.

Garbo, L. (2016). Adam Smith's last teachings: dialectic wisdom. *Journal of the History of Economic Thought*, vol. 38(1): 41–54.

Haakonssen, K. (1981). *The Science of the Legislator: the natural jurisprudence of David Hume and Adam Smith.* Cambridge: Cambridge University Press.

Hanley, R.P. (2008). Commerce and corruption: Rousseau's diagnosis and Adam Smith's cure. *European Journal of Political Theory*, vol. 7(2): 137–58.

Heilbroner, R.L. (1973). The paradox of progress: decline and decay in the Wealth of Nations. *Journal of the History of Ideas*, vol. 34(2): 243–62.

Heilbroner R.L. (1982). The socialization of the individual in Adam Smith. *History of Political Economy*, vol. 14(3): 427–39.

Hill, L. (2006). Adam Smith and the theme of corruption. *The Review of Politics*, vol. 68(4): 636–62.

Hill, L. (2012). Adam Smith on *thumos* and irrational economic 'man'. *European Journal of the History of Economic Thought*, vol. 19(1): 1–22.

Himmelfarb, G. (1984). *The Idea of Poverty; England in the Early Industrial Age.* New York: Alfred A. Knopf.

Hollander, S. (1977). Adam Smith and the self-interested axiom. *Journal of Law and Economics*, vol. 20(1): 133–52.

Hont, I. (2006). The early Enlightenment debate on commerce and luxury. In: *The Cambridge history of eighteenth-century political thought*, Volume 1, Goldie, M. and Wokler, R. (eds), Cambridge: Cambridge University Press, pp. 379–418.

Hont, I. (2015). *Politics in Commercial Society; Jean-Jacques Rousseau and Adam Smith.* Edited by B. Kapossy and M. Sonenscher. Cambridge/London: Harvard University Press.

Horne, T.A. (1981). Envy and commercial society: Mandeville and Smith on "Private Vices, Public Benefits". *Political Theory*, vol. 9(4): 551–69.

Hume, David (1981). *A Treatise of Human Nature.* Edited by L.A. Selby-Bigge; second edition. Oxford: Clarendon Press.

Hume, David (1987). *Essays, Moral, Political, and Literary.* Edited by E.F. Miller; revised edition. Indianapolis, IN: Liberty Press.

Hundert, E.G. (1994). *The Enlightenment's Fable: Bernard Mandeville and the discovery of society.* Cambridge: Cambridge University Press.

Hundert, E.G. (2003). Mandeville, Rousseau and the political economy of fantasy. In: *Luxury in the Eighteenth Century: debates, desires and delectable goods*, Berg, M. and Eger, E. (eds), Basingstoke: Palgrave, pp. 28–40.

Hurtado Prieto, J. (2004). Bernard Mandeville's heir: Adam Smith or Jean Jacques Rousseau on the possibility of economic analysis. *European Journal of the History of Economic Thought*, vol. 11(1): 1–31.

Ignatieff, M. (1990), *The Needs of Strangers.* London: Hogarth Press.

Jack, M. (1978). One state of nature: Mandeville and Rousseau. *Journal of the History of Ideas*, vol. 39(1): 119–24.

Lovejoy, A.O. (1961). *Reflections on Human Nature*. Baltimore: The John Hopkins Press.

Mandeville, Bernard (1988[1724]). *The Fable of the Bees or Private Vices, Publick Benefits*. Edited by F.B. Kaye; 2 volumes. Indianapolis, IN: Liberty Classics.

Meek, R.L. (1954). Adam Smith and the classical concept of profit. *Scottish Journal of Political Economy*, vol. 1(2): 138–53.

Mehta, P.B. (2006). Self interest and other interests. In: *The Cambridge Companion to Adam Smith*, Haakonseen, K. (ed.), Cambridge: Cambridge University Press, pp. 246–69.

Montes, L. (2003). Das Adam Smith problem: its origins, the stages of the current debate, and one implication for our understanding of sympathy. *Journal of the History of Economic Thought*, vol. 25(1): 63–90.

Montesquieu, Charles de Secondat, (1989[1748]). *The Spirit of the Laws*. Translated and edited by A.M. Cohler, B.C. Miller and H.S. Stone. Cambridge: Cambridge University Press.

Muller, J.Z. (1995). *Adam Smith in his Time and Ours: Designing the Decent Society*. Princeton, NJ: Princeton University Press.

Nieli, R. (1986). Spheres of intimacy and the Adam Smith problem. *Journal of the History of Ideas*, vol. 47(4): 611–24.

O'Neal, J.C. (1986). Rousseau's theory of wealth. *History of European Ideas*, vol. 7(5): 453–67.

Otteson, J. (2002). Adam Smith's marketplace of morals. *Archiv fur Geschichte des Philosophie*, vol. 84(2): 190–211.

Pack, S.J. (1991). *Capitalism as a Moral System: Adam Smith's critique of the free market economy*. Aldershot: Edward Elgar.

Paganelli, M.P. (2010). The moralizing role of distance in Adam Smith: The Theory of Moral Sentiments as possible praise of commerce. *History of Political Economy*, vol. 42(3): 425–41.

Raphael, D.D. (1975). The impartial spectator. In: *Essays on Adam Smith*, Skinner, A.S. and Wilson, T. (eds), Oxford: Clarendon Press, pp. 83–99.

Rasmussen, D.C. (2008). *The Problems and Promise of Commercial Society: Adam Smith's response to Rousseau*. University Park, PA: The Pennsylvania State University Press.

Rasmussen, D.C. (2013). Adam Smith and Rousseau: Enlightenment and counter-Enlightenment. In: *The Oxford Handbook of Adam Smith*, Berry, C.J., Paganelli, M.P. and Smith, C. (eds), Oxford: Oxford University Press, pp. 57–78.

Robertson, J. (2005). *The Case for the Enlightenment: Scotland and Naples 1680–1760*. Cambridge: Cambridge University Press.

Rosenberg, N. (1960). Some institutional aspects of the Wealth of Nations. *Journal of Political Economy*, vol. 18(6): 557–70.

Rosenberg, N. (1968). Adam Smith, consumer tastes, and economic growth. *Journal of Political Economy*, vol. 76(2): 361–74.

Rosenberg, N. (1990). Adam Smith and the stock of moral capital. *History of Political Economy*, vol. 22(1): 1–17.

Ross, I.S. (1995). *The Life of Adam Smith*. Oxford: Clarendon Press.

Rothschild, E. (2002). *Economic Sentiments: Adam Smith, condorcet and the Enlightenment*. Cambridge/London: Harvard University Press.

Rothschild, E. and A. Sen, (2006). Adam Smith's economics. In: *The Cambridge Companion to Adam Smith*, Haakonssen, K. (ed.), Cambridge: Cambridge University Press, pp. 319–65.

Rousseau, J.J. (1964). *The First and Second Discourses*. Edited by R.D. Masters. New York: St Martin's Press.

Rousseau, J.J. (2011[1752]). *Preface to Narcisse, or the Lover of Himself.* Translated by Samuel Webb from Oeuvres completes de J.J. Rousseau, retrieved from www.marxists.org/reference/subject/economics/rousseau/narcisse, 4–6-2013.

Sagar, P. (2016). Smith and Rousseau, after Hume and Mandeville. *Political Theory*, published online June 29. https://doi.org/10.1177/0090591716656459.

Schumacher, R. (2016). Adam Smith and the "rich country-poor country" debate: eighteenth-century views on economic progress and international trade. *European Journal of the History of Economic Thought*, vol. 23(5): 764–93.

Smith, Adam (1976a[1759]). *The Theory of Moral Sentiments.* Edited by A.L. Macfie and D.D. Raphael. Oxford: Clarendon Press.

Smith, Adam (1976b[1776]). *An Inquiry into the Causes and Nature of the Wealth of Nations.* Edited by R.H. Campbell and A.S. Skinner. Oxford: Clarendon Press.

Smith, Adam (1977). *The Correspondence of Adam Smith.* Edited by E.C. Mossner and I.S. Ross. Oxford: Clarendon Press.

Smith, Adam (1978). *Lectures on Jurisprudence.* Edited by R.L. Meek, D.D. Raphael and L.G. Stein. Oxford: Clarendon Press.

Smith, Adam (1980[1755]). Letter to the Edinburgh Review. In: *Essays on Philosophical Subjects*, Ross, I.S. (ed.), Oxford: Clarendon Press.

Verburg, R. (2000). Adam Smith's growing concern on the issue of distributive justice. *European Journal of the History of Economic Thought*, vol. 7(1): 23–44.

West, E.G. (1971). Adam Smith and Rousseau's discourse on inequality: inspiration or provocation? *Journal of Economic Issues*, vol. 5(2): 56–70.

Winch, D. (1996). *Riches and Poverty: an intellectual history of political economy in Britain 1750–1834.* Cambridge: Cambridge University Press.

Winch, D. (1997). Adam Smith's problem and ours. *Scottish Journal of Political Economy*, vol. 44(4): 384–402.

Zak, P. (2008). *Moral Markets: The Critical Role of Values in the Economy.* Princeton, NJ: Princeton University Press.

5 Self-interest after Smith
From passion to behavioural assumption

Turn of the tide

In the last decade of the eighteenth century a page was turned. Ideas, beliefs, sentiments and preoccupations were caught in a maelstrom of revolutionary developments. Frames of reference and hence interpretations and meanings changed. All this greatly affected political economy. There is a world of difference between Smith's *The Wealth of Nations* and Malthus's *Essay on Population* (Rothschild 2002). As a matter of course it affected the ideas on commerce, wealth and virtue that had preoccupied the eighteenth century. The vision of society that had been developed at the time emphasised how, animated by man's passions, the exchange of ideas, ways, goods and knowledge not only created wealth but also refinement of tastes, manners and morals. Industry, commerce and the arts advanced together and were all part of a civilising process. Dissenting voices like Rousseau's told a less hopeful narrative, claiming the incompatibility of commercial society and virtue. As the commercial spirit spread and infected human relationships, virtue and manners were believed to corrode, undermining the polity and its benefits. Proponents and opponents varied in their assessments of commercial society according to their ideas about the interaction of antagonistic forces operating in society. After all, human nature harbours a love of society, compassion and a need for approbation but also a bent for dissension and domination, and given the chance, a proclivity for using illegitimate and fraudulent means to satisfy wants. As a consequence, social forces move between cooperation and cohesion on the one hand, and conflict and dissension on the other.

The optimism usually attributed to the philosophers of the Enlightenment may be associated with the belief in the possibility to balance out these antagonistic forces and direct their dynamic interaction towards cooperation, trust and progress. This belief was built upon the idea that man's passions were natural and good rather than destructive. Nevertheless, man's passions may easily lead him astray. Fortunately the second building-block of the optimism of the age helped out. Taking in the idea of some providential order in social phenomena which can be known, the eighteenth century developed the idea of the constructability of society once such knowledge was put into the service of humanity. Philosophers searched for patterns in the interaction of passions and institutions safeguarding the social utility of the passions for the common good.

In the context of the debate on commercial society, the concept of interest became the gravitational force from which to understand the social universe. In the course of two centuries, 'interest' had shifted from collectivity to the individual and from the political domain to the economic sphere. In the eighteenth century, self-interest was seen as originating in self-love – man's natural care for his own well-being – cohering with other passions. "[B]ound up with and overlaid by other psychological propensities" (Winch 1996: 107), self-interest was seen to hold a neutral middle position between pride and praiseworthiness and between greed and public spiritedness, that is, if set in an appropriate institutional environment. Self-interest was first and foremost about balancing passions and sentiments. This equally applied to self-interest in the context of exchange relations. Passions are ubiquitously involved in the motivational forces of economic behaviour (desire for gain, vanity), in restraints upon behaviour ('reputation'), with reason being subservient in figuring out the best way to realise the objectives set by man's passions and imagination. Hence the idea of interest as the rational, innocuous form of greed, checked by considerations of need and utility. Crucial to this transposition of self-love and greed into self-interest was the development of the idea of mutual gain of trade and commerce. The cross fertility involved in trade and commerce implies that individuals and nations advance together, whereby everyone has a stake in cooperation.

The concept of self-interest in Smith is part of this language of commerce, virtue and liberty. *The Wealth of Nations* was a milestone in the debate on the nature and growth of commercial societies as a process of civilisation. Self-interest is about identity. It is relational, context-bound, in flux, and virtuous if it strikes a balance between extremes of various passions. Moreover, self-interest is the '*trait d'union*' between passions and institutions. In this framework of thought, self-interest is a strong and calm passion predominant among the passions, supported by socialisation, institutional encouragement and restraint. Although institutions develop through a process of trial and error over the centuries, the idea of politics is to make laws and institutional arrangements that provide a structure of incentives and disincentives so as to create a positive-sum society in which man's self-interest works for the benefit of all. Without the proper institutional framework of society, the pursuit of self-interest may produce malevolent social outcomes. Given man's unsociable sociability and changing circumstances, any balance is temporal, tentative and never self-evident.

Conditions and ideas, however, changed in a maelstrom of revolutionary developments. Economic activity, output and population increased in Britain in the last quarter of the eighteenth century as industrialisation took off. The last decade saw how the French Revolution digressed into terror and war, how wartime conditions coupled with bad harvests and increasing demand led to scarcity and soaring food prices, whereby, amidst prosperity, growing numbers were unable to provide for themselves and forced to apply for public relief. As Winch observed: "Smith's followers confronted a society and an intellectual world that was different from that envisaged by Smith" (1996: 8). Political economy came to be seen in a new frame of reference and was made to serve new purposes. For some, political economy became a vehicle for their ideas of reform. Others rose against political economy as an affront to humanity or as a vehicle of aristocratic class interests in its defence of the status quo. Either way, political economy found itself in the frontline of debates on society, progress, (in)equality and reform, which was bound to influence its development as a science. All of these developments reverberate in the changing conceptual contents and role of self-interest in political economy. This chapter aims to describe the vicissitudes of the concept of (self-)interest after Smith in English classical political economy. The following section relates how the debate on order, reform and progress was fired up in the 1790s, challenging political economy and the gravitational force and beneficial effects of self-interest. Defending Smith's 'system of optimism' against conservative and radical allegations, Malthus reframed political economy by highlighting laws of nature and conditions of scarcity and diminishing returns, reaffirming the primacy of self-interest (discussed in the third section). In the decades that followed, political economy detached itself from issues of morals and politics. For various reasons the Philosophical Radicals (fourth section) and the Oriel Noetics (fifth section) developed political economy into an abstract-deductive science in which self-interest was made to serve as a psychological assumption from which all reasoning ensued in determining unequivocal consequences (sixth section). Stripping self-interest of the usual behavioural checks and balances, however, did away with the theory of limits that separated self-interest from greed (seventh section). Finally, conclusions are drawn.

A new frame of reference unfolding

The eighteenth-century vision of commercial society, its assumptions, benefits and Smithian political economy were taken to task from 1789 onwards as ink started to flow in assessing the unfolding processes of democratisation and industrialisation. Initially, the prospects held out by revolutionary developments in France appealed to many. The old order, with its curtailments of freedom, its inequalities and lack of promises of progress and happiness, was no God-given and immutable entity, but a man-made product and therefore subject to improvement and reconstruction by applying reason and scientific principles. Happiness was within reach for all. However, endorsement soon turned into alarm and it was not long before conservative, anti-revolutionary forces were up in arms. Upon the winds of change, a new climate of opinion emerged in Britain in the last decade of the eighteenth century. Supporters and opponents discussed the merits of the French Revolution and the feasibility of reform and progress (Butler 1993). Views clashed on human nature, the role of institutions, politics and the relationship between commerce and virtue. Political economy was caught up in the debate between conservative and radical forces, represented here by two of its most prominent spokesmen, Edmund Burke and William Godwin.

Edmund Burke (1729–97), an Irishman who built a career as a statesman and political philosopher in England (Bromwich 2014), penned down his passionate aversion to the turn of events across the Channel in *Reflections on the Revolution in France* (1976[1790]). Against the enlightened view of the immanent victory of reason through rational reform, he argued that human behaviour is governed by habit and tradition. People are driven by their passions and need the guiding and restraining hand of rules and institutions. Established institutions, traditions and customs are the proven ways to get things done properly and as such represent the accumulated experience and reason of ages. It is an illusion to think that society can be reformed upon abstract principles; individual reason is far too limited to perform such a practical task. Consequently,

> it is with infinite caution that any man ought to venture upon pulling down an edifice which has answered in any tolerable degree for ages the common purposes of society, or on building it up again, without having models and patterns of approved utility before his eyes.
>
> (Burke 1976[1790]: 152)

Casting aside traditional values and social structures to build up society anew on abstract principles could only yield dire bull-in-a-china-shop consequences. The Scottish school, following Montesquieu, had wrongly supposed that trade and commerce brought about a process of civilisation, promoting refinement, polished manners and enlightenment. This view, Burke contended, mistakes the effect for its cause: "Even commerce, and trade, and manufacture, the gods of our oeconomical politicians, are themselves perhaps but creatures; are themselves but effects, which, as first causes, we choose to worship" (*ibid.*: 174). Instead, it is the "historical edifice of manners", build upon "clerical learning and feudal chivalry", on which "the possibility of commerce" depends (Pocock 1986: 199). If this edifice of manners is "trodden down under the hoofs of a swinish multitude" (Burke 1976[1790]: 173), property and commerce would wither away, drying up the benefits of material and moral growth. Against the feverish zeal of radicals to reconstruct society, Burke lamented the loss of chivalric manners, the true source of development and civilisation. Chivalry was destroyed by "this new conquering empire of light and reason" (*ibid.*: 171). The philosophy of this empire had shown itself to be "the offspring of cold hearts and muddy understandings, and which is as void of solid wisdom, as it is destitute of all taste and elegance" (*ibid.*: 171). It will not work if laws and institutions are constructed upon considerations of utility, force and private interest without some sense that individuals are part of a larger whole: "Nothing is left which engages the affections on the part of the commonwealth" (*ibid.*: 172). With much sense of drama, Burke proclaimed: "the age of chivalry is gone. – That of sophisters, oeconomists, and calculators, has succeeded; and the glory of Europe is extinguished for ever" (*ibid.*: 170).

In the conservatives' view, political economy became a likely suspect on which to pin part of the blame for the onslaught on traditional order and its values (Coleman 2004: 33). Political economy – Quesnay, DuPont de Nemours, Turgot and Smith – had been instrumental in unleashing the forces of rationalisation, individualisation and secularisation. As such it had called up forces antagonistic to social order and had contributed "to separate and tear asunder the bonds of . . . community, and to dissolve it into an unsocial, uncivil, unconnected chaos of elementary principles" (Burke 1976[1790]: 195). Conservative philosophers found the reduction of society to a mechanical system composed of functional parts hard to stomach. They typically argued that society was to be seen as an organic whole. The way these parts interact, rely upon each other and suffer together could in no way be accounted for on the basis of a mechanical philosophy ruled by reason and self-interest. Burke identified the 'oeconomists' with the mechanistic and constructivist philosophy that he held responsible for the "new conquering empire of light and reason", through which a spirit of calculation and self-regard reigned in society.

While abhorred by conservative thinkers, the idea of reforming society on the basis of transparent principles was paramount in the minds of utopian thinkers like Condorcet and Godwin. A new order was shaping up under the influence of democratisation and industrialisation, displacing the traditional order and its hierarchical structure that had given the propertied classes the power and means of control to preserve their privileged position. The time was rife to update order on the basis of scientific knowledge of the principles and mechanisms through which society worked, and in the firm conviction of humanity being guided by enlightened reason.

In *An Enquiry Concerning Political Justice* (1793), the minister and political philosopher William Godwin (1756–1836) (Locke 1980) took up the challenge to respond to Burke. Chivalry? Aristocratic society has produced an institutional system of property, injustices and inequalities through which people were oppressed and enslaved. "Indeed 'the age of chivalry is' not 'gone!' The feudal spirit still survives, that reduced the great mass of mankind to the rank of slaves and cattle for the service of a few" (1793 II: VIII.II.800). Instead of passions, it is institutions that are up to no good, and government in particular. Man and society are perfectible, if only institutions of 'divide and rule' like property, marriage and government would be removed from society and were no longer able to exercise their coercing obstruction to the growth of reason. Establishing a system of equality in an anarchistic, non-political society and enlightening people by reason, people would be content, altruistic and just. Instead of taking self-love as the basic trait of human nature, Godwin argued that self-love and egoism are a reflection of the state of society and its institutions, which can be remedied by applying the principles of reason and equality to reform society.

With equal passion Godwin set out to destroy Burke's claims about the historical edifice of manners from which the benefits of prosperity and luxury were supposed to result, criticising Smith's 'system of optimism' in his stride. He considered the division of labour "the offspring of avarice" (*ibid.*: VIII. VI.859), while accumulation was founded upon rivalry and vanity. He denied prosperity and luxury the status of 'public benefits' and objected to the way institutions shaped incentives and opportunities to generate these bitter fruits. Inequality, upheld by law and government and rooted in the abuse of power and fraud, amounts to "the perpetual spectacle of injustice", leading men astray in their desires by fixing the mind on the acquisition of wealth. "The ostentation of the rich perpetually goads the spectator to the desire of opulence" (*ibid.*: VIII.II.802), at the expense of real virtues like sobriety, integrity, industry and benevolence.

> To acquire wealth and to display it, is therefore the universal passion. The whole structure of human society is made a system of the narrowest selfishness . . . Wealth is acquired by overreaching our neighbours, and is spent in insulting them.
>
> (Godwin 1793 II: VIII.II.802)

In undermining virtue and promoting avarice and rivalry, the benefits of luxury are illusory while the system of property, cooperation and commerce, upheld by government through which these so-called benefits are secured, only produce the social evils of poverty and misery. Godwin described a system of property and accumulation, driven by greed to rival one another, designed to appropriate at the expense of others, creating conditions of wealth for some and poverty for most. The rich man appropriates the fruits of the work of others for purposes of display and vanity. In squandering labour to produce luxuries, "he will be found, when rightly considered, their enemy" (1823[1797]: 159). Manners? The whole system, with no benefits to boast of, rests upon and promotes selfishness.

The good news is that these social evils are remediable and selfishness can be replaced by benevolence, if conditions of equality are established. Godwin reaffirmed the reformer's message of hope by claiming that the misery, unhappiness and vices of man are products of an unequal and unjust society. These social evils are man-made so they can be unmade. What if we build a system that rules out exclusion from the benefits? If society was reformed and its inequality-producing institutions like property and marriage abolished, misery and poverty would be banished from society and benevolence would rule among men. Godwin proposed a system of equality in which everyone would have the right to security of subsistence. He acknowledged that such a system might induce population growth. However, population pressure would not be a threat if property rights did not restrict agricultural production, hampering the operation of the principle of population, whereby population would adjust to its natural level, i.e. the level of the means of subsistence.[1] Moreover, by no means is luxury necessary as an incentive to industry and growth of population.[2] Commerce and wealth are the outgrowth of a society, set by conditions of inequality and dependence, and driven by greed and vanity. If Mandeville and Rousseau were right in pointing out the necessity of luxury and inequality, and therefore the vices of greed and vanity to arrive at an age of polished manners and humanity, we are not stuck forever. "We may throw down the scaffolding, when the edifice is complete" (Godwin cited in Waterman 1991: 49).

A curtain was drawn in the 1790s. A new climate of opinion developed as conservative and radical forces discussed order, reform and progress. The debate struck at the root of political economy as it had shaped up in the eighteenth century. It questioned the positive-sum society, in which all would share in the growth of wealth, knowledge and virtue: its driving forces, its cause-and-effect relationships and its benefits. It put constituent concepts and ideas of political economy in a new context, changing their meaning.

In the second part of the eighteenth century, the excitement over Mandeville's confronting claims about the incompatibility of wealth and virtue had died away and most agreed that self-interest or self-love was no more than a natural, proper and healthy regard for man's own well-being, and as such neither reason for moral indignation nor moral acclaim. Undermining the interdependence of passions and institutions, however, the debate upset this hard-won consensus on the moral neutrality of self-interest. Burke distrusted man's passions and emphasised the need for institutional restraints for their control. By contrast, Godwin identified coercion and institutional restraints as the prime obstacles to the perfectibility of man, and called for their removal. A new frame of reference was built, one which had no use for the concept of interest as a balance of sentiments, of which its constructive and beneficial nature depends on the positive interaction with its institutional environment.

Once more self-regard became an issue, as the notion of self-interest was knocked off its pedestal. "A preoccupation with egoism emerged in the wake of the French Revolution partly because the Revolution seemed to discredit the Enlightenment's favoured positions, including its trust in self-interest" (Coleman 2004: 140). Egoism, linked to individualism, autonomy and independence, was seen to destroy communitarian values, honour and compassion and the established order and authority. To emphasise its pejorative or depreciative meaning, egoism was contrasted with compassion and altruism, setting the parameters for the challenge. Political economy was drawn into this challenge given the prominent position of self-interest, whereby it represented a suitable target for criticism. Rallying against self-interest meant rallying against political economy. The more self-interest was interpreted in terms of selfishness and egoism, the more political economy was seen to conflict with common humanity and compassion, and the more the idea of self-interest as being uniform and invariable was considered unacceptable. Egoism reflected the state of society rather than providing an adequate description of human nature. This point of view effectively called into question the idea that self-interest, or the drive to better one's condition, can be taken as the uniform and invariable principle of human nature from which the natural order of things may be understood. And if the principles of political economy by which the mechanical operation of society was explained were to be questioned, then how could its conclusions be trusted, let alone its acclaimed beneficial effects of growth of wealth, knowledge and virtue?

Although on opposite sides of the argument, Burke and Godwin held self-interest in ill repute. Burke's case for tradition and authority was built upon the fear of sapping the social ties and moral fibre of society, infusing society with vulgar self-interest through its rational reconstruction. Godwin argued that the cold-hearted selfishness of men is only permanent in a society driven by the vices cultivated by an institutional structure geared towards preferment and inequality. Both authors considered the other a representative of an ideology of selfishness, yet both dismissed the validity of the principle of self-interest to explain human action and society. When Thomas Robert Malthus joined the argument with his *Essay on the Principle of Population* (1798), he presented a third way "between Godwin's wholesale repudiation of institutions on the one hand, and an ultra-Burkean defence of the *ancient regime* on the other" (Waterman 1991: 144). Political economy was set up in a new décor.

Malthus's third way

Waterman qualified Malthus's attack upon Godwin's system of equality in the first *Essay* (1798) as "the centre-piece of the entire book" (1991: 40). It wasn't that Malthus did not sympathise with the ideal:

> it is impossible to contemplate the whole of this fair structure without emotions of delight and admiration, accompanied with an ardent longing for the period of its accomplishment. But, alas! that moment can never arrive. The whole is little better than a dream, a beautiful phantom of the imagination.
>
> (Malthus 1798: X.2)

Even worse, reform along the lines suggested by Godwin would result in a social equilibrium, in which, on the conditions set out by Godwin, people are worse off than with the status quo. To make his point, Malthus asked the reader to join him in a thought experiment of what would happen if Godwin's utopia were established. Private property and the institution of marriage, government, and thereby the (presumed) causes of vices and misery, are removed, equality has been established and the spirit of benevolence rules. Such a system is favourable to propagation and, given that population tends to increase faster than the means of subsistence, more labour is needed to generate enough subsistence. Give diminishing returns in agriculture, food production in the next period is unable to keep up with population growth and food per capita declines. The spirit of benevolence disappears and the law of self-preservation and man's selfish nature reassert themselves. In order to regulate things, institutions like private property and marriage are re-established. Governed by laws of nature, population growth sets in motion a process towards a new equilibrium which, instead of improvement, implies a physical and moral deterioration.

This short exercise is enough to show that Godwin is barking up the wrong tree. Malthus faulted Godwin for "attributing almost all the vices and misery that are seen in civil society to human institutions" (*ibid.*: X.2). The real causes of evil, Malthus submits, are the laws of nature and the passions of mankind. Basic characteristics of human nature together with basic facts of life produce regular tendencies following from the nature of things. Given the instinct to propagate, the struggle for existence is one such basic fact of life. The constant tendency of populations to increase beyond the means of subsistence naturally creates pressure of population and necessity, triggering self-preservation and self-interest. If population oversteps its mark, the checks of misery and vice equalise the forces of population and those of subsistence. Society is far less a man-made, social construction that can be reformed at will than utopian writers would like to think; the whole idea of improvement and perfectibility is a chimera. Any plan of reform that does not start from these laws of nature is bound for disaster.

Moreover, the key to unlock the laws of society is the principle of self-interest. It is a mistake to think that the natural goodness of man would reassert itself once institutions such as private property were abolished from society, removing the necessity to act selfishly out of considerations of self-preservation. It is an illusion to think that human nature will smell like roses once social circumstances have changed. In Smithian fashion, Malthus posits the view that self-love is "the master-spring, and moving principle of society" (*ibid.*: X.2). It may be softened but never replaced by benevolence and for good purpose too. For it is self-love that activates people to improve their condition and unintentionally shapes a process of growth and civilisation.

> It is to the established administration of property, and to the apparently narrow principle of self-love, that we are indebted for all the noblest exertions of human genius, all the finer and more delicate emotions of the soul, for every thing, indeed, that distinguishes the civilized, from the savage state; and no sufficient change, has as yet taken place in the nature of civilized man, to enable us to say, that he either is, or ever will be, in a state, when he may safely throw down the ladder by which he has risen to this eminence.
>
> (Malthus 1798: XV.6)

Malthus reaffirmed Smith's emphasis on the human drive to better his condition, and defended Smith's system of natural liberty within a framework of law and order against Godwin (Winch 1993). Institutions like private property and marriage are necessary to trigger man's self-love to act responsibly. Therefore Godwin was wrong to suppose that we can discard self-love and institutions and live happily ever after once a threshold stage of civilisation is reached by inappropriate means: it is the combination and interaction of self-love and institutions of property and marriage that create the preconditions for improvement.

With his rebuttal, "the *Essay on Population*, by deflecting both popular and scientific attention from the benign effects of wealth and wealth-creation to the seemingly malign consequences of resource scarcity and diminishing returns, created a whole new climate of opinion" (Waterman 2004: 119). Using population pressure as wrecking-bar to break down Godwin's argument, Malthus' third way zeroes in on interrelations between population growth, poverty, productivity, wage rates and economic growth, shifting emphasis from moral-political arguments to natural-economic laws (McNally 2000). Political economy is set in a whole new frame as Malthus, "not at all averse to making the flesh creep" (Robbins 1953: 75), describes in vivid colours the evil consequences of unrestrained population growth following from the inescapable logic of the two unequal ratios. Although his argument against Godwin made him emphasise the tendency for population to outrun food production in the absence of institutions to restrain population (Hollander 1986: 204), there was enough in the *Essay* to suggest that Malthus denied the possibility of improvement. As a consequence, he was seen to claim the inevitability of misery and vice and the futility of reform, spoiling the hope for infinite progress by claiming the reign of unconquerable laws of nature that turn each effort at improvement into Sisyphean labour.

From the second edition of the *Essay* (1803) onwards, Malthus more explicitly allowed a way out by adding another (preventive) check on population growth: moral restraint, or the rational decision to postpone marriage until one was able to afford a family without vice.[3] The extent to which misery and vice are inevitable depends on whether "self-love as the moving principle of society" (1798: XV.6) is activated, and institutions exist that promote conduct that takes long-run consequences into account. By setting forth the conditions under which the tendency of population to produce misery and vice could be subverted, Malthus felt that he underpinned rather than denied the possibility of improvement, sharing Hume's and Smith's belief in the benefits of commerce and manufactures:

> most of the effects of manufactures and commerce on the general state of society are in the highest degree beneficial. They infuse fresh life and activity into all classes of the state, afford opportunities for the inferior orders to rise by personal merit and exertion, and stimulate the higher orders to depend for distinction upon other grounds than mere rank and riches. They excite invention, encourage science and the useful arts, spread intelligence and spirit, inspire taste for conveniences and comforts among the labouring classes; and above all, give a new and happier structure to society, by increasing the proportion of the middle classes, that body on which the liberty, public spirit, and good government of every country must mainly depend.
>
> (Malthus, Observations on the Effects of the
> Corn Laws 1970[1814]: 118)

Although sharing conservative overtones, Malthus steered clear of Burke's reversed relationship between wealth and happiness/virtue. Neither did the social significance of institutions mean that all existing institutions were beyond criticism as pillars of accumulated wisdom and experience that uphold society. They may still mismanage incentives or be biased to certain interests and fail to prevent zero-sum outcomes. Malthus was well aware of the pitfalls of the established system of private property, law and institutions in its unwholesome effects upon the health, happiness and virtue of the labouring classes. He therefore argued that the key to politics and morals was the art of optimising:

> Many of the questions both in morals and politics seem to be of the nature of the problems of *de maximis et minimis* in Fluxions; in which there is always a point where a certain effect is the greatest, while on the either side of this point it gradually diminishes.
>
> (Malthus 1970[1814]: 119; italics in original)

The legislator's work of creating the conditions for positive-sum outcomes is never done.

Malthus, as well as the other English classical economists, propagated the superiority of a system of economic freedom – organising production through the institutions of private property and the market to the end of consumption – on the assumption of a suitable framework of law and order (Robbins 1953). They sought improvements by extending and diffusing knowledge from "a sense of mission" (Grampp 1973: 360). As reformers, they critically examined the rules that defined the limits and latitude of freedom within which the free pursuit of self-interest could be expected to coordinate with the public good. At the same time, they inquired into the principles of economic action. This framework of thought distinguishes between the science of political economy and the science of politics and morals. The legislator aims to remedy or ameliorate undesirable outcomes, redesigning the motivational structure of society by trial and error. Consequently, the legislator's agenda and non-agenda are not fixed but change with changing circumstances.

Malthus aimed to counter Godwin's arguments in his first *Essay*, but he soon realised that his arguments had wider implications, which changed the décor in which political economy was set. For the argument of the two ratios and the evil consequences of unrestrained population growth in the face of scarcity of land and diminishing returns in agriculture also undermined the system of optimism by opening the possibility of a conflict between 'wealth' and 'happiness/virtue' and thereby "a conflict between the concerns of political economy strictly delimited, and those of a more general science of morals and politics" (Winch 1983: 63). Indeed, after defending Smith's system, Malthus pointed at a probable error in Smith's reasoning, arguing that Smith had been too hasty in considering an increase in wealth to be smoothly transformed into an improvement in the standard of living of the labouring classes. Smith's analysis allows for the possibility of rising wages and increasing population if the rate of capital accumulation exceeds the rate of growth of labour supply. Capital accumulation increases the funds available for paying wages, pushing wages upward. As a consequence, capital accumulation is the key factor in Smith's growth model and hence his insistence upon parsimony. As long as capitalists were not allowed to regulate the market by monopoly power, by conspiracy and/or rent-seeking, Smith's envisioned a positive-sum society in which the operating principles of a market economy would bring advance to all.

By contrast, Malthus reasoned that if more units of capital and labour are applied to agriculture in response to the evermore-pressing need to produce more food for a growing population, marginal product will fall (diminishing returns). Competition among labourers will drive down real wages (tending towards the subsistence level). Competition among employers will drive down the return to capital to the point where capital accumulation stops (at which point return to capital and labour equals marginal product) (Waterman 2012). With the proportion between population (labour supply) and resources (the wages fund) as the crucial ratio to be influenced to bring about material and immaterial improvement, the only way to improve the condition of the labouring classes is to diminish the birth rate by controlling passion and to practice moral restraint. The extent to which wealth can be transformed into virtue and happiness depends upon the habits of the labouring classes. These habits may be influenced by way of education (making people understand the consequences of their own conduct), duly supported by the legislator in creating a supportive institutional framework. Political economy is assigned the crucial task of exposing how population growth, poverty, productivity, wage rates and economic growth interrelate, showing how the various elements interact within a system of economic freedom. If people adjust their behaviour to the laws of nature uncovered by political economy, classes would be able to advance together.

Malthus concluded the first *Essay* with two chapters in which he explained his views on the telos or purpose of these laws of nature in the face of their attending misery and vice.[4] Malthus explained that God allowed the physical and moral evils that the laws of population brought about, to trigger the mind into activity. "Evil thus challenged men to shape their own destiny" (LeMahieu 1979: 471).[5] Malthus enraged many by claiming the necessity of misery and by the harshness with which he sometimes presented his contemporaries with the basic facts of life.[6] Denying the needy the right to subsistence, to compassion, to life, only showed with perfect clarity the depraved nature of political economy. Illustrating the change of climate that had developed, political economy came to be seen as reducing human beings to self-interested competitors on a course of misery and vice, and presenting "a hideous chain of paradoxes at apparent war with religion and humanity" (journal commentary quoted in Waterman 2004: 119). If Malthus had intended to uplift the status of political economy, his efforts were counterproductive.

Ricardian economics, Bentham's utilitarianism and the Philosophical Radicals

Robbins argued that the English classical school was "the first reform movement" to have developed "a comprehensive body of economic analysis" (1953: 176), on which its proposals for reform were built. Focusing exclusive attention on the science of political economy and abstracting from issues of politics and morals, it was David Ricardo who separated what Malthus had merely distinguished. Constructing a body of knowledge and positive facts, however, requires a purpose or goal for which it is meant to work (Robbins 1953: 177). For the Philosophical Radicals that goal was set out and explained by Bentham's utilitarianism. Under the energetic and inspiring leadership of James Mill, Bentham's 'science of politics and morals' was brought together with Ricardian political economy to further their political programme of reforming society to maximise happiness. In the first quarter of the nineteenth century, a group of reformers took hold of political economy in order to turn it into a vehicle for their ideas of reform: the Philosophical Radicals, a band of Bentham devotees, including James and John Stuart Mill, David Ricardo, Francis Place and others.

Ricardo had no use for the subtleties of the distinction between wealth and happiness, and considered questions on the relationship between wealth and happiness outside the province of political economy. Narrowing down his field of inquiry to the science of political economy proper, Ricardo took Smith's analytical model of the economic system and its explanation of economic growth for granted. However, some principles had been muddled over, so Ricardo set out to correct these deficiencies. Ricardo's fame as an economist had much to do with the way he made complex processes accessible. Cutting complex economic processes to a few well-defined strategic variables, and abstracting from their social and political context to fish out their systematic nature, he devised an analytical model and reasoned his way towards conclusions and prescriptions (Deane 1982). Underscoring Smith's emphasis on capital accumulation as the engine of the growth process and hence the strategic role of profits, Ricardo took the vicissitudes of the profit rate as the key to sustainable modern growth. However, inquiring into the long-term trend in profits only made sense within an integrated theory of the distribution of national product into rents, wages and profits. Ricardo mopped up Smith's inadequate views on rent and Malthus's inquiry into the question of whether wages and population can rise together, when he described in the preface of *On the Principles of Political Economy and Taxation* (1981[1817]: 5) the "principle problem in political economy" as "[t]o determine the laws which regulate this distribution" of produce between the three social classes in society, viz. landowners, capitalists and labourers".

Reasoning from Malthus's principle of population and diminishing returns in agriculture, Ricardo argued that population growth required more and more land to be turned into grain fields. Increasingly land would become less suitable and fertile, raising costs of production and hence the price of provisions and the wage rate. Farmers would see their profits fall. Conditions of scarcity of fertile land and diminishing returns under the pressure of population would gradually but inevitably bring capital accumulation to a halt, driving the economy into a stationary state.

In the hands of Ricardo and Mill, political economy moved away from the Smithian approach. "The transformation in method and epistemology as between *The Wealth of Nations* and Ricardo's *Principles*", Hutchison wrote, "seems sufficiently profound, extreme and consequential, as to justify the adjective 'revolutionary'" (1978: 26, 54).[7] Ricardian/Millian political economy had "little or no room for judgements of probabilities or qualifications, or for weighing up, or striking a balance between, contrasting tendencies, or for broadly political considerations" (Hutchison 1978: 45). On the contrary, the irresistible logic in the chain of reasoning from certain principles about the mechanics of wealth and scarcity was precisely what made political economy a perfect instrument of reform.

All classical economists, starting from the notion of some natural order in economic processes, pursued knowledge of the natural laws governing the economy. Yet the antagonism on method between its practitioners that was to develop into a full battle between Menger and Schmoller towards the end of the nineteenth century, was alight already in the era of classical economics (O'Brien 1975). One group followed in the steps of the Scottish school and its philosophical-historical approach, emphasising historical analysis and empirical investigation as techniques of analysis to build theoretical generalisations about economic reality. The second group, build up around David Ricardo and James Mill, employed the method of deductive logic to draw conclusions from *a priori* assumptions ('strong cases').[8] Given its focus on abstract reasoning, internal consistency and logical step-by-step inference, political economy is seen to partake in the characteristics of a mathematical science.

Although Malthus was a trained mathematician, he rejected the mechanical philosophy and geometrical method in favour of the historical-inductive method applied by Smith and the Scottish school. He tried to give counterweight to Ricardo and argued in his *Principles of Political Economy* (1968[1820]: 4) that "[t]he principal cause of error, and of the differences" of opinion among political economists concerned "a precipitate attempt to simplify and generalize". Such attempts usually do not admit the operation of more causes than one, combined with a "disinclination to allow of modifications, limitations, and exceptions to any rule or proposition", and "an unwillingness to bring their theories to the test of experience" (*ibid.*: 6, 8). The rise of theoretical economics, with Ricardo as the first 'pure' theorist, not only narrowed the scope of political economy. It also created a domain of inquiry, defined by hypothetical premises in which relationships between variables were established by logic rather than empirical observations. Drawing away from the real world, political economy set itself on a track separate from other social sciences.

Setting up political economy as a theoretical framework of deductive logic concerning the causes of wealth split up the 'how' from the 'why' of the economic system. It separated the science of political economy (the 'how') from the science of politics and morals (the 'why'). Bentham's utilitarianism was the answer to the latter. Whatever else it may be, Bentham's utilitarianism was a doctrine that proposed a way to solve the problem of how to prevent zero-sum or negative-sum outcomes as the unintended consequence of discrete acts of interacting individuals. It worked out a system that eliminates such outcomes by simple decision rules by which to calculate positive-sum outcomes, individually as well as collectively through the guiding hand of the legislator. As such it was brilliantly simple and a logical step in the debate. If previous systems, in being dependent upon the careful balancing of passions interacting with the institutional framework, only result in uncertain outcomes and questions of tangencies, perhaps it works if actions and institutions are scrutinised for their sum result in advance by applying the test of utility.

The English philosopher, reformer and eccentric Jeremy Bentham (1748–1832) built his ethical doctrine, (classical) utilitarianism, from ideas derived from Gay, Hartley, Helvetius, Hutcheson, Hume and Smith. Central to utilitarianism is the belief that human action is motivated by the desire to obtain pleasure and to avoid pain (psychological hedonism). Bentham defined 'interest' in these terms. An individual has an interest in something, if he expects to be able to derive pleasure from it or if it helps to prevent pain. He linked this notion of interest directly to 'utility':

> By utility is meant that property in any object, whereby it tends to produce benefit, advantage, pleasure, good, or happiness . . . or . . . to prevent the happening of mischief, pain, evil, or unhappiness to the party whose interest is considered.
>
> (Bentham 1982[1789]: 12)

The more value is attached to this pleasure or pain, determined in terms of quantities of pleasure and/or pain, the higher its utility and the stronger the interest. Given this exclusive focus on pleasure and pain, Bentham is usually thought to assume that man is essentially egoistic.[9]

Bentham's utilitarianism is also an ethical doctrine. It proclaims that happiness is the ultimate end of human action and thereby the ultimate measure of right and wrong. Consequently, the principle of utility is a moral standard by which actions, existing practices, laws and institutions can be measured as to their contribution to society's end, the happiness of its members. The nature of Bentham's ethics is consequentialist. The utilitarian claims that an action is not intrinsically good or bad. Instead, the value of an action depends on its consequences, viz. the way it affects the happiness of people in terms of pleasure and pain. Pecuniary interest, in itself neither good nor bad, may be judged as avarice if it turned out to have harmful consequences (*ibid.*: 130). That action which maximises the surplus of pleasures over pains (ethical hedonism) is morally right.

Emphatically Bentham argues that utilitarianism is not a purely individualistic doctrine: behaviour should be directed at maximising social happiness, the sum of pleasures of all individuals in society: "It is the greatest happiness of the greatest number that is the measure of right and wrong", as Bentham wrote in *Fragment on Government* (1823: vi). Having tied all human motivations to a single principle to be applied to the end of happiness, Bentham thought he had laid the foundations for the construction of a science of human happiness.

However, people may be ignorant or confused about their interests or biased in weighting their own pleasures and pains against those of others. How to align personal interest to the public interest? Bentham assigned this task to the legislator, who seeks to influence human choice to maximise happiness in society. Moral calculus offers the legislator a method to decide whether intervention is necessary (the agenda of government) or whether interests can be left free to play (the non-agenda). In the former case, the legislator (re)constructs interests (by creating or adding/subtracting pleasures or pains through benefits and sanctions) to influence people's calculations in their self-regarding acts, so that these acts accord with the public interest, i.e., the greatest happiness of the greatest number. For this reason, Halévy (1972) describes Bentham's utilitarian science of politics and morals as a science of the legislator who creates an artificial identity of interests by manipulating utilities. The legislator sizes up practices, laws and institutions by measuring their utility in promoting happiness. The fact that institutions and practices have existed for a long time, *pace* Burke, does not prove their value, but neither, *pace* Godwin, is it necessary to remove them from society. They can be screened by applying the test of utility.

Bentham subdivided the aim of the legal system, i.e. maximising happiness, into four subsidiary goals: subsistence, abundance, security and equality. He argued the primacy of security (of a person, his property, reputation and condition) as 'precondition to' rather than 'component part of' the pursuit of happiness. In the absence of security (without the ability to form stable expectations about the future), the other goals would never be realised. He also tried to develop maxims about the way goals are interrelated, noting for instance that growth of abundance improves conditions of equality. Within such a framework of legislative principles and civil code, Bentham discussed the science of political economy as being concerned with the goals of subsistence and abundance. He argued that government should abstain from intervening in the economy and best follow a policy of laissez-faire, granting economic freedom, given that each man is the best judge of his own interest. Bentham acknowledged that if wealth increased beyond mere subsistence and given diminishing marginal utility of wealth, his principle of happiness would support a policy of redistribution. Recognising the inherent conflict between the principles of security and equality, he claimed superiority of the principle of security (except in circumstances of dire need).

It was James Mill (1773–1836) who brought people and ideas together, who 'organised' the alternative vision of the Philosophical Radicals, and who became the driving force of their reform programme. James Mill did the marketing of Bentham's utilitarian views. He convinced Ricardo to write down his views on political economy, coaching him along the way, becoming "the evangel of the Ricardian movement, its St. Paul" (Grampp 1973: 360 n. 3). He mixed Bentham's views on government with ideas on government and liberty he had learned as a student from Dugald Stewart. As his son John Stuart wrote in his *Autobiography*: "he was a great centre of light to his generation. During his later years he was . . . the head and leader of the intellectual radicals in England" (Mill 1873: 205). James Mill argued that all humans seek happiness. Given nature's scanty provision of the means of happiness, people have to work for it. However, man has many desires and, loving his ease, has a natural inclination to take from others what he desires. In his *Essay on Government* (2015[1828]), Mill claimed that the chief task of government is to prevent encroachment upon the fruits of one's labour (and hence property) by others. In true Hobbesian style, Mill proclaimed this desire for power to be boundless, and therefore only the community as a whole can be relied upon not to abuse its power. Based on self-evident laws of human nature, Mill built a science of government by logical inference and deduction. He amplified Bentham's view that rulers are far more likely to further their own interests than to promote the happiness of the community, and given these 'sinister interests', only a regime of representative democracy would give rulers the incentive to act in the interests of the community.

In the same undiluted, uncompromising way, with the full force of deductive logic behind it, Mill presented a schoolbook-version of Ricardian economics in his *Elements of Political Economy* (1821). Starting from some self-evident axioms about human nature, Mill reduced political economy to a set of logical propositions, taking the pupil by the hand to demonstrate the unquestionable truth of his conclusions. Setting political economy up as a closed, mechanical model, Mill tried to detach it from its historical, institutional social and moral context, developing political economy into a branch of deductive logic (Mazlish 1975: 99). In this world, inhabited by economic man driven by selfish interests, the happiness of the labouring classes depends upon the growth of the productive powers of the instruments of production. Although only growth allows society to advance beyond a zero-sum game,[10] this is only temporary. Growth of the productive powers of the instruments of production depends upon the increase of capital. Arguing in Ricardian fashion that "rent may be left altogether out of the question" (1965[1844]: 70), Mill describes a zero-sum game between profits and wages ("whatever . . . increases the share of the one diminishes that of the other, and *vice versa*" (*ibid*.: 70)). Discussing wages first, Mill argued:

> Universally, then, we may affirm, that, other things remaining the same, if the ratio which capital and population bear to one another remains the same, wages will remain the same; if the ration which capital bears to population increases, wags will rise; if the ratio which population bears to capital increases, wages will fall. From this law, clearly understood, it is easy to trace the circumstances which, in any country, determine the condition of the great body of the people.
>
> (Mill 1965[1844]: 44)

Demonstrating on the basis of psychological premises and logic that capital does not tend to increase as fast as population, Mill claims to have demonstrated beyond doubt that wages have a tendency to fall. It is of the utmost importance, Mill urges, to find the means of limiting the birth rate (*ibid.*: 65), when the return on capital is still high and a large surplus remains. Mill follows Hume and Smith in praising the middle ranks as the most active in pursuing knowledge and ways to better their condition and contribute to wisdom, virtue and happiness.

> the men of middling fortunes, in short, the men to whom society is generally indebted for its greatest improvements, are the men, who, having their time at their own disposal, freed from the necessity of manual labour, subject to no man's authority, and engaged in the most delightful occupations, obtain, as a class, the greatest sum of human enjoyment. For the happiness, therefore, as well as the ornament of our nature, it is peculiarly desirable that a class of this description would form as large a proportion of each community as possible.
>
> (Mill 1965[1844]: 64)

Mill worked with unflagging zeal to win people over to the Philosophical Radicals' reform programme. Political reform should be focused unto the middle ranks as the bearers of civilisation and democratisation by a more general suffrage (emphasising that the lower classes follow the lead of the middle ranks). Material progress first required population growth to be limited by birth control and, on that condition, would produce a tendency towards more equality (which was not to be had at the expense of security of property). If the dissemination of knowledge would lead to the association of pleasure and pain with public benefits, individuals would learn to coordinate their privately motivated actions with the public interest.

In Philosophical Radicalism, political economy was developed into a strict science, separated from the science of politics and morals, setting up a mechanical, abstract model of the economic world. This new theoretical world required a matching abstract man: economic man. Mechanical man, moving on the principle of self-interest, inhabited this mechanised world of production and consumption. In plain words Bentham wrote:

> That principle of action is most to be depended upon, whose influence is most powerful, most constant, most uniform, most lasting, and most general among mankind. Personal interest is that principle: a system of economy built on any other foundation, is built upon quicksand.
>
> (Bentham in Stark 2004: 433)

Ricardo took self-interest as basic to all reflections on political economy, presenting conclusions deduced from the premise of self-interest as ironclad laws of nature.

These two features are strongly related. The Radicals sought to create a social science modelled after the exact sciences, allowing measurement, geometry and mechanics. Science was seen to explain things by reduction, by breaking phenomena into simple abstract elements without circumstantial frippery. In the case of political economy and in the science of the legislator, these simple elements were individuals driven by self-interest (measured in terms of quantities of pleasures and pains). Allowing other motives and passions into the picture, as well as emergent properties not reducible to individual entities, would undermine the whole project of creating an exact, social science (Halévy 1972: 467). Moreover, Halévy continued, the Utilitarians sought to rehabilitate egoism as "the necessary condition of all the social virtues" (1972: 477). Man must attain a certain level of well-being or happiness before he will care for others, and given that this includes the command over external goods, it requires man to possess sagacity, prudence and all other egoistical virtues. Egoism

> is the moral code of a new era which Bentham and James Mill are promulgating. It is no longer the religious or aristocratic, ascetic or chivalrous morality which makes current antipathies and sympathies the sentimental rule of its practical judgments, which exalts the rare and showy virtues, and recommends to the masses, in the interest of a governing class, humility or sacrifice. It is a plebeian or rather a bourgeois morality, devised for working artisans and shrewd tradesmen, teaching subjects to take up the defence of their interests; it is a reasoning, calculating and prosaic morality. The morality of the Utilitarians is their economic psychology put into the imperative.
>
> (Halévy 1972: 477–8)

Philosophical radicalism, as John Stuart Mill was to dub the doctrine of reform founded upon Bentham's utilitarianism and Ricardian political economy, (1) separated political economy from the science of morals and politics; (2) while within political economy, the two qualities of self-interest – ruling principle of human action and analytical method to understand economic processes – were increasingly seen as complementary elements.

The practitioners of political economy tread on a large number of toes with their views. Malthus had already affronted the friends of humanity by his harsh judgements of the labouring poor and their bend to blindly follow their instincts, as well as by his unacceptable theodicy. The Radicals made things worse by turning political economy into a vehicle for a reform programme that called for representative democracy, which questioned the established authority of the church and the aristocracy, held disdain for art and aesthetics and propagated a morality of cold calculation to further private interest.

Christian theology, the Oriel Noetics and methodology of political economy

The Philosophical Radicals made political economy subservient to their utilitarian views on happiness and virtue by which they challenged Christian beliefs. As a consequence, the schism between political economy and Christian theology that had been created by Malthus's theodicy of the first *Essay* flared up again in the 1820s. Political economy was regarded by many "with a mixture of dread and contempt – as a set of arbitrary and fanciful theories, subversive of religion and morality" (Whately cited in Waterman 2004: 121). In Oxford, under the guidance of Richard Whately,[11] an attempt was made to defend political economy against the unholy direction in which it seemed to develop in the hands of the Philosophical Radicals and 'disinfect' it from the prejudices and misapprehensions that plagued its conclusions and reputation.

Whately's pupil and friend, William Nassau Senior (1790–1864), was appointed to the newly established Drummond Chair of Political Economy in Oxford for this purpose. In his *Introductory Lectures on Political Economy*, delivered in 1826, Senior divided political economy into a theoretic and a practical branch. The theoretic branch was argued "to rest on a very few general propositions, which are the result of observation, or consciousness, and which almost every man, as soon as he hears them, admits, as familiar to his thoughts" (1966[1827]: 7). The practical branch seeks "to ascertain what institutions are most favourable to wealth" and is "a far more arduous study" because it depends on "so many antagonist springs" (*ibid.*: 8). Many of the complaints raised against political economy, Senior held, could be traced back to the failure to distinguish them. Senior also dismissed the argument that wealth is an inferior subject of study. Given the detrimental effects of poverty on the human character and the state of society, "the pursuit of wealth . . . is, to the mass of mankind, the great source of moral improvement" (*ibid.*: 12), and therefore its study a noble enterprise.

Getting himself elected to succeed Senior to the Drummond Chair, Whately set himself the task of strengthening the argument. In his *Introductory Lectures on Political Economy* (1832) Whately adopted the following strategy: (1) the first axe to grind was the view that political economy is unfavourable to religion; (2) he next criticised the utilitarian answer to the 'why' question; and finally (3) he showed that political economy and Christian theology were natural allies.

His first objective was met by severing the 'how' question from the 'why' question. To this purpose Whately argued the need to distinguish religious truth from scientific truth, and to stay away from "the erroneous principle . . . of appealing to Revelation on questions of physical science": "Scripture is not the test by which the conclusions of Science are to be tried" (1832: II.3). Theology and science (like political economy) are "distinct, incommensurable and non-competing fields of inquiry" (Waterman 2004: 123). Political economy is analytical, abstract, value-free, deals with (national) wealth and is not concerned with the connexion of wealth to virtue or happiness. It has nothing to say on the telos or purpose of human efforts and is to be regarded as an instrument by which to pursue these ends efficiently. Narrowing down its proper province, abstracting from links with human values, and emphasising its ahistorical, abstract-theoretical nature, political economy produces scientific knowledge, which should be carefully distinguished from religious knowledge, but which is instrumental in achieving the ends proposed by religious truth and moral principles (Waterman 1991: 208–10).

The objective to rescue political economy from being turned into a convenience to further utilitarian ends by the Philosophical Radicals was met by pointing out the inadequacy of the utilitarian telos. Whately first argued the necessity of a moral sense that informs us of the difference between good and evil. Without a notion of the good as an end, people are unable to make calculations of utility to this end. Next he argued that the utilitarian claim of happiness as the ultimate end will not do because there is no way of knowing beforehand what the consequences of actions are in terms of happiness, whereby such a consequentialist ethic is defective.

Trying to prove that political economy and Christian theology are natural allies, Whately next addressed another lingering issue which might be seen to bring political economy and theology into conflict: the question of the compatibility of national wealth and virtue, denied by 'Mandevillians'. He posits that progress got momentum with security of property, division of labour and some basic knowledge of arts, triggering the drives of emulation and gain to exert themselves. The dynamics of human drives and institutions towards the good of all is presented as the invisible hand of Providence. Indeed, "by the wise and benevolent arrangement of Providence, even those who are thinking only of their own credit and advantage, are, in the pursuit of these selfish objects, led, unconsciously, to benefit others" (1832: VI.19). It should be realised that selfishness, injustice and envy are individual dispositions and cannot "be attributed to national wealth" (1832: VI.18) and so do not reflect on political economy. Moreover, these dispositions are part of human nature and are as much present in savage communities as in wealthier nations. In fact, in wealthier nations there is much more scope for promoting the public interest by pursuing one's own interest (1832: VI.29), while "the counteracting and restraining principles, of Prudence, Morality, and Religion" (1832: VII.11) will have more power, the more society is advanced. Whately concluded that "there seems every reason to believe, that, as a general rule, advancement in National Prosperity . . . must be favourable to moral improvement" (1832: VII.17).

Whately emphasised the scientific, ahistorical, value-free nature of political economy. It studies national wealth as a means without pretending to being able to make claims about happiness or virtue. In treating wealth, political economy in no way encourages avarice (1832: II.1), while selfishness is of all times and places. Thus he repositioned and immunised the science of political economy.

Senior elaborated on the methodology of economics in *An Outline of the Science of Political Economy* (1836). In this book he focused exclusively on pure economics at the expense of the art of political economy. The political economist's

> conclusions, whatever be their generality and their truth, do not author-
> ize him in adding a single syllable of advice. That privilege belongs to
> the writer or the statesman who has considered all the causes which may
> promote or impede the general welfare of those whom he addresses, not
> to the theorist who has considered only one, though among the most
> important, of those causes. The business of a Political Economist is neither
> to recommend nor to dissuade, but to state general principles.
>
> (Senior 1965[1836]: 3)

Senior started from four (inductive or empirical) "general propositions, the result of observation, or consciousness, and scarcely requiring proof, or even formal statement . . . and . . . inferences are nearly as general, and, if he has reasoned correctly, as certain, as his premises" (*ibid.*: 2–3). He aimed to develop an analytical apparatus of an exact science with universal validity. Senior fur-ther developed his ideas in later writings. Distinguishing between the art and science of political economy, he argued in *Four Introductory Lectures on Political Economy* that although "[i]n the progress of human knowledge art precedes science" (1966[1852]: II.19), in due course the practice of art will grow increasingly dependent upon science. As a science, political economy is concerned with the laws of mind. The distinction between physical and mental sciences was important because their premises are drawn from different sources: observation, consciousness and hypothesis. In contrast to physical sci-ences (which draw primarily from hypothesis and observation), mental sciences found their premises on consciousness (*ibid.*: II.26–27). Political economy is a moral science, concerned with the sensations, faculties, and habits of the human mind (*ibid.*: II.22), and to be regarded as a positive science. He disa-greed with Ricardo and Mill that political economy was a hypothetical science; it was unnecessary and therefore undesirable to work with arbitrarily assumed premises (*ibid.*: IV.63; Depoortère 2013). Substituting a few empirical, general propositions for hypothesis would provide "an equally firm foundation for our subsequent reasonings, and have put a truth in the place of an arbitrary assumption" (Senior 1966[1852]: IV.62). This way conclusions would have greater certainty than hypothetical economics with its assumptions and models would admit.

In his essay *On the Definition of Political Economy*, published in 1836, Mill may be said to have formalised this evolving methodology of political econ-omy. He first criticised received definitions of political economy for failing to distinguish between science and art. Although closely related, science and art are "essentially distinct". "The one deals in facts, the other in precepts. Science is a collection of *truths*; art, a body of *rules*, or directions for conduct" (CW IV: 312).[12] Arguing his way towards a definition of political economy as a science,

Mill separates analysis from prescription, the study of the laws which govern economic phenomena from rules or means to effect certain ends. Political economy "teaches us how things take place of themselves, not in what manner it is advisable for us to shape them, in order to attain some particular end" (CW IV: 313).

Mill next considers the method of inquiry proper to political economy. The road of controlled experiments in human affairs being impassable, the moral sciences, including political economy, cannot rely on the inductive method but instead are dependent on the method *a priori*, by which is meant "reasoning from an assumed hypothesis" (CW IV: 325). Consequently Mill characterised political economy as a hypothetical or abstract science, logically deducing the implications of assumed psychological premises regarding the production and distribution of wealth. This mode of investigation is giving credence considering that, as Mill writes in the sixth book of his *System of Logic*, dealing with the logic of the moral sciences, "different species of social facts are in the main dependent, immediately and in the first resort, on different kinds of causes; and therefore not only may with advantage, but must, be studied apart" (CW VIII: 900). This is the case with political economy, which concerns itself only with "such of the phenomena of the social state as take place in consequence of the pursuit of wealth" (CW IV: 321).

Whatever the differences on the ultimate end of human action in commercial society between the Oriel Noetics and the Philosophical Radicals, they saw eye to eye in their view of political economy as a deductive science.[13] Carving out a separate domain, immune to questions of theology and metaphysics, value-free in order to be freed from controversy over the telos of human action, they adopted a methodological approach founded upon *a priori* assumptions, deductive logic and abstract truth. In this enterprise the primacy of the concept of self-interest was unchallenged but fundamentally renovated.

The concept of self-interest: from passion to behavioural assumption

Self-interest in the eighteenth century was one of the passions smoothened by socialisation and institutional restraint. Rooted in self-love (pride) and greed, self-interest involved a balance of sentiments. It was the *trait d'union* between passions and institutions and, taken in this sense, morally neutral. After Adam Smith, however, political economy travelled along a bumpy road. This was not only because the rise of a new department of science generated a natural tendency to define and settle its basic principles, subject matter and method of inquiry. Political economy was also caught in the middle of the debate on reform, order and progress, influencing its development as a science. Especially its 'mechanical philosophy', its reliance on 'selfish motives' and its views on public benefits raised critical voices. Responding to these challenges, political economy developed a new frame of reference and was made to serve new purposes, which resonated in the changing meaning and role of self-interest.

No doubt the need to break down complex processes into manageable proportions in the face of the bewildering complexity of the transformation of society happily combined with the need to define and pin down the subject matter and method of political economy. Narrowing down the scope of political economy to wealth, leaving behind claims about the relationship between wealth and happiness/virtue, political economy carved out a sphere of human action that was presented as a logical and mechanical world, governed by natural forces and principles. Side-tracking historical, institutional and moral considerations, the science of political economy sought to describe these forces and principles and to explain their logic. These aims made demands on the behaviour of the economic agent inhabiting such a world and self-interest became political economy's key assumption about behaviour, from which to make its deductions.

How to derive definite and exact conclusions about economic behaviour from the multiplicity of motives, circumstances, values, impulses and passions, knowledge and expectations? Surely psychology enters into the assumptions about human behaviour but doing justice to the variability and diversity of human behaviour – "the agency of so variable a being as man" Malthus writes in his *Principles* (1968[1820]: 1) – would make it impossible to arrive at definite conclusions. Instead of one among many other passions, self-interest became the basic premise to describe and explain economic behaviour. Self-interest served the purpose of providing some fundamental assumption or principle through which economic behaviour was separated from non-economic behaviour (Hennipman 1945). Laws of economic behaviour can be formulated on the assumption that self-interest rules supreme over economic behaviour, pinning behaviour down in its course of action. Ricardo wrote: "It is self-interest which regulates all the speculations of trade; and where that can be clearly and satisfactorily ascertained, we should not know where to stop if we admitted any other rule of action" (1981[1810]: 102). Dugald Stewart posited as a maxim known by introspection that "private interest may be safely trusted to as a principle of action universal among men" (quoted in Waterman 2004: 136). According to Malthus, self-love was "the moving principle of society" (Waterman 1991: 107). Senior was equally convinced. The proposition "that every man desires to obtain additional wealth with as little sacrifice as possible . . . is assumed in almost every process of economic reasoning" (Senior 1965[1836]: 27–8). And to drive his point home: "In short, it is in Political Economy what gravitation is in Physics . . . the ultimate fact beyond which reasoning cannot go, and of which almost every other proposition is merely an illustration" (*ibid.*: 28).

Despite such exclamations of adherence to the general principle of self-interest, clearly the classical economists took self-interest to mean pecuniary interest, the profit motive or the desire for money. In its general meaning, the claim that people act out of self-interest is insufficient to pin down behaviour to a predictable course of action and would be unfit for its intended purpose of deducing unequivocal results of economic action. In his *Principles of Political*

Economy (PPE), John Stuart Mill argued before expounding his theory of value that he was only concerned with those cases

> in which values and prices are determined by competition alone. In so far only as they are thus determined, can they be reduced to any assignable law. The buyers must be supposed as studious to buy cheap, as the sellers to sell dear.
>
> (PPE I.III.I.5: 532)

Senior further explained that amidst the most diverse desires people can have, "[m]oney seems to be the only object for which the desire is universal; and it is so, because money is abstract wealth" (1965[1836]: 27). In formulating scientific principles, political economy does not consider the whole of man and his motley collection of motives, as Bagehot put it, "not with man, the moral being, but with man, the money-making animal" (1895: 102).

This is the (in)famous concept of economic man. Mill explained that political economy qualifies as a species of social facts in the main caused by the desire for wealth, operating on the psychological law that "a greater gain is preferred to a smaller" (CW VIII: 901). Therefore a class of social phenomena can be distinguished and a department of science constructed that studies this class by utilising the fact that they depend mainly on just this one class of circumstances to allow for the effects of modifying circumstances next. Political economy abstracts from other human passions or motives (except for two auxiliary assumptions which follow the desire for wealth like its shadow[14]) and

> considers mankind as occupied solely in acquiring and consuming wealth, and aims at showing what is the course of action into which mankind, living in a state of society, would be impelled if that motive . . . were absolute ruler of all their actions.
>
> (Mill CW VIII: 902)

Stripped of the countervailing influences of other passions that had seemed to justify the transformation of greed into self-interest in the eighteenth century, 'greed' was reintroduced as the desire for wealth as a behavioural assumption. Mill hastened to add that no economist was ever so absurd as to suppose that this is an accurate description of man but

> this is the mode in which science must necessarily proceed. When an effect depends on a concurrence of causes, these causes must be studied one at the time, and their laws separately investigated, if we wish, through the causes, to obtain the power of either predicting or controlling the effect; since the law of the effect is compounded of the laws of all the causes which determine it.
>
> (CW VIII: 902)

Political economy does not claim that man is driven by a burning desire to acquire wealth in all departments of human affairs. Man is not greedy; political economy takes *economic* man to be greedy in explaining the basic functioning of a market economy. Surely he is much more, and all kinds of other motives will have their part to play in his actual behaviour, but in a scientific account of economic life it is a pretty good approximation of the truth. Given that premises may be "totally without foundation in fact", however, conclusions derived from deductive analysis are only true "*in the abstract*; that is, they are only true under certain suppositions" (CW IV: 326). Mill points out that such abstract truth needs to be corrected by allowing the influence of the effects of other motives as soon as the results of the political economist's analysis are applied to a particular case. The concept of self-interest was refitted in political economy's new theoretical frame and reworked from passion to behavioural assumption.

Paradoxically, tailoring self-interest as the pursuit of pecuniary gain or the acquisition of wealth did away with the charge of egoism. Self-interest had come to be seen as interchangeable with egoism or selfishness, undermining the neutrality of self-interest. Consequently, political economy was reproached for being founded upon morally depraved motives. Narrowing interest down to one specific interest, pecuniary interest or the profit motive, implied that economic action is assumed to be directed at an intermediary goal in the service of other goals. Ultimately wealth or money is only a means. Self-interest is neutral in the sense that it only defines the goal of economic activity (pecuniary wealth). It does not say anything about the purposes of wealth (wealth is not a goal in itself, but a means to some other end) and it does not say anything about the motives for wanting wealth (which may be egoistic or altruistic). Self-interest may serve objectives of widely different moral worth but is in itself ethically neutral.

The cutting edge of romanticism

On the rising status of political economy as a science, could self-interest safely leave behind its low-born origins of greed and self-love? Not quite. Despite the efforts of Whately and the other Oriel Noetics to appease Christian theology and political economy, political economy kept arousing controversy. Especially the English romantic poets and critics, including Coleridge, Southey, Wordsworth, Hazlitt, Carlyle and Ruskin, continued to vehemently attack political economy of the utilitarian creed. They took political economy as unwelcome sign of the times, propagating false pretentions of truth and undermining the framework of values, duties and rights by which society was much more than a mere collection of individuals. Romantic critics reserved most scorn for the Utilitarians for reducing the community to its constituent individuals and the individual to a mere calculator of pleasures and pains, their sum total to be manipulated towards collective happiness. Carlyle considered laissez-faire the "freedom of apes" and utilitarianism "a philosophy for pigs" (cited in Grampp 1973: 366).

The romantic writers lamented the rise of industrial and mechanised society and its mechanisation of the human mind, destroying all imagination, aesthetic sense and compassion. "Men are grown mechanical in head and heart, as well as in hand . . . Their whole efforts, attachments, opinions . . . are of a mechanical character", Carlyle wrote in *Signs of the Times* (cited in Ryan 1981: 85). The romantic critics took political economy as the religion of mechanical society. It was faulted for its mechanical mode of reasoning by decomposing society into its component elements, abstracting from irregular and temporary disturbances. Especially the idea of building explanations of social phenomena from uniform principles of human nature and the working out of this idea in the reduction of explanations of economic behaviour to pecuniary interest or the profit motive was an affront. This method of abstraction and deduction failed to capture the fact that individuality can only exist within a framework of social relations. As Coleridge wrote: "an abstract conclusion in a matter of political economy, the premises of which neither exist now, nor ever will exist within the range of the wildest imagination, is not a truth but a chimera–a practical falsehood" (Coleridge cited in Ryan 1981: 84).

These reductionist moves enraged the romantic writers, castigating political economy with venomous intent.[15] In Rousseauist fashion, they argued that mechanical man in a mechanical world would become estranged or alienated, while traditional values such as duty and honour were replaced by the monetary value set by the market, reducing "all human relations to the cash-nexus", promoting, as Carlyle had it, "Mammon-worship" (Ryan 1981: 85): "Is there no value, then, in human things, but what can write itself down in a cash-ledger?" (Carlyle cited in Dixon 2006: 35).

Many have described the rift that opened between political economists and romantic poets. They all express the idea of a fault-line (Winch 2009), the great divide (Bronk 2009) or two cultures (Snow 1959). John Stuart Mill, raised to preach the utilitarian creed, proved unable to enjoy a world conceived in terms of efficiency and utility alone, banning out aesthetic passions and sentiments, imagination and dreams. Later he was to write two essays, *Bentham* and *Coleridge*, in which he juxtaposed their antagonistic modes of thought, urging the need to combine both points of view to arrive at true understanding.

Mill argued that Bentham had failed to do justice to the complexity of human motivation by interpreting human nature in terms of man's selfish interest, committing "the mistake of supposing that the business part of human affairs was the whole of them" (CW X: 100). Moreover, Mill objected to Bentham's narrow and rational view of institutions and laws, neglecting the influence of culture, tradition and the binding forces of society. Third, although praising Bentham for his method of detail, viz. breaking up topics into their constituent elements to make analysis possible, Mill faulted Bentham's lack of imagination and his inclination to take the part for the whole. In Mill's view, what was lacking in Bentham was highlighted in Coleridge and vice versa. Mill praised Coleridge for his appreciation of the value of existing institutions (even if they outlived their purposes), for assigning the state educational and moral tasks, and his insistence that social cohesion in society cannot be built upon shared interests alone but requires common values, social affections and institutions. Nevertheless, though deficient to deal with all human affairs, Bentham's method and outlook would serve perfectly to build the science of political economy. Indeed, if it is true that Mill came a long way in bridging the rift between rationalism and romanticism, this does not hold regarding political economy.

It may be argued that Mill should not have bothered anyway because the romantic critics besieged a fortress political economists had already abandoned. Rejecting industrial society and the way it turned social relationships into relations of exchange, they turned the *doux commerce* thesis upside down: industrial, commercial society is destructive of civilisation and virtue. Commercial society was, Owen wrote, a "thoroughly selfish system", under which "there can be no true civilisation" (cited in Ryan 1981: 82). Coleridge's complaint about "the lack of suitable 'correctives of the commercial spirit' in the form of religion and respect for tradition that can act as a 'countercharm to the sorcery of wealth'" (Bronk 2009: 44) does indeed seem to revive the eighteenth-century debate of wealth and virtue. Given the retreat to the *science* of political economy, a move which side-tracked all issues relating to the relationship between wealth and happiness/virtue and which refashioned self-interest for methodological purposes, political economists had left these issues outside their province. Moreover, any charge that political economy takes "the human being merely as a covetous machine" (Ruskin 1997[1862]: 167) misrepresents this abstraction in the cause of science.

However, it would be a mistake to think that the romantic critics were simply barking up the wrong tree. Classical political economy was framed after Smith's 'system of natural liberty and justice', in which individuals were free to pursue their interests within an appropriate framework of morality, law and order. Whereas Smith had spent much time on the (historical) interaction of both domains in the development of classical thought, the science of political economy and the science of morals and politics were increasingly differentiated, separating (pecuniary) self-interest from the social affections, duties, rights, etc. as the one motive to explain economic behaviour. Not all of the romantic critique on the model of (natural) science of the political economists and its basic assumption of self-interest can be disposed of as spiteful though eloquent rhetoric.

First, separating self-interest from the social affections is part and parcel of the mechanical mode of reasoning employed in political economy. This method of decomposing the whole into parts to arrive at conclusions tore something essential apart from the object of study that can never be regained in synthesis. In other words, the social affections "alter the essence of the creature under examination the moment they are added; they operate, not mathematically, but chemically, introducing conditions which render all our previous knowledge unavailable" (Ruskin 1997[1962]: 167). It simply does not add up:

It is not possible to derive a precise prediction of behaviour by simply adding together the effects of the general "economic" tendency to self-interested behaviour (including opportunism and doing as little as possible to achieve one's goal) and the effects of the more Romantic social tendencies (or "disturbing causes") of trust, loyalty and the pursuit of excellence (which imply the suspension of self-interest). The particular cultural compounds of (or trade-offs between) such conflicting motivational factors are forged by tradition, norms and leadership. They will vary from place to place, and they can be revealed only by observation.

(Bronk 2009: 55)

Separating self-interest from the social affections, moreover, produces conceptual inconsistencies following from the incompatibility of theoretical frames. This is the other side of the coin: if it is added up, it does not fit. The science of politics and morals takes economic relationships as expressions of a particular set of changeable social, political and moral relationships, while these same relationships in political economy are uniform and invariable. In similar vein, self-interest in the domain of politics and morals refers to the balancing of sentiments moulded by institutional circumstances, while the science of political economy defines self-interest in terms of the desire for wealth as the omniscient drive of economic man.

Second, separating self-interest from the social affections also implied that self-interest in political economy was no longer about the balancing of often-contrary sentiments. Appointed as "absolute ruler of all their actions" (Mill CW VIII: 901), pecuniary interest or the desire for wealth lost the countervailing forces of other motives and drives to keep it within bounds, which had been the crux of one of the central arguments for the social utility of greed. In *Analysis of the Phenomena of the Human Mind* (1829), James Mill's remarked: "The motive which leads to the acquisition of wealth, great as is the part which it plays in human life, has no appropriate name. Avarice, Rapacity, like the words Gluttony, and Lust, are only names for cases of excess" (1967[1869] II: 266). With one motive proclaimed as 'absolute ruler', however, any distinction between the mean and the excess is blurred. In the absence of countervailing passions within the province of political economy, there is no way to distinguish between self-interest and greed.

The concept of self-interest was fitted to the requirements of the deductive logic of political economy by abstracting from other motives than the desire for wealth, as well as from its social and moral context. Consequently self-interest became indistinguishable from greed. This implied the absence of a mechanism to keep self-interest within the bounds of propriety and to prevent harm to others. Consequently, it is impossible to conclude that self-interest is beneficial except by invoking a moral logic, that is, by assuming the existence of an appropriate framework of law, morality and order whereby requirements of behavioural and moral conditioning of self-interest are assumed to be met. Therefore the beneficial effects of self-interest cannot be determined upon abstract principles alone, but require consideration of "the varieties of circumstance" (Ruskin 1997[1862]: 169):

> It is impossible to conclude, of any given mass of acquired wealth, merely by the fact of its existence, whether it signifies good or evil to the nation in the midst of which it exists. Its real value depends on the moral sign attached to it . . . Any given accumulation of commercial wealth may be indicative, on the one hand, of faithful industries, progressive energies, and productive ingenuities: or, on the other, it may be indicative of mortal luxury, merciless tyranny, ruinous chicane.
>
> (Ruskin 1997[1862]: 187)

Political economy erroneously pretends that there is an economic logic separate from its moral logic. Given that this economic logic is built by removing the disturbing influences of behavioural and institutional factors, the whole burden of the argument of the social utility of greed comes to rest upon the competitive system. In this vein Mill wrote in his *Principles*:

> only through the principle of competition has political economy any pretension to the character of a science. So far as rents, profits, wages, prices, are determined by competition, laws may be assigned for them. Assume competition to be their exclusive regulator, and principles of broad generality and scientific precision may be laid down, according to which they will be regulated.
>
> (Mill PPE I.II.IV.1: 292)

Although he defended the system of competition against the Owenite cooperative system for enlisting self-interest in the cause of human welfare, even Mill was not thrilled about "the trampling, crushing, elbowing, and treading on each other's heels" (PPE II.IV.VI.1: 322). Despite (and perhaps thanks to) favourable conditions in terms of equality and justice, Mill saw America as an example of a stage of society in which "the life of the whole of one sex is devoted to dollar-hunting, and of the other to breeding dollar-hunters" (*ibid.*: 323). This perfectly illustrates the fundamental mismatch between the economic logic of commercial society and its moral logic, of which political economy on its own premises is incapable of taking notice. Indeed, how reasonable is it to expect the social and benevolent affections to blossom, if its precondition – wealth – is achieved by encouraging self-interested behaviour unrestrained by public spiritedness?

Conclusion

The concept of self-interest in Adam Smith was part and parcel of a long debate on passions, interests, virtue and order that accompanied the transformation of state and society with expanding trade and commerce. From the 1790s onwards, however, political economy was given a new décor and had to meet new demands. The concept of self-interest was redecorated as well. As political economy was challenged in the debate on order and reform and sought to achieve its scientific pretensions, the emphasis shifted from art to science, defining the business of the political economist "to state general principles" (Senior 1965[1836]: 3). In its focus on logical relationships between strategic variables, detached from their historical, moral and social context, political economy was given a much stronger analytical (than descriptive) orientation. Separating the 'how' from the 'why', political economy was presented as a positive and value-free science.

The concept of self-interest changed along with political economy. From part of human nature and psychology, self-interest became a behavioural premise within an analytical model that uses deductive logic to develop laws. Converted from passion into behavioural assumption, self-interest was singled out as motive from which conclusions could be drawn about the consequences of behaviour. This renovated concept of self-interest, previously defined by its relationship with passions and institutions, was not only defined with a view to its methodological purpose, but also taken as strictly linked to contributions to increase wealth (utility). With this narrowly defined science of political economy, references to civilisation, manners, virtue and happiness as public benefits of trade, commerce and manufacturing were put outside the province of political economy.

Nevertheless, restructuring the assumptions from which political economy was to proceed to fulfil its pretensions as a science dismantled the checks and balances that had separated self-interest from greed. Mill admitted the love of money to be one of "the strongest, most general, and most persistent passions of human nature' (Mill's notes to his father's *Analysis* 1967[1869] II: 234(n)). Although "[t]here is nothing originally more desirable about money than about any heap of glittering pebbles . . . the desire to possess it is often stronger than the desire to use it", whereby "money is desired not for the sake of an end, but as part of the end. From being a means to happiness, it has come to be itself a principal ingredient of the individual's conception of happiness" (CW X: 235–6). Mill claims that "the utilitarian standard . . . tolerates and approves" such desires "up to the point beyond which they would be more injurious to the general happiness than promotive of it" (CW X: 237). Many felt, however, that the economic and the moral logic of commercial society were not as forthcomingly parallel as hoped for. On the contrary, Owen argued, the manufacturing system sacrificed humanity to selfish gain, while commercial competition necessarily created "a covered civil warfare" between trades and professions (1991[1840]: 358).

Human greed, entering through the back door again, raised the same old questions (although most questions were relegated to the domain of morals and politics). Not in the least because optimistic beliefs about mutual benefits, cooperation and progress were extinguished in ironclad generalisations about conditions of scarcity and diminishing returns. These generalisations predicted that improvements in the condition of the labouring poor were wasted due to the increase in numbers, an inevitable tendency towards a stationary state and a zero-sum game between profits and wages. So much for the positive-sum society in which all would share in the growth of wealth, knowledge and humanity. As Southey wrote in *Colloquies*:

> [A] people may be too rich; because it is the tendency of the commercial, and more especially of the manufacturing system, to collect wealth rather than to diffuse it . . . great capitalists become like pikes in a fish-pond, who devour the weaker fish; and it is too certain that the poverty of one part of the people seems to increase in the same ratio as the riches of another.
> (Southey cited in Nisbet 1980: 24–5)

The question of whether the rich were rich because the poor were poor was to keep troubling the nineteenth century.

Notes

1 If not, there still is an abundance of land that could be cultivated, while, with further refinement, man comes more and more to prefer intellectual pursuits over physical pleasures, diminishing the appetite between the sexes.

2 Neither holds the fear that men would sink to idleness in a system of equality, that is, "if they be not excited by the stimulus of gain", on the supposition that "[t]he present ruling passion of the human mind is the love of distinction" and that "the love of praise hurries us on to the most incredible achievements". For it is not true that a system of equal property leaves the mind unoccupied. "Men, no longer able to acquire the esteem or avoid the contempt of their neighbours by circumstances of dress and furniture, will divert the passion for distinction into another channel" and "will seek the noblest course, and perpetually fructify the seeds of public good" (Godwin 1823[1793] II:VIII.IV: 824–6).

3 Although Malthus's argument changed course with the second edition, the change of perspective is less pronounced than is usually assumed. The first *Essay* allows room for countervailing passions to check the power of population, while Malthus was not very optimistic about the extent to which moral restraint would be practised (Levy 1978: 280; Hollander 1986: 210; Waterman 1991: 138–9).

4 In his theodicy, Malthus considered social evil to be natural and inevitable (in contrast to Godwin who argued that social evil was man-made and therefore remediable). How could misery and vice be necessary if, as Malthus held in line with Newton, God had created a universe on the basis of fixed laws with a view to man's welfare? He explained that only necessity and privation can arouse man's mind, develop his reason and bring him to act to better this condition. LeMathieu has observed that Malthus transformed "the problem of evil" into a "theory of incentive" (1979: 469). Malthus's claim and explanation brought schism between political economy and Christian theology, as the former seemed to proclaim scarcity, the necessity of misery and vice, selfishness, while denouncing virtue, in particular charity (Waterman 2004: Chapter 7). Malthus's views were pimped up to defuse this conflict. From the second *Essay* onwards, his theodicy was replaced by the view (developed over the years by Paley, Copleston and Sumner (see Waterman 1991)), that human life is all about

trial and discipline with a view to eternity (Waterman 2004: 129). Divine wisdom puts man under the strain of the principle of population and the consequent rise of private property and inequality to form moral character and practice virtue.

5   Although Malthus later adjusted his views, in the first *Essay* he posited "the benefi-cial economy of evil", arguing that evil and distress are the final cause of civilisation, happiness and benevolence (LeMathieu 1979: 471, 469).

6   Especially the following passage brought about vitriolic responses: "A man who is born into the world already possessed . . . has no claim of right to the smallest portion of food, and in fact to be where he is. At nature's mighty feast there is no vacant cover for him. She tells him to be gone, and will quickly execute her own orders if he does not work on the compassion of some of her guests" (Malthus, the second (1803) edition of the *Essay*).

7   Hutchison especially calls attention to the influence of James Mill in this devel-opment, putting Smith's theories in a "much starker and more unqualified form" (1978: 29). Hutchison denounces Mill for betraying his Scottish roots. A similar, unfavourable assessment of Mill is given by Torrance (2006). For a more balanced judgement see De Marchi's 'The case for James Mill' (1983).

8   In his famous passage on Ricardian Vice, Schumpeter wrote about Ricardo's way of reasoning: "His interest was in the clear-cut result of direct practical significance. In order to get this he cut that general system to pieces, bundled up as large parts of it as possible and put them in cold storage – so that as many things as possible should be frozen and 'given'. He then piled one simplifying assumption upon another until, having really settled everything by these assumptions, he was left with only a few aggregative variables between which, given these assumptions he set up simple one-way relations so that, in the end, the desired results emerged almost as tautologies" (Schumpeter 1954: 472).

9   This assumption has given rise to severe criticism. To Bentham's defence, however, it may be argued that he does list benevolence among the pleasures, whereby the self-regarding and other-regarding nature of pleasure is difficult to discern (*Introduction* 1982[1789]: Chapter V).

10   Thus Mill wrote: "there can be no alteration in the quantity of produce which the one receives, but by an alteration in the quantity which the other receives; unless in that one case, in which the productive powers of the instruments of production have undergone alteration" (Mill 1965[1844]: 78).

11   Richard Whately (1787–1863) belonged to the so-called Oriel Noetics, a group of Oxford dons educated at Oriel College, who pursued an intellectual life build on logic and reason, which also included Copleston, Nassau Senior, Arnold and Newton. Whately was a prominent scholar and administrator, who threw his weight around in matters of theology, politics and political economy. He succeeded Senior as Drummond Professor of Political Economy in 1831, vacating the chair within a few months to become Archbishop of Dublin (Rashid 1977).

12   Except for Mill's *Principles of Political Economy* (PPE) and his *Autobiography*, refer-ences are to *The Collected Works of John Stuart Mill*, vol. IV (On the Definition of Political Economy *in Essays on some unsettled Questions of Political Economy* (1844); vol. VIII (On the Logic of the Moral Sciences in *A System of Logic* (1843); and vol. X: Utilitarianism (1861), and the essays on Bentham (1838) and Coleridge (1840).

13   'Cambridge' disagreed. Founded upon different views on natural theology, Richard Jones and William Whewell opposed the abstract-deductive method in which Oriel Noetics and Philosophical Radicals concurred for its religious and political implications (Maas 2008).

138   *Self-interest after Smith*

14 Mill mentions the aversion to labour and desire for present enjoyment, while Senior lists the love of ease and the desire for distinction.
15 James Bonar, the author of Ruskin's obituary in the *Economic Journal* wrote: "Political economists, with the doubtful exception of Adam Smith were cordially hated by Ruskin" (1900: 274). See Winch (2009: Chapter 4) for an attempt to explain Ruskin's aversion to political economy and John Stuart Mill in particular.

References

Bagehot, W. (1895). *Economic Studies*. London: Longmans, Green.
Bentham, J. (1823). *Fragment on Government*. Second, enlarged edition. London: Wilson and Pickering.
Bentham, J. (1982[1789]). *An Introduction to the Principles of Morals and Legislation*. Edited by J.H. Burns and H.L.A. Hart. London/New York: Methuen.
Bentham, J. (2004). The psychology of man. In: *Bentham's Economic Writings*, Stark, W. (ed.), London/New York: Routledge, pp. 419–50.
Bonar, J. (1900). Obituary of John Ruskin. *Economic Journal*, vol. 10(38): 274–5.
Bromwich, D. (2014). *The Intellectual Life of Edmund Burke: from the sublime and beautiful to American independence*. Cambridge, MA: The Belknap Press of Harvard University Press.
Bronk, R. (2009). *The Romantic Economist; Imagination in Economics*. Cambridge: Cambridge University Press.
Burke, Edmund (1976[1790]). *Reflections on the Revolution in France*. London: Pelican Books.
Butler, M. (ed.) (1993). *Burke, Paine, Godwin, and the Revolution Controversy*. Cambridge: Cambridge University Press.
Coleman, W.O. (2004). *Economics and its Enemies; two centuries of anti-economics*. New York: Palgrave Macmillan.
De Marchi, N. (1983). The case for James Mill. In: *Methodological Controversy in Economics: Essays in Honor of T.W. Hutchison*, Coats, A. (ed.), Greenwich: JAI Press, pp. 155–84.
Deane, P. (1982). *The Evolution of Economic Ideas*. Cambridge: Cambridge University Press.
Depoortère, C. (2013). William Nassau Senior and David Ricardo on the method of political economy. *Journal of the History of Economic Thought*, vol. 35(1): 19–42.
Dixon, R. (2006). Carlyle, Malthus and Sismondi: the origins of Carlyle's dismal view of political economy. *History of Economics Review*, vol. 44: 32–8.
Godwin, William (1793). *An Enquiry Concerning Political Justice, and its Influence on General Virtue and Happiness*. Two volumes. London: Robinson. http://oll.libertyfund.org/titles/godwin-an-enquiry-concerning-political-justice-vol-ii (27–01–2016).
Godwin, William (1823[1797]). Of avarice and profusion. In: *The Enquirer: reflections on education, manners, and literature, part II, essay II*. Edinburgh/London: Anderson/Simpkin & Marshall.
Grampp, W.D. (1973). Classical economics and its moral critics. *History of Political Economy*, vol. 5(2): 359–74.
Halévy, E. (1972). *The Growth of Philosophical Radicalism*. London: Faber and Faber.
Hennipman, P. (1945). *Economisch motief en economisch principe* (Economic motive and economic principle). Amsterdam: Noord-Hollandsche Uitgevers Maatschappij.
Hollander, S. (1986). On Malthus's population principle and social reform. *History of Political Economy*, vol. 18(2): 187–235.

Hutchison, T.W. (1978). *On Revolutions and Progress in Economic Knowledge*. Chapter 2: James Mill and Ricardian economics: a methodological revolution? Cambridge: Cambridge University Press,

LeMathieu, D.L. (1979). Malthus and the theology of scarcity. *Journal of the History of Ideas*, vol. 40(3): 467–74.

Levy, D. (1978). Some normative aspects of the Malthusian controversy. *History of Political Economy*, vol. 10(2): 271–85.

Locke, D. (1980). *A Fantasy of Reason: the life and thought of William Godwin*. London: Routledge & Kegan Paul.

Maas, H. (2008). "A hard battle to fight": natural theology and the dismal science, 1820–50. *History of Political Economy*, vol. 40(suppl.): 143–67.

Malthus, T.R. (1798). *An Essay on the Principle of Population*. London: J. Johnson. First edition. www.econlib.org/library/Malthus/malPop1.html (27–01–2016).

Malthus, T.R. (1968[1820]). *Principles of Political Economy*. New York: A.M. Kelley Publishers.

Malthus, T.R. (1970[1814]). Observations on the effects of the Corn Laws. In: *The Pamphlets of Thomas Robert Malthus*. New York: A.M. Kelley Publishers.

Mazlish, B. (1975). *James & John Stuart Mill; Father and Son in the Nineteenth Century*. New Brunswick/Oxford: Transaction Books.

McNally, D. (2000). Political economy to the fore: Burke, Malthus and the Whig response to popular radicalism in the age of the French Revolution. *History of Political Thought*, vol. 21(3): 427–47.

Mill, James (1965[1844]). *Elements of Political Economy*. Third edition. New York: A.M. Kelley.

Mill, James (1967[1869]). *Analysis of the Phenomena of the Human Mind*. Edited and annotated by J.S. Mill, two volumes, New York: A.M. Kelley Publishers.

Mill, James (2015[1828]). *An Essay on Government*. Cambridge: Cambridge University Press.

Mill, John Stuart (1857). *Principles of Political Economy*. Fourth edition. London: Parker & Son.

Mill, John Stuart (1873). *Autobiography*. Second edition. London: Longmans et al.

Mill, John Stuart (1963–91). *The Collected Works of John Stuart Mill*. Edited by J.M. Robson. Toronto: University of Toronto Press/London: Routledge and Kegan Paul. Available at http://oll.libertyfund.org/titles.

O'Brien, D.P. (1975). *The Classical Economists*. Oxford: Clarendon Press.

Owen, Robert (1991[1840]). *A New View of Society and Other Writings*. London: Penguin Books.

Pocock, J.G.A. (1986). *Virtue, Commerce, and History*. Chapter 10: The political economy of Burke's analysis of the French Revolution. Cambridge: Cambridge University Press, pp. 193–212.

Rashid, S. (1977). Richard Whately and Christian Political Economy at Oxford and Dublin. *Journal of the History of Ideas*, vol. 38(1): 147–55.

Ricardo David (1981[1817]). On the principles of political Economy and taxation. In: *The Works and Correspondence of David Ricardo*. Volume 1. Cambridge: Cambridge University Press.

Ricardo, David (1981[1810]). The high price of bullion; Appendix. In: *The Works and Correspondence of David Ricardo*. Volume 3. Cambridge: Cambridge University Press.

Robbins, L. (1953). *The Theory of Economic Policy in English Classical Political Economy*. London: Macmillan & Co. Ltd.

Rothschild, E. (2002). *Economic Sentiments; Adam Smith, condorcet and the Enlightenment.* Cambridge/London: Harvard University Press.

Ruskin, John (1997[1862]). *Unto This Last and Other Writings.* London/New York: Penguin Books.

Ryan, A. (1974). *J.S. Mill.* London/Boston: Routledge & Kegan Paul.

Ryan, C.C. (1981). The fiends of commerce: Romantic and Marxist criticisms of classical political economy. *History of Political Economy*, vol. 13(1): 80–94.

Schumpeter, J.A. (1954). *History of Economic Analysis.* London/Boston: Allen & Unwin.

Senior, N.W. (1965[1836]). *An Outline of the Science of Political Economy.* New York: A.M. Kelley.

Senior, N.W. (1966[1827–1852]). *Selected Writings on Economics: a volume of pamphlets 1827–1852.* New York: A.M. Kelley Publishers.

Snow, C.P. (1959). *The Two Cultures and the Scientific Revolution.* Cambridge: Cambridge University Press.

Stark, W. (2004). *Jeremy Bentham's Economic Writings.* Critical edition based on his printed works and unprinted manuscripts. Volume 3. London/New York: Routledge.

Torrance, T.S. (2006). James Mill as economist: theory dominated by deductive method. In: *A History of Scottish Economic Thought*, Dow, A. and Dow, S. (eds), London and New York: Routledge, pp. 146–62.

Waterman, A.M.C. (1991). *Revolution, Economics & Religion; Christian political economy 1798–1833.* Cambridge: Cambridge University Press.

Waterman, A.M.C. (2004). *Political Economy and Christian Theology since the Enlightenment.* New York: Palgrave Macmillan.

Waterman, A.M.C. (2012). Adam Smith and Malthus on high wages. *European Journal of the History of Economic Thought*, vol. 19(3): 409–29.

Whately, Richard (1832). *Introductory Lectures on Political Economy.* London: B. Fellowes. www.econlib.org/library/Whately/whtPE.html (22–01–2016).

Winch, D. (1983). Higher maxims: happiness versus wealth in Malthus and Ricardo. In: *That Noble Science of Politics: a study in nineteenth-century intellectual history*, Collini, A., Winch, D. and Burrow, J. (eds), Cambridge: Cambridge University Press, pp. 63–90.

Winch, D. (1993). Robert Malthus: Christian moral scientist, arch-demoralizer or implicit secular utilitarian? *Utilitas*, vol. 5(2): 239–53.

Winch, D. (1996). *Riches and Poverty: an intellectual history of political economy in Britain, 1750–1834.* Cambridge: Cambridge University Press.

Winch, D. (2009). *Wealth and Life: essays on the intellectual history of political economy in Britain, 1848–1914.* Cambridge: Cambridge University Press.

6 The wheels of 'greed, and the war amongst the greedy'

Despite the foundational importance of human greed in establishing political economy as a science, the term greed practically disappeared from economic discourse in the nineteenth century. Senior is a case in point. In his *Outline of the Science of Political Economy* (1965[1836]: 27), Senior's first principle of economics was that "every man desires to obtain additional wealth with as little sacrifice as possible". He defined wealth in terms of money, "the only object for which the desire is universal", and given that money allows the satisfaction of the most diverse wants and needs, "the desire for wealth must be insatiable" (*ibid.*: 27). Self-interest, the desire for wealth, acquisition, accumulation and insatiability took the place of greed and avarice, to which Senior added that the political economist "is bound, like a juryman, to give deliverance true according to the evidence, and allow neither sympathy with indigence, nor disgust at profusion or at avarice" (*ibid.*: 3). Such a representation opened the way for a formalisation of political economy as a separate department of science. Abstracting from other human passions or motives, as Mill put it, political economy does not concern itself with the whole of man's nature in the social state but only insofar as he is motivated by the pursuit of wealth at the least possible effort (CW IV: 321).

Senior's and Mill's motivational reductionism in defining political economy did away with the range and diversity of human passions and motives that had been the crux of one of the central arguments on which the case for the logic of greed was build. As a calm, persistent and rational passion, human greed was deemed capable of taming the wild and destructive passions, the very quality for which money-making or human greed had been acclaimed in the eighteenth century (Hirschman 1977). Singling out this desire for wealth as the driving motive of economic behaviour destroyed the argument of the subservience of human cupidity to human welfare, or at least it relegated these issues to beyond political economy's province. Within this new conception of political economy, the burden of the claim of the subservience of greed to welfare shifted towards the system of interdependence and (free market) competition.

In the seventeenth and eighteenth centuries, trade and commerce, previously held to be corrupting, were upgraded into the very basis of national health and wealth. Whereas religious and moral precepts had failed to goad men's passions into compliance and cooperation, and repressive systems had proven to be vehicles of elite interests, trade and commerce seemed to be capable of generating growth of knowledge, wealth and refinement. Extending the division of labour and creating a system of interdependence, commercial society advanced welfare and sociability. Interdependence was seen to secure the beneficial nature of commercial society. Given that people depend on each other to satisfy their needs, they are bound to share benefits (albeit not equally) to preserve conditions of cooperation on which everyone's welfare depends. Given the inherent restraint such a system of interdependence implies, competition is a positive force in the dynamics of growth of wealth. It delivers positive-sum outcomes to the extent that this internal regulatory mechanism in market exchanges is allowed to work.

However, the natural laws that governed the system of interdependence seemed to produce results that defied claims of benign providence. If this system generated unprecedented wealth and, as Ricardo's labour theory of value indicated, wealth was created by human labour, how then can labour be in such miserable conditions in the presence of so much mechanical power to produce wealth? What providential order? Misgivings questioned the system of self-interest and competition, and its promise of elevating moral character in a capitalistic society as a natural by-product of material prosperity. Many felt cheated by the adverse consequences of the growth of industrial, mechanised society – inequality, poverty and alienation – and much anger was directed at the extenuating spokesman of this process, the political economist. Previously held claims – the positive force of competition, the positive-sum nature of capitalist society and the immaterial benefits of material prosperity – were closely scrutinised and criticised. This chapter aims to show the development of the socialist argument, starting with the views of Robert Owen. The second section deals with the utilitarian Owenite, William Thompson, who defended his views before the Cooperative Society in London against John Stuart Mill. The section that follows is devoted to Friedrich Engels, and then the views of Marx are discussed. A concluding section rounds off this chapter.

Robert Owen

Robert Owen (1771–1858) worked his way up from a draper's apprentice to the manager and co-owner of a cotton mill and yarn factory. In 1797, the successful entrepreneur entered into a partnership to purchase New Lanark Mills, a factory village in Scotland. He married the daughter of the founder and previous owner of the mills two years later and took up residence in New Lanark as its general manager in 1800 (Taylor 1982). Convinced that human character is a product of social environment – for better or worse, the key idea in his well-known *A New View of Society* (1991[1813–16]) – Owen turned the factory village into a model community, arguing that higher wages, education and improvements in working/living conditions would increase rather than decrease productivity, output and profit. Trying to persuade others to follow his example through the spoken and the written word, he became an influential figure in early English socialism.

Owen was greatly concerned about the manufacturing system. He lamented the way machinery took the place of manual labour and the consequent depreciation of the value of labour. In *Observations on the Effect of the Manufacturing System* (1991[1815]: 95), Owen fulminated even more against the new spirit this system brought along; a spirit governed by the "principle of . . . immediate pecuniary gain, to which on the great scale every other is made to give way". Arousing the acquisitive passion and a desire for injurious luxuries, the system generated "a disposition which strongly impels its possessors to sacrifice the best feelings of human nature to this love of accumulation" (*ibid.*: 95). This spirit of gain at the expense of others creates conditions of rivalry, inequality, fraud and misery. Owen dismissed the idea that the division of labour created a framework of mutual dependence and cooperation, within which competition was a creative and positive force, harmonising interests for the good of all. Instead the division of labour set workers apart, putting their private interests "perpetually at variance with the public good" (*ibid.*: 282). In Owen's perception, competition created "a covered civil warfare" (*ibid.*: 358). True to his conviction that "the character is formed *for* and not *by* the individual" (*ibid.*: 305), however, it is the system that is at fault (*ibid.*: 96). In his autobiography Owen noted:

> I am thoroughly convinced that there can be no superior character formed under this thoroughly selfish system. Truth, honesty, virtue will be mere names, as they are now, and as they ever have been. Under this system there can be no true civilisation.
>
> (cited in Ryan 1981: 82)

Private property and inequality of rank, wealth and knowledge, Owen argued, correlates with poverty, ignorance and vice, breeding "envy, jealousy, a desire to possess, by any means in their power" (1991[1815]: 361). Competition is inevitable in such a setting. Private property, competition and greed are a package deal, with competition as the principle or mechanism driving the system towards excess and abuse. Founded upon opposing interests, competition as a mode of production and distribution of wealth necessarily brings out the worst in men and destroys happiness and well-being. Pointing out the systematic nature of greed in a system of private property and competition, Owen realised that to eradicate greed required a radical transformation of society by establishing a system of common property and communal living. To drive home his argument, Owen presented his views by drawing a contrast between the 'system of competition' and the 'system of cooperation'. Substituting competition for cooperation, discord for unity, and selfishness for benevolence is only possible by casting anew relations of property and the organisation of economic functions in society. And so he worked on a 'model of social harmony' (Goodwin 1978), fusing together individual and collective interest and benevolence and enlightened selfishness, because given man's sociability, "individual happiness can be increased and extended only in proportion as [man] actively endeavours to increase and extend the happiness of all around him" (Owen cited in Goodwin 1978: 31). Political economy was wrong to adopt the principle of individual competition as the cornerstone of its scientific inquiry, and in claiming that

> man can provide better for himself, and more advantageously for the public, when left to his own individual exertions, opposed to and in competition with his fellows, than when aided by any social arrangement which shall unite his interests individually and generally with society.
>
> (Owen 1991[1815]: 276)

Owen castigated political economy for selling this principle as scientific truth while it is instrumental in creating conditions of poverty and misery. None of the evils of the manufacturing system brought forth by the mechanism of competition were necessary to arrive at its benefits. The present system was "the most antisocial, impolitic, and irrational, that can be devised" and it is ludicrous to suppose it to be "a more advantageous principle on which to found the social system, for the benefit of all, or of any, than the principle of union and mutual co-operation" (*ibid.*: 276). Recognising that political economists were his main adversaries, but aware that the language of political economy was a useful vehicle to attract attention (Claeys 1987a: 49), Owen argued that his system of a community of property and equality would generate more wealth more efficiently than a system of competition and private property.

The economic logic of Owen's proposals is most fully explained in his *Report to the County of Lanark* (1991[1820]). Here he argued that "manual labour, properly directed, is the source of all wealth, and of national prosperity" (*ibid.*: 250). Labour would have to be remunerated by its actual value (rather than fluctuating monetary value). Pinning down the natural value of labour to ascertain the value of its products would do away with the zero-sum system of deceitful bargaining. Abolishing "the system of individual rewards, punishments, and competition" (*ibid.*: 304), which had created artificial distinctions of class and rank in flagrant contradiction to the fact that "all men, by nature, have equal rights" (*ibid.*: 344), would establish equality of wealth and rank and allow all unproductive, wasteful and ill-directed efforts to be put to productive use. Serving justice, such a system would remove poverty from society. Devising detailed plans to create self-managed communities of workers or cooperatives, Owen presented a view of a new society in which all would share in the benefits of the productive power of the manufacturing system.

Owen's views inspired the rise of the Owenite or cooperative movement, committed to form self-sufficient communities of workers based on cooperative ownership and profit sharing to remedy the evils of industrial society. Private property, selfishness and inequality/poverty were seen as intimately related, with competition being the centrifugal force in which all evil parts and effects spun together. The reformer and Chartist leader William Lovett argued that rather than "despotic power and corrupt legislation", it is competition that called forth "selfish, cunning, and rapacious feelings", as it implied clashes of interest in a zero-sum game (Claeys 1989: 142). With competition as "the pivotal concept in Owenite criticisms of the economy" (*ibid.*: 142), the movement also increasingly came to cast its criticisms in economic terms (touching upon questions of productive/unproductive labour, exchange and value). Taking labour to be the foundation of all wealth, these socialist writers emphasised that industrial society was built on exploitation, creating a mass of impoverished workers in sharp contrast to the growing riches of capitalists and landowners. That is why the methodology adopted by political economy of narrowing its focus to production growth by men driven to accumulate is wholly inadequate: it failed to consider distributional effects from the point of view of justice, which were essential to well-being in society given prevailing conditions of misery and poverty. Consequently, "the play of economic forces must be rationalized, organized, and moralized" (Pankhurst 1991: 91). Cooperation was to be established as a social form, taming self-interest "by destroying the conditions in which it thrives" (Goodwin 1978: 78).

Thompson's inquiry to reconcile security with equality

These features clearly light up in the work of the acknowledged leader of the cooperative or Owenite movement, William Thompson (1775–1833). This Irish landowner professed to be ashamed to belong to the idle classes and sought to redeem himself by improving the conditions of the tenants of his estate. He was deeply influenced by the ideas of Godwin, Owen and Bentham. Bentham invited him to stay at his place in London, where Thompson stayed almost five months before he moved on. Thompson tried to align Benthamite principles with the argument for Owen's system of mutual cooperation in his best-known work, his *Inquiry into the Principles of the Distribution of Wealth Most Conducive to Human Happiness* (1824), written to demolish the idea of the necessity and blessings of inequality of wealth. Thompson became the most prominent spokesman of the movement at the London Cooperative Society. This society of workers sought to disseminate the views of Robert Owen and organised several debates in 1825 between Owenites and Utilitarians. John Stuart Mill, 19 years old at the time, stepped into the ring against Thompson to defend the point of view of the political economists.

In the introduction to the *Inquiry*, Thompson argued that if utility or happiness is the measure of society and its institutions, and wealth is the most important means of happiness, wealth should be considered in its effects upon happiness, and in its political and moral as well as its material or economic effects. Mere accumulation or possession of wealth on which political economy focuses does not yet constitute utility, as it fails to consider the effects on happiness of how wealth is parcelled out among men in society. "It is not the mere possession of wealth", Thompson urges, "but the *right distribution* of it, that is important to a community" (1824: ix). That is why Thompson speaks of 'social science' as distinct from pure political economy. Founded upon the principle of utility, social science aims to discover that form of distribution most conducive to the happiness of all.

Following Bentham, Thompson applies the principles of security and equality to define the key question of social science. People are motivated to generate wealth to the extent to which they may enjoy the fruits of their labours (security). In the entire use of the products of labour, security triggers the maximum incentive. However, given that people have an equal capacity for pleasure, wealth should be equally distributed to extract the most happiness from wealth in society. The dilemma social science aims to solve is "*how to reconcile equality with security;* how to reconcile *just distribution with continued production*" (ibid.: xiv; italics in original). Calling attention to the immense increase in the productive powers of nations, industry and knowledge, Thompson attributes the "misery in the midst of all the means of happiness" to a vicious distribution of wealth. The existing arrangement of distribution "is to enrich a few at the expense of the mass of the producers" (*ibid.*: xvi), which cries out for an inquiry into modes of distribution and the extent to which these modes are consistent with the aims of wealth, political utility and morality. In the *Inquiry*, three economic systems are discussed in order to discover which system performs best: "labor by force", "labor by unrestricted individual competition" and "labor by mutual co-operation" (*ibid.*: xviii).

Investigating the natural laws of a just distribution of wealth, Thompson agrees with Owen that wealth is created by labour. Labour gets its strongest stimulus to produce wealth as means of happiness by its free use and by retaining the entire use of its products. To extract the maximum of happiness for both parties, moreover, any exchange must be voluntary. He sings the moral praises of voluntary exchange in terms reminiscent of the *doux commerce* thesis. With 'the art of exchange' gradually triumphing over the law of the jungle in the development of society, as Claeys summarised Thompson's view:

> Apprehension, distrust, envy and rapine were then replaced by an appreciation of the "nursery of social virtue", whereby satisfaction and pleasure elicited mutual sympathy, sociability and benevolence. Exchange was the most essential agency of human civilisation.
>
> (Claeys 1987a: 94)

Notwithstanding the advance made possible by voluntary exchange, the existing arrangement interferes. Direct force, fraud or unequal laws with the natural laws of distributive justice create a system in which wealth accumulated in the hands of a few. Such a system of great inequality is attended by moral, economic and political evils.

Dealing with the moral effects first, Thompson pointed out the negative-sum nature of the unequal distribution of wealth between the rich and the rest of the community. Wealth is created by labour and therefore accumulated wealth can only be derived from deductions from the products of the individual labours of the rest of the community. Given zero marginal utility of wealth for the rich, such a system diminishes the total sum of happiness in society. Worse, the system of forced inequality "engenders positive vices in the possessors of these excessive shares of wealth" (Thompson 1824: 187). At the same time, it "excites the admiration and the imitation, and in this way diffuses the practice of the vices of the rich, amongst the rest of the community" (*ibid.*: 191). This way "[a]n over-anxious pursuit of wealth" has become "the moving spring of society" (*ibid.*: 193), while the resulting "slavish selfishness" (*ibid.*: 194) has extinguished sympathy and benevolence.

Discussing the economic evils of excessive inequality next, Thompson argued that spending patterns by the rich are usually unproductive. Given their conspicuous nature, they are often wasteful by directing resources away from the production of articles which may satisfy ordinary wants and comforts of society. Under the political evils of excessive wealth Thompson listed "the usurpation of the powers of legislation, as well as of the executive and judicial authority, by those unqualified by education to exercise them aright, and with interests hostile to the general or national interest" (*ibid.*: 210).

Capitalism generates insecurity and inequality. Within capitalism, "[t]o inequality of wealth there is no bound: it becomes the ruling passion: the distinction which it confers, the envy which it excites, urge men to acquire it by any means: talents, virtue are sacrificed to it" (*ibid.*: 170). Greed ruled. Capitalism was a system of exploitation. Although the idle classes have no right to the fruits of the labour of others, Thompson argued with reference to Ricardo's labour theory of value, they appropriate the lion's share supported by conventions and/or legislation.

> A universal and always vigilant conspiracy of capitalists . . . exists every where, because founded on a universally existing interest, to cause the laborers to toil for the lowest possible, and to wrest as much as possible of the products of their labor to swell the accumulations and expenditure of capitalists.
>
> (Thompson 1824: 171)

The second system, of 'labor by unrestricted individual competition', constitutes a major improvement over such a system of restraint and force because greed is restrained by competition. A free market system satisfies the principle of security by way of "free labor, entire use of its products, and voluntary exchanges" and creates "abundant production, and development of all the active faculties" (*ibid.*: 367). All benefit but, as Thompson comes to conclude, it still fails the test of equality. A system based on competition leaves the seeds of selfishness and conflict intact, since the principle of competition itself harbours certain evils. The greatest evil is that competition brings along private property, inequality and rivalry. It pushes men towards selfishness and "a constant temptation to sacrifice the interests of others to his own" (*ibid.*: 370):

"Get wealth, if possible, honestly; but at all events get wealth" (*ibid.*: 193). Competition crowds out benevolence and cooperation. It is not a sufficient condition to ensure positive-sum outcomes in terms of happiness.

Judged by the principles of security and equality, Thompson claims superiority of Owen's system of 'labor by mutual co-operation'. It not only removes the evils of forced inequality, as does 'labor by individual competition', but also the evils attending the latter system, by killing the beast of greed (and pride). Owen had proven that it did not take the profit motive to encourage productive effort. Mutual cooperation in the full awareness that the general interest and the interest of the individual coincide, and with benefits voluntarily shared equally, generates full gains by doing away with all sorts of wastes following from the efforts to outdo others. At the end of his inquiry Thompson proposed a planned, cooperative society. One made up of mutually coordinated, self-managing communities, where the distinction between the owners of capital and the suppliers of labour collapses, where wealth is controlled and shared, and the acquisitive passion and the desire for distinction are put to rest.

Owen and Thompson argued that private property, competition and greed are a package deal, identifying competition as the operating mechanism of the system. Both accounts develop into a juxtaposition of the system of individual competition and the system of cooperation. Both claimed that benefits are only shared and evils avoided in the latter system. Property relations are identified as the most important condition determining the possibility of positive-sum outcomes. This is disputed: it matters to the assessment of the beneficial effects of the competitive system whether one takes the historically evolved property relations as a given or not. If the former, as Hunt pointed out, the worker may be said to benefit from exchange, although he is cheated out of his fair share, because a low wage is better than starvation (Hunt 1979: 146).

It was against these ideas that Mill responded in debates organised by the London Cooperative Society between Utilitarians and Owenites. Mill came prepared to the meetings, but only delivered his second speech. Prominent in both speeches was the idea that competition is not the big bad wolf (and neither was the labourer little red riding hood).

Mill first riposted to reaffirm the mutual benefits involved. Wealth is a product of labour, "but not of unassisted labour" (CW XXVI: 309): it takes two to tango. He dismissed the counterargument that capital itself is the produce of labour by arguing that labour was aided by capital, and that originally capitalists had been diligent labourers who had saved part of the produce of their industry. Mill made clear that he cares for much more than accumulation of wealth. His greatest and exclusive concern was the condition of the labouring poor. He would like to see all have as many comforts and joys as possible. Key issue is the remuneration of labour, which depends on competition. It all comes down to the ratio between labour and capital. According to Mill, the population tends to grow faster than capital, whereby wages have a tendency to fall. Any plan to improve the condition of labour without some regulation of numbers is futile. Moreover, establishing an equal distribution of wealth within a competitive system would only bring back the same inequalities within a few years and so, Mill impressed upon his audience, establishing equality requires renouncing private property.

Attending the second of the Chancery Lanes debates on cooperation, the once-more fully prepared Mill had his say. He insisted that he was equally distressed by the evils in society, but denied that these were necessary consequences of the competitive system. Many of the acclaimed benefits of the cooperative system – a very great degree of happiness, good government, good laws, a good administration – are equally compatible with a competitive system. The cooperative system not only suffers likewise from taxes and tithes. If much is made of crossing out the deductions from the produce of labour from profits and rents, it should also be realised that these deductions amount to no more than one tenth. Fat lot of good that would do.

Mill next discussed Thompson's objections against competition. First, he argued that competition does not rule out benevolence; there is competition for everything – for good as well as ill. Neither does competition obstruct the apportioning of demand and supply. Instabilities are inherent to commerce and usually regulate themselves. Mill made short shrift with the presumed evil of the competition of machinery to manual labour, arguing that mechanisation would increase the demand for labour in the long run. Last, he denied that competition implies rivalry (as long as the population is properly regulated). But what about the disadvantages of the proposed cooperative system? Mill offered four objections, starting with the view that a cooperative system fails to provide proper incentives to exertion and work if it basically benefits others. Second, Mill noted a problem of accountability: "what is every body's business is nobody's" (CW XXVI: 320). Third, Mill objected to the system's universal regulation, arguing that "it is infinitely better to attain a given end by leaving people to themselves than to attain the same end by controlling them" (ibid.: 321). Last, the cooperative system was too expensive, drawing away funds from more productive uses. In his closing words Mill insisted that he was not to be thought an enemy of Owen's system, but considered it "neither the only nor the best chance" (ibid.: 324) at human improvement and that he put his money on the principle of self-interest. Given its strength and potency,

> it is surely not very wise to court opposition from it, when you might have it on your side. Let things be so arranged that the interest of every individual shall exactly accord with the interest of the whole – thus much it is in the power of laws and institutions to effect; and, this done, let every individual be so educated, as to know his own interest – Thus by the spontaneous action of a vast number of agents, every one drawing in the direction of his own happiness, the happiness of the whole will be attained.
> (CW XXVI: 324)

So Mill had several axes to grind: (1) competition is not to be identified with negative/zero-sum outcomes; (2) the contrast drawn between the system of cooperation and the system of competition is misleading;[1] and (3) there is no package deal: the competitive system tends towards greater equality, without the need to radically reform society and its institutions by abolishing private property and inequality. Most importantly, (4) competition is not a malevolent mechanism, and if in present times selfishness abounds, do not throw out the child with the bathwater.

In his essay *Civilization* (1836), Mill identified the progress of civilisation with advancements in cooperation. And it is the division of employments that "is the great school of co-operation" (CW XVIII: 123), showing advances in security, knowledge, wealth and humanity. One effect of the growth of civilisation, Mill argued, is an ever-stronger focus on "the individual's money-getting pursuits" (*ibid.*: 129). The advance of civilisation implies that we rely upon others to secure most of our concerns, directing our energy towards wealth, distinction, charity and virtue. Only the desire for wealth is universal, and

> wealth being, in the case of the majority, the most accessible means of gratifying all their other desires, nearly the whole of the energy of character which exists in highly civilized societies concentrates itself on the pursuit of that object.
>
> (CW XVIII: 129–30)

Moreover, commercial dealings increasingly take place in an impersonal context without the benefit of the correcting influence of public opinion. As a consequence, there is the growth of 'puffing' in "a state of society where any voice, not pitched in an exaggerated key, is lost in the hubbub. Success, in so crowded a field, depends not upon what a person is, but upon what he seems" (*ibid.*: 133). Cooperation may help out. The fall in profit rates had slashed the number of small dealers and small producers, concentrating businesses in the hands of large capitalists. Yet Mill did not believe competition was extinguished. Nor should a general association be entrusted with managing the community's resources. Mill believed that competition would be limited by "the progress of the spirit of cooperation" (*ibid.*: 136).

Mill may also have learned from the debates to recognise the importance of the question of a just distribution of wealth. In his *Principles of Political Economy* (1848), Mill argued that laws of distribution are human institutions, which can be changed any way a society sees fit. Mill considered this insight to be his most important contribution to political economy (Pankhurst 1991: 151). He added that they are not arbitrary, and that within a system of competition its outcomes are sure as ever. Mill acknowledged that political economists in England focused exclusively on competition as regulator of the division of produce. This is understandable, because it is only on this assumption that laws that explain how rents, profits, wages and prices are regulated can be laid down (PPE I: 292). After all, political economy is a hypothetical science. In actual affairs, distribution is often more the result of custom. He repeated his basic stance against the socialists, rejecting their "declamations against competition" (PPE II: 354). Yes, there are inconveniences in competition and there is ground for moral objections, but it is not true that competition is the sole cause of all economic evils. Again he pointed out that the merit of competition should be judged against its opposite, monopoly. Most forms of competition are beneficial to labour. They are indispensable, although perhaps not the best conceivable stimulus to action and progress. Dispensing with the qualifications once he drew his conclusions, Mill argued that competition is no baneful and anti-social principle, as the socialists would have it: "I conceive that, even in the present state of society and industry, every restriction of it is an evil, and every extension of it . . . is always an ultimate good" (PPE II: 356).

Friedrich Engels

Friedrich Engels (1820–95) was the son of a wealthy German manufacturer. His parents expected him to join the family firm and were distressed by their son's radical views and revolutionary activities. In 1842 they send him to Manchester where his father co-owned a factory. Engels was shocked by the factory system, the condition of the working class in England and the oppressive nature of economic forces in society. In Manchester he contacted British socialists and attended lectures at the Owenite Hall of Science. His education in political economy through the lectures and works of Watts and Thompson is apparent in his first essay *Outlines of a Critique of Political Economy* (1844). He wrote the piece for the *Deutch-Französische Jahrbücher*, which greatly impressed its editor, Karl Marx. Many of the themes Marx and Engels were to develop in later years already featured in Engels's *Outlines* (see Hollander 2011: Chapter 1; Claeys 1987a; Muller 2003: 178–81).

The essay opens with a short historical sketch of political economy – defined as "science of enrichment born of the merchants' mutual envy and greed" (Engels 1844: 1). Here Engels argued that although the Smithian system was an advance over mercantilism, it was only half a step forward. 'New economics' failed to question the basic premise in analysis, private property, and had to resort to sophistry and hypocrisy to cover up its inherent contradictions. Engels's central aim in the *Outlines* is twofold: (1) to show the contradictions in the analysis of political economy's basic categories (like value, rent, population); and (2) to expose that all deliberations in political economy are premised on competition as the necessary consequence of private property.

The first consequence of private property is trade. Never mind that trade in the eighteenth century was humanised and argued to be mutually beneficial and promoting bonding. Underneath trade, selling and buying is a zero-sum game in which interests are strictly opposed, leading to rivalry, mistrust, unlawful action and deception. Trade, Engels emphasised, is "legalised fraud" (*ibid.*: 5). Another such a contradiction pops up in value theory. Economists usually suppose that abstract value (distinguished from exchangeable value) is regulated by cost of production based on the argument that no-one would sell without covering costs. The argument introduces selling and hence the concept of exchange and "the circumstance of competition" (*ibid.*: 7) and muddles over the distinction between abstract (or real) value and exchangeable value. The same confusion surrounds the idea that abstract value is regulated by utility. This also applies to the concept of self-interest. Self-interest is never innocent in the context of a world of monopoly and private property. As Muller captured Engels's disgust:

> The work of Adam Smith and his disciples obscured what Engels found morally scandalous: capitalism was built on avarice and on selfishness. If the key maneuver of Enlightenment thinkers such as Smith was to call attention to the potential social benefits of what had been previously stigmatized as "greed" and "pride", the first countermaneuver of socialist critics such as Engels was to restigmatize self-interest as greed.
>
> (Muller 2003: 178)

Private property and competition are omniscient in the political economy's analysis, without any effort on the part of the economist to question these concepts. Competition is "the economist's principal category – his most beloved daughter, whom he ceaselessly caresses" (Engels 1844: 14). Engels argued that private property creates opposition and discord. It splits production into nature (soil) and human activity. The latter in turn is dissolved into labour and capital. Next each of these three elements becomes fragmented. Therefore "private property isolates everyone in his own crude solitariness" (*ibid.*: 14) and since each has identical interests, competition necessarily follows. Taking position against these premises, Engels aimed to destroy both the moral and the economic logic of competition.

Engels argued that the mercantile system has "paraded its mean avarice" with a certain artless Catholic candour but that with Smith, 'the *economic Luther*', Protestant hypocrisy entered economics (*ibid.*: 5). It is true, as Smith asserted, that commerce humanises but only because it serves private interest. In true Mandevillean style, Engels pointed out the hypocritical and egoistical foundation of this so-called "humanity of trade":

> Naturally, it is in the interest off the trader to be on good terms with the one from whom he buys cheap as well as with the other to whom he sells dear. A nation therefore acts very imprudently if it fosters feelings of animosity in its suppliers and customers. The more friendly, the more advantageous. Such is the humanity of trade. And this hypocritical way of misusing morality for immoral purposes is the pride of the free-trade system.
>
> (Engels 1844: 6)

Like Mandeville, Engels disqualified any moral benefit that is rooted in private vices: true morality is never instrumental to private advantage, and honestly,

"When have you been moral without being interested, without harbouring at the back of your mind immoral, egoistical motives?" (*ibid.*: 6). Competition is based on self-interest and puts self-interested individuals at war with one another, transforming "mankind into a horde of ravenous beasts (for what else are competitors?) who devour one another" (*ibid.*: 6).

Engels equally found fault with the economic logic of competition that political economists boast about. Competition is self-destructive: given that every competitor desires to control the market for private advantage, competition necessarily resolves into monopoly. The contradiction involved in competition is that "each cannot but desire the monopoly, whilst the whole as such is bound to lose by monopoly and must therefore remove it" (*ibid.*: 15). In the context of private property, competition is a system of power. Free competition is an impossibility. Moreover, if competition is to benefit all, it does not deliver. Engels argued that because of competition, demand and supply continually adjust but never correspond. This creates perpetual fluctuations and regular trade crises, attended by misery and poverty, which were all unnecessary "if they were to organise production" (*ibid.*: 16). Given price fluctuations, buying and selling with an eye to profit involves an element of gambling and "everyone must become a speculator – that is to say . . . must enrich himself at the expense of others, must calculate on the misfortune of others" (*ibid.*: 17). Claeys concluded that "Engels essentially adopted the conclusions of Owenite political economy" (1987a: 179), showing that in all key terms of political economy "everything comes down to competition" (Engels 1844: 14), and hence as effects of private property. Private property, splitting up production into distinct categories, creates competition: labour is set up against labour, capital against capital, and landed property against landed property. Competition is "the cunning right of the stronger" (*ibid.*: 13). This law of the stronger will lead to centralisation of property "until the world is divided into millionaires and paupers" (*ibid.*: 23). Whatever scheme is dreamt up to remedy these inequalities, the only workable solution is "a total transformation of social conditions, a fusion of opposed interests, an abolition of private property" (*ibid.*: 23).

Thompson had juxtaposed different types of society and aimed to show the material and moral superiority of the system of cooperation. Engels put these three systems in a historical perspective. He identified competition as the basic mechanism through which private property and greed create conditions of misery and inequality. While agreeing and extending Engels's moral critique of political economy, and making use of Engels's hints at capitalism's contradictions and mystifications, Marx sought to demolish the economic logic on which the political economist's acclaim of competition rested.

Marx's analysis of the 'war amongst the greedy'

An appeal to reason and/or morality was not going to persuade the ruling class to transform society. Therefore, Karl Marx (1818–83) saw the early socialist utopians as dreamers. Luckily, transformation would not have to await the benevolence of the ruling class: capitalism would work its own demise and transformation. But people had to be aware of what was going on. Political economy threw dust in everyone's eyes. Economists claimed to have established the natural laws that governed economic phenomena without recognising the historical contingency of the basic categories of their analysis. Things are not what they seem. Failing to distinguish between appearance and essence, the economist's laws only appeared to bring harmony, directing inherent tendencies within capitalism towards wealth, freedom and equality. To get a grip on the complexity and variety of reality, Marx adopted Hegel's method of breaking down complex relationships into essences through abstraction and simplification, studying their interconnections and synthesising these elements dialectically, thus building up a comprehensive understanding of the whole. Marx lavishly used abstractions himself, so it is not abstraction as a method of analysis to which he objected in political economy. Marx criticised economists for taking the world at face value. And appearances are deceptive indeed, as surface appearances often turn out to be contrasted and reversed at a deeper level. Marx shared the idea with Mandeville that a look behind the façade of society is necessary to understand the actual driving forces of man and society. In ignorance of the essences and their interconnections, political economy coughs up pre-cooked conclusions without much explanation to show for. It seeks to discover the principles of exchangeable value, rent, profit and wage, without comprehending that these basic categories of political economy move to the rhythm of their underlying forces.

This is where Marx's materialist conception of history comes in. Society changes as people develop more complex forms of productive activity to secure the means of subsistence. Marx held that social structure, social conflict and change are conditioned, not causally determined, by the material mode of production. History reveals different epochs on the basis of different configurations of production and organisation modes. Within each stage of society, the organisation of material life and means of production give rise to relations of production or class structure of society. These relations of production are the ground rules and roles by which the game is played. They reflect the social relationships shaped by conditions of ownership of and control over the means of production. Therefore, class relations are inherently antagonistic, as control of the means of production by one class allows exploitation of the other. To Marx, history is a continuing story of exploitation. He discussed how capitalism emerged from feudal society as a new mode of production based on capital and wage labour and investigated the mechanisms of reproduction. For "every social process of production is, at the same time, a process of reproduction" (Marx 1867: 401). Continuity of the capitalist system requires the continuous reproduction of the class structure, enabling the upward march of capital by exploiting labour. From Marx's perspective, it is an insult that political economy takes for granted 'the facts' of private property, competition, division of labour, exchange, the social categories of labour, capital and land and the distribution of wealth into rents, wages and profits. These basic categories of political economy are not natural categories, universal across place and time, but contingent upon historical and material conditions. Marx insisted that the economists had failed to recognise that capitalism is a historically specific form of property and production. Capital is in all modes of production an instrument of production produced by past labour. Specific to the capitalist mode, however, is "the power of capital to yield profits", with capital as "the source of income and power to the dominant social class" (Hunt 1979: 181). The same goes for property; there is nothing natural or self-evident about private property. Forms of property and property rights vary with different stages of society, shaping social relations in defining power, privileges and sanctions for each stage in the material conditions of production (Hunt 1990: 77). The basic categories of political economy cannot be taken for granted as a starting-point for analysis.

Emphasising the historical character of capitalism, in *Capital* (1867) Marx aims to provide a theoretical analysis of the capitalist mode of production rather than a moral critique:

> Marx does not advance a moral "right" to an unscathed existence or something similar against the impositions of capitalism. Instead, he hopes that with the growing insight into the destructive nature of the capitalist system (which can be established without recourse to morality), the working class will take up the struggle against this system – not on the basis of *morality*, but rather on the basis of its own *interest*. Not, however, on the basis of an interest of a better situation within capitalism, but rather on the basis of an interest in a good and secure life, which can only be realized by transcending capitalism.
>
> (Heinrich 2004: 36)

Marx sought to expose the hidden suppositions, growing contradictions and zero-sum nature of the economic logic of capitalism. Probing into the hidden, inner logic of capitalism, looking in the 'machine-room' behind the façade, reveals the antagonisms, inconsistencies and mystifications within the capitalist mode of production. They prove that the acclaimed beneficial results of the bourgeois economy political economists boasted about is framed by the assumptions and presumed self-evident truths on which their analysis rests. Marx set out to show that political economy's claim regarding the benign operation of competition is untenable on its own terms. Without any pretension of being able to capture the full flavour of Marx's analysis and assessment of capitalism, I focus on the wheels of "*greed, and the war amongst the greedy*" (Marx 1844: 28).

Competition plays a pivotal role in Marx's account of capitalism and partakes in the confusion the political economists have created. The latter stick to the surface view of competition, emphasising its centripetal forces, a mechanism of social coordination founded upon equality and freedom. Underneath, however, the centrifugal forces of competition rule, showing competition to be a coercive and exploitative mechanism, which increases inequality (see also Fornäs 2013: 254). Contrary to what political economists claim, competition does not produce a beneficial result for all. Moreover, the mechanism of competition is itself a historical category. It reflects rather than instigates the dynamics of value, money and capital in evolving forms of production. Therefore, competition can never be the starting point of analysis. As Marx explained in the *Grundrisse*, written in 1857 and 1858 and containing preliminary studies for the argument in *Capital*: "Competition generally, this essential locomotive force of the bourgeois economy, does not establish its laws, but is rather its executor" (1857: 476). Competition is the mechanism through which the laws of motion of capitalism work. Given that the circulation of capital is the 'supercharger' of the capitalist mode of production, "a scientific analysis of competition is not possible, before we have a conception of the inner nature of capital" (1867: 222).

And do not be fooled by the praise of competition in the name of liberty either. Free competition, Marx emphasised, is not to be opposed to a system of limits and barriers. While it did remove limits and barriers, it was only those that proved detrimental to the development of capital. "It is not individuals who are set free by free competition; it is, rather, capital which is set free" (1857: 573). However crucial in understanding the laws of motion in capitalism, "[c]ompetition merely *expresses* as real, posits as an external necessity, that which lies within the nature of capital" (*ibid.*: 574). That is why it is ludicrous to claim that free competition is the natural consequence of and condition for human freedom. The same goes for equality. The act of exchange between two individuals, taken in isolation, may be said to involve two equivalents or express the idea that exchange establishes equality. Exchange, however, is a social act, and always involves differences in power, knowledge and opportunities. Marx denied the liberal conception of competition as the opposite pole of monopoly or power (Palermo 2016). Competition generates a tendency towards monopoly and is set by conditions of power. It also propels capitalism towards its transformation. As Marx observed: "The analysis of what free competition really is, is the only rational reply to the middle-class prophets who laud it to the skies or to the socialists who damn it to hell" (1857: 575). The framing of classical economics is all wrong, underscoring the need to beat political economy on its own turf.

Marx starts *Capital I* (1867) from an inquiry into the nature of a commodity and immediately plunges into value theory. Each commodity represents value. It may be used to satisfy a need (use value) or to exchange it for some other commodity (exchange value). The exchange value of a quantity of a commodity is expressed in terms of a quantity of some other commodity. Marx argued that the equivalence expressed in this comparison of quantities of different commodities implies a common element. He adopted the view of the classical economists that exchange value between commodities is determined by the quantity of homogeneous labour used in production. Value is a product of abstract labour, assumed to be applied under prevailing conditions of production, skills and intensity, and stripped of all qualitative differences, varying only in quantity, i.e., labour time. Exchange relations between commodities are regulated by value, the socially necessary labour time required to produce a commodity.

Value, being immaterial, needs a means of representation. In the development of exchange relations, one commodity first assumes the role of universal equivalent or money commodity, moving to the institution of money to represent value next. With money starting to circulate, the value of all other commodities is measured and expressed by money.

The circulation and exchange of commodities gave rise to the circulation of money, and money in turn created capital. Money breaks up exchange into two acts (selling and buying), represented by Marx by the formula C–M–C. In this process, value changes form twice: from commodity (particular) to money (universal) and into commodity again. Split into two, exchange allows holding on to the money received from the sale as a reserve fund (hoarding). Such reserves also allow a split between the purchase and its payment, creating relations between debtor and creditor. The rise of creditor–debtor relations signify the emergence of a new form of circulation in which money is exchanged to get money. The exchange relation C–M–C is changed into M–C–M, in which money assumes the function of capital and becomes "the end and aim of a sale" (*ibid.*: 88).

So capital arrives at the scene as people start to use money to make money and money becomes a means to create surplus value. For Marx capital is a process: setting money to work to increase value. The capitalist is driven by a "boundless greed after riches" (*ibid.*: 107), for which purpose he throws his money into circulation again and again to chase after value. In *Grundrisse*, Marx argued that money is 'the general form of wealth', but being a commodity capable of being appropriated and accumulated, it "changes into the lord and god of the world of commodities" (1857: 150).[2] Like money, greed is a historical category. As general wealth is individualised in money form, money is "not only the object but also the fountainhead of greed. The mania for possessions is possible without money; but greed itself is the product of a definite social development, not *natural*, as opposed to *historical*" (*ibid.*: 151).

Capital is the process of valorisation, value chasing after value, changing form between commodities and money in the process. If the circulation of money developed out of the circulation of commodities, the circulation of capital emerges from the circulation of money. As this historical process evolves, the rule of capital is established, defining the terms of its relation to labour. Marx described the development of the capitalist forces of production as a process in which the inner logic (as well as its contradictions) of capitalism coagulate as capital takes control. Gradually the elements got into place and created that mix of initial conditions that set the capitalist system in motion. Capital started to circulate. "[T]he owner of the means of production and subsistence meets in the market with the free labourer selling his labour-power" (1867: 120). In other words, labour has become a commodity bought and sold in the market, whereby the capitalist gains control over the labour he contracts, as well as its product.

And a very special commodity it is, because labour alone is capable of creating value. Labour is a life-giving substance but it needs capital to reproduce itself, just like capital needs labour to reproduce itself and grow. These needs clash. Capital and labour are antagonistic: "Capital is dead labour, that, *vampire-like*, only lives by sucking living labour, and lives the more, the more labour it sucks" (*ibid.*: 163). The resulting competition between capital and labour, between personified capitals, and between labour and labour, turned greed into a necessity and structural characteristic of capitalism. In order to lay bare the intricacies of capital and "the secret of profit making" (*ibid.*: 123), Marx says, we need to leave the noisy sphere at the surface ruled by

> Freedom, Equality, Property and Bentham. Freedom, because both buyer and seller of a commodity, say of labour-power, are constrained only by their own free will . . . Equality, because each enters into relation with the other . . . and they exchange equivalent for equivalent. Property, because each disposes only of what is his own. And Bentham, because each looks only to himself. The only force that brings them together and puts them in relation with each other, is the selfishness, the gain and the private interests of each. Each looks to himself only, and no one troubles himself about the rest, and just because they do so, do they all . . . work together to their mutual advantage, for the common weal and in the interest of all.
>
> (Marx 1867: 123)

All mere pretence. Upon entering into "the hidden abode of production", "Mr Moneybags" and "the possessor of labour-power" change appearance and turn into antagonists and representatives of capital and labour respectively: "The one with an air of importance, smirking, intent on business; the other, timid and holding back" (*ibid.*: 123). Marx argues that capitalists chase after value by seeking to maximise surplus value, the difference between the use value of labour power (its product) and the exchange value of labour power (wage). Value is a product of labour, the putting to work of labour power. Not that the labourer has a choice: to survive he needs to buy access to the means of production with the one thing marketable he has. The capitalist buys labour power and secures the product of labour for himself by paying the cost of reproduction.

To Marx labour is so central to human existence that man defines or realises himself through labour. Labour defines man in relation to nature (and the means of subsistence), to his fellowmen and to the product of his labour. The capitalist mode of production founded upon labour as a commodity under the control of the capitalist deprives the labourer of these self-defining qualities of labour and alienates him. The capitalist buys labour power and appropriates the value it creates. "The worker puts his life into the object; but now his life no longer belongs to him but to the object. . . . the greater this product, the less is he himself" (1844: 29). Marx (1844) concluded that private property is originally the necessary consequence of alienated labour, although the relationship between private property and alienation turns reciprocal. The labourer's estrangement is inextricably linked to appropriation by the capitalist.[3] This is where competition comes in. Competition is the necessary consequence of private property and estranged labour (ibid.: 34), as appropriation and the conditions of production set up rivalry between capital and labour.

Marx first discussed competition in the context of the basic conflict between capital and labour about the length of the working day, the number of extra hours in the working day after the labourer has produced his reproduction value. "He [the capitalist], like all other buyers, seeks to get the greatest possible benefit out of the use-value of his commodity" (1867: 163). The worker, by contrast, equally eager to strike the best deal, demands a normal working day to be able to restore his labour power. "There is here, therefore, an antinomy, right against right, both equally bearing the seal of the law of exchanges. Between equal rights force decides" (ibid.: 164).

According to Marx (1844), the worker necessarily loses in the struggle between capitalist and worker. The price of labour is determined by demand and supply, with labourer and capitalist having opposite interests. Inequalities in power to secure class interests put workers at a great disadvantage. Moreover, specialisation implies that workers are not able to apply their labour elsewhere or offer their labour where its price is highest. Adding to the subordinated position of the worker vis-à-vis the capitalist is that the labourer is far more dependent upon the capitalist than the other way around, while institutional barriers deny workers the chance to make a fist as a pressure group. The unilateral dependence of workers upon wage income to secure provision does not help either. Workers are worse off even in an advancing state of society, let alone in a stationary or declining state. They get the short end of the stick: (1) growth implies overwork and premature death; (2) growth means capital accumulation with all its destructive consequences: increased dependency (reduction to a mere machine, a bond servant of capital), competition and poverty (starvation or beggary for a section of the workers). If force decides, Marx concluded, "Victory goes necessarily to the capitalist" (ibid.: 3), stretching the length of the working day to overexploitation. Although capital itself suffers if labour is overexploited (shortening the lifetime of labour power means raising the rate of replacement), competition among individual capitalists prevents acting on this interest of capital. A surplus population lends a helping hand to capital here and allows the capitalist to press on, regardless of the effects on the health and well-being of its workers. "Après moi le déluge! is the watchword of every capitalist" (1867: 181). This cannot be pinned on the capitalists: "Free competition brings out the inherent laws of capitalist production, in the shape of external coercive laws having power over every individual capitalist" (ibid.: 181).

Given the limitations on the creation of surplus value by the limited hours in a working day and the limited supply of labour, capitalists seek other ways to increase surplus value. As soon as an individual capitalist finds a way to increase productivity by innovation (organisational improvements, new technology, etc.), which cuts the socially necessary labour time to reproduce labour, he can extract additional surplus value. Other capitalists, now confronted with a comparative disadvantage, are pressed to adopt the new technology as well, whereupon all capitalists enjoy the increase in relative surplus value. "Hence there is immanent in capital an inclination and constant tendency, to heighten the productiveness of labour, in order to cheapen commodities, and by such cheapening to cheapen the labourer himself" (*ibid.*: 224). Innovations are a permanent source of relative surplus value. This includes organisational forms. Marx next analysed how cooperation, framed within the manufacture under the direction of capital, is appropriated by capital to pocket its benefits at the expense of labour.

Capital accumulation allowed the introduction of the manufacturing system. Manufacture concentrated the labour process, organising cooperation between workers in a framework controlled by capitalists,[4] allowing gains in productivity. This enabled capitalists to appropriate the surplus value that cooperation generated. Manufacture marked the transition from the feudal stage of society to the capitalist stage, setting the interaction of elements and conditions in motion.

First the division of labour takes off. Putting handicraft workers together, their usual productive activities are simplified, subdivided into detail processes and assigned to different workers. The resulting increasing returns to scale generate additional surplus value by reducing the labour time necessary for the reproduction of labour power. Specialisation also implies a deskilling process, whereby the value of labour power falls, increasing the surplus value extracted by capital (*ibid.*: 244). Given the growing uniformity of labour, competition among workers increases, reducing bargaining power. Having no alternative to procure the means of subsistence, workers lose the advantage of knowledge and skills to capital (Tinel 2013). Subdividing the production process, moreover, requires coordination and structuring at the different detail processes. Consequently, a pre-ordered, continuous and regular process develops, set by quantitative rule. As the production process fragments, instruments must be adapted to the requirements of the detail processes, paving the way for the use of machinery. Marx referred to Babbage, who had argued: "When each process has been reduced to the use of some simple tool, the union of all these tools, actuated by one moving power, constitutes a machine" (quoted in Tinel 2013: 261). As a consequence, the production process achieves a certain autonomy. This autonomy is not absolute in manufacturing because it still is "a productive mechanism whose parts are human beings" (Marx 1867: 238), whereby expansion is necessarily limited.

For expansion to become limitless, the production process needs to be mechanised further, substituting human labour for machinery. This is what happens as manufacture is replaced by the factory system or modern industry. The factory system propels the process of mechanisation to the next stage, adapting and subordinating labour to machinery. Division of labour is objectified

(Tinel 2013): the productive mechanism is no longer based on the combination of labour (subjective), but found in the combination of detail machines, imposing technical, numerical and sequential requirements upon the production system. Machinery instead of human labour becomes the regulating element of the production process (Ricoy 2003: 56), perfecting the logic of the process (Marx 1867: 380). "[M]odern industry has a productive organism that is purely objective, in which the labourer becomes a mere appendage to an already existing material condition of production" (*ibid.*: 268).

This is the ultimate humiliation as man by his labour is forced to recreate again and again the chains by which he is fastened to a system which dehumanises him (*ibid.*: 716; Tinel 2013: 270). With the advance of machinery as an organising element of production, labour becomes ever more uniform, creating greater flexibility, elasticity and hence gains in productivity, expanding production and the accumulation of capital as well as competition among workers. The last step was taken when modern industry took it upon itself "to construct machines by machines" (Marx 1867: 267), generating autonomous technical change which continually promotes expansion of production.

Naturally, these developments assume an expanding social division of labour and an expanding system of exchange or sphere of circulation of commodities and money (Smith's extent of the market). Marx argued that division of labour in society and division of labour in industry are correlated and advance together. With all these elements interacting – mechanisation, division of labour, expanding productivity and exchange system – the system is fully geared to the production of capital through the extraction of surplus value. This way "capital and its self-expansion appear as the starting and the closing point, the motive and the purpose of production" (1894: 176). To Marx the accumulation of capital and the development of the forces of production go hand in hand, and depend on the expansion of markets and demand. To secure such expansion, capitalism must constantly create new needs. Appetites are triggered and new needs created to trick others into dependence and sacrifice to enrich oneself. Sacrificing his humanity, the more man needs, the more he needs money. Consequently, "[t]he need for money is . . . the true need produced by the economic system", and given the constant drive to accumulate, *"[e]xcess* and *intemperance* comes to be its true norm" (1844: 49; italics in original). For each capitalist, competition is a must in order to survive and as such a coercive mechanism, forcing capitalist to accumulate. As Marx exclaimed: "Accumulate, accumulate! That is Moses and the prophets!" (1867: 418).

In the case of labour, the ongoing process of growth and accumulation leads to an intensification of competition among workers with all sorts of harmful effects (violence, wage cuts and beggary and starvation for some). In the case of capitalists, competition destroys itself, as wealth and capital are increasingly concentrated into the hands of an ever-smaller group of capitalists. Competition puts both capitalists and labourers between the devil and the deep blue sea.

In the process of accumulation, capitalists compete by cheapening commodities through increasing productivity and the scale of production. Consequently, "the larger capitals beat the smaller" (*ibid.*: 441). Given the ongoing increase in output without matching effective demand, periodically crises occur which tend to become ever more severe.

One has to probe into the hidden world to understand what makes capitalism tick. By differentiating between essences and their representations, Marx uncovered the dynamics of contradictions operating beneath the surface, increasingly bent to the rule of capital. The same duality can be observed in competition, the mechanism by which the forces of production develop. At the surface, competition absorbs these contradictions (between capital and labour, between capitals, and between labourers), bringing about a state of unity (establishing equilibrium between supply and demand and the tendency towards an equalisation of the rate of profit across industries). Underneath this surface appearance of competition, competition is the (increasingly nasty) muscle man, acting in the service of the rule of capital, forcing capitalists and labourers alike into behaviours in the service of accumulating capital. Greed sums up the mind-set of this muscle man. As Palermo added:

> Competition . . . operates as an external coercive force governing an increasingly wide spectrum of social relations and presenting itself as an autonomous force . . . Competition becomes a social standard, a normative benchmark that imposes its logic in every act of social life and far beyond the realm of commodity production.
>
> (Palermo 2016: 277)

Both expressions of competition are intrinsically related. The point of view of competition held by classical political economy is short-sighted and wholly inadequate. Yet, it forms the basis of the claim that cooperation through the mechanism of competition is mutually beneficial. In reality, however, growth of production and capital is accompanied by dehumanisation, deskilling and immiserisation, as such increasingly undermining the conditions under which greed may be said to be self-interest. It simply is not true that reciprocal dependence in living by exchange is mutually beneficial:

> The economists express this as follows: Each pursues his private interest and only his private interest; and thereby serves the private interests of all, the general interest, without willing or knowing it. The real point is not that each individual's pursuit of his private interest promotes the totality of private interests, the general interest . . . The point is rather that private interest is itself already a socially determined interest, which can be achieved only within the conditions laid down by society and with the means provided by society; hence it is bound to the reproduction of these conditions and means. It is the interest of private persons; but its content, as well as the form and means of its realisation, is given by social conditions independent of all.
>
> (Marx 1857: 87)

Starting from these social conditions, capitalist society is not the scene of unintended, private contributions to the public good, but the scene of class conflict driven by the antagonism between capital and labour. In the capitalist system, greed is a system property infecting capitalists and labourers.

> It establishes an accumulation of misery, corresponding with accumulation of wealth. Accumulation of wealth at one pole is, therefore, at the same time accumulation of misery, agony of toil slavery, ignorance, brutality, mental degradation, at the opposite pole, *i.e.*, on the side of the class that produces its own product in the form of capital.
>
> (Marx 1867: 451)

On the suppositions of the political economists themselves, then, a liberal market society is increasingly characterised by (1) a tendency towards monopoly as capitalist power is ever more centralised; and (2) growing wealth for the few and growing misery for the many (Harvey 2010: 289). Using the same basic suppositions, Marx shattered the dream of a positive-sum society built on greed by pointing out the zero/negative-sum outcomes of the system.

In *Capital II* (1885), Marx turned his attention to the process of the circulation of capital, which in the analysis of the process of production of surplus value of *Capital I* had been assumed to run ever so smoothly (Arthur and Reuten 1998; Harvey 2013). This time Marx abstracted from the intricacies and dynamics of this process of producing surplus value, assuming that commodities are sold at their values, that the system is closed and that there are no productivity gains through technological and organisational change.

The circulation process consists of three separate but interdependent circuits of capital. Capital is value in motion, taking different forms in the process of generating surplus value. Money buys labour power and means of production (first circuit; money capital), which are used to produce commodities (second circuit; productive capital), but next have to be (transported and) sold to be converted back into money (realising surplus value as M' > M; commodity capital). The money then allows the process to start again. So capital passes from money through commodity to money again in the process of valorisation.

In these transformations, all kinds of obstacles and barriers may arise that obstruct circulation. Individuals may hoard money instead of spending what they receive. To some extent hoarding is a necessary part of the process. Organisational change and new technologies create instabilities in the circulation process and as the capital intensity of production increases, more money capital must be kept in reserve to deal with these adjustments. This raises the question of effective demand: where does the demand to buy the surplus value come from? If more and more surplus value is produced by paying labour less and less, the consequent lack of effective demand may threaten the capacity to realise surplus value through sales. However, keeping effective demand high by paying more, threatens the capacity to extract surplus value in production.

All these contradictions and obstacles to the continuity of the circulation process freeze up capital and make capital unproductive. As the argument unfolded (Campbell and Reuten 2002), Marx showed that credit becomes essential to overcome these barriers in expanding the capacity to create and capture surplus value. Shortening the time capital is tied up in circulation, being unproductive, cuts costs. It pays to have a class of merchants who specialise in selling commodities and converting them into money, although the profit of commercial capital comes out of the surplus value created by productive capital.

> A definite part of the total capital dissociates itself from the rest and stands apart in the form of money-capital, whose capitalist function consists exclusively in performing these operations for the entire class of industrial and commercial capitalists . . . The movements of this money-capital are, therefore, once again merely movements of an individualised part of the industrial capital engaged in the reproduction process.
>
> (Marx 1894: 216)

Limits due to problems of synchronisation between buying and selling are first dealt with by commercial credit, "the credit which the capitalists engaged in reproduction give to one another" (*ibid.*: 344). Commercial credit alone, however, is incapable of accommodating the growth of capitalist production and banking/financial institutions are created to help out. The banking and credit system develops to circumvent the limits and barriers to (the growth of) capital. These institutions concentrate and centralise money capital, assuming a separate social function of mobilising money as potential capital and managing money capital. With the development of the banking and credit system, the social character of capital takes full effect:

> It places all the available and even potential capital of society that is not already actively employed at the disposal of the industrial and commercial capitalists so that neither the lenders not users of this capital are its real owners or producers. It thus does away with the private character of capital . . . By means of the banking system the distribution of capital as a special business, a social function, is taken out of the hands of the private capitalists and usurers.
>
> (Marx 1894: 452)

As capitalism matures, it is the division of capital into separate functions that allows the further growth of capital. At the same time, however, the credit system evokes processes that exacerbate the inherent instability of a capitalist monetary economy. Money can be used as capital, as means to produce surplus value. Money becomes a commodity with an exchange value (interest) and a use value (production of surplus value). As capital, money appears to have magical powers by being able "to create ever more money in and by itself"

(Harvey 2013: 173). As such, it tends to distort and mystify the laws of motion of capital, even to the point of endangering its continuity.

Money capital has a market price – interest – but no natural price (around which the market price fluctuates). There is no law by which the natural rate of interest can be determined and consequently the rate of interest is "lawless and arbitrary" (Marx 1894: 241), set by competition between the class of industrial capitalists and that of financial capitalists over the share of interest out of the surplus value. Marx saw profit and interest as antagonistic. Although interest depends upon the profit of productive capital, there is a tendency for financial capital to become autonomous.

> Capital appears as a mysterious and self-creating source of interest – the source of its own increase . . . While interest is only a portion of the profit, *i.e.*, of the surplus-value, which the functioning capitalist squeezes out of the labourer, it appears now, on the contrary, as though interest were the typical product of capital, the primary matter, and profit, in the shape of profit of enterprise, were a mere accessory and by-product of the process of reproduction. Thus we get the fetish form of capital and the conception of fetish capital.
>
> (Marx 1894: 266–7)

The belief that money itself is productive allows the building of a make-believe world. In the zeal for enrichment and accumulation, again and again finance capital (the market value of shares) gets out of step with productive capital (the real value of physical assets). This excess is what Marx called fictitious capital; make believe capital. The socialisation of capital allows capital to turn ficti-tious, whereby it appears as if money itself is "the source of its own increase" (*ibid.*: 266). Although necessary to further the accumulation of capital, the credit system comes at a price: "if capital accumulation depends upon a paral-lel accumulation of credit moneys and credit instruments, then it necessarily produces a fetish monster of its own design, based on faith, confidence and expectation, that periodically lurches out of control" (Harvey 2013: 213). Once capital assumes a fictitious character, it becomes limitless. Creating an illusion of productive serviceability, the credit system develops "the incentive of capitalist production, enrichment through the exploitation of the labour of others, to the purest and most colossal form of gambling and swindling" (Marx 1894: 318; Eltis 1991). The credit system changes the game and raises the stakes. It establishes a web of financial interdependencies between capitalists, which on the one hand allows capitalists to reach further and boost their com-petitive drive, while on the other hand their fate and prospects get entwined. Any disturbance in the process of production and circulation ploughs its way through the entire economy. "In times of crises, the financial system functions as a transmission mechanism that generalizes problems in any given sector to the entire economy" (Shuklian 1991: 208). The only resistance to illusions and disillusions was to be expected from human institutions, the central bank and the regulatory authorities, although they can never balance out an inherently unstable system bound for periodic eruptions as expectations and confidence contract and break up.

The financial system, expanding on capital that is wrongly believed to represent real value, tends to overreach itself in its quest for profit. Marx described the financial system as a house of cards, which is built up and extended until it mocks the law of gravitation too much in stretching beyond belief the imbalance between interest-bearing capital and productive capital and its lightness becomes unbearable. Dealing with make-believe capital, with money as mere figures on paper or screen, with no apparent relation to what goes on in production facilities and factories (exploitation and alienation), it is but one small step to an amoral universe, playing the game of high finance of keeping the gains and pushing around the risks, without reference to what is right or wrong (Luyendijk 2015).

Reasoning from the same assumptions as the bourgeois economists, Marx reached an opposite conclusion. Bourgeois economists had argued that the socialisation of greed under the rule of competition smoothens the accumulation of capital to build up productive capacity for the benefit of all. Marx held that the evolving relations of capitalist production created a system in which the socialisation of capital turned greed truly systemic to the benefit of a shrinking class of capitalists by the enforcing power of competition. As Harvey concluded, Marx's critique of bourgeois economics amounted to a "devastating reversal of the Smithian vision of 'the benefit of all' that derives from the hidden hand of market exchange" (Harvey 2010: 290).

Opposite narratives

Chapter 5 focused on how political economy remodelled itself as a deductive science developing a mechanical, abstract model of the economic world. With a matching economic man, solely driven by self-interest. A science aiming to explain the principles of the production of wealth. Focusing on the abstract principles that govern economic phenomena, assuming the desire for wealth to be the ruling passion, and leaving aside processes of social and institutional conditioning, the science of political economy had put its money on the principle of competition to claim the beneficial conditions and effects of commercial society.

This chapter discussed how socialists rallied and charged against competition as a mode of production and distribution. In the development of English socialist thought, from Owen to Marx, two tendencies can be discerned: (1) at first the notion of competition is very much tied up with claims about civilisation, manners and virtue – issues which were widely discussed within the eighteenth-century conception of political economy. Then competition came to be seen as the pivot of the argument and consequently the citadel against which socialists marched; (2) there is a growing preponderance of economic arguments in the socialist critique of competition.

Increasingly attacking political economy on its own terms, socialists per-ceived the claim that competition was mutually beneficial as untenable. The 'war amongst the greedy', as Marx had termed competition, is an inherently destructive mechanism. Predefined by property relations conditioning relations between capital and labour, it is through this – supposedly providential – mechanism that the riches of the few are built upon the poverty of the many. Marx sought to demolish any claim that competition went hand in hand with 'benefits for all', freedom and equality. The system of interdependence is not a benign framework which sets competition unto the track of mutual benefit and cooperation, but a malevolent framework forged by economic necessity that heightens rivalry. Competition is not the friendly, beneficial and support-ive counterpart of monopoly, but capital's enforcer to realise enrichment by a happy few.

The charges brought against capital, competition and greed on political economy's own terms were expected to make economics change its ways. And so it did: it took evasive action.[5] The labour theory of value was ditched to get rid of its undesirable implication that labour was exploited by capital. Capital was reframed to lose any suggestion of its reign over labour by point-ing out capital's original contribution to output, justifying its remuneration. Competition was redefined. Rather than rivalry among men as a process to outdo others in economic gain, competition stood for a hypothetical situa-tion or market structure, described by way of a set of conditions under which equilibrium results. Moreover, the claim that greed was systemic was cir-cumvented by a focus on individual decision-making. It took a paradigmatic shift to make this happen, but it allowed 'Freedom, Equality, Property and Bentham' largely to be reaffirmed. It started four years after Marx published *Capital I* when Jevons's *Theory of Political Economy* (1965, 1871) heralded the era of neoclassical economics.

Notes

1 Although he took a stance against the socialist's system of cooperation, Mill later took the trouble of studying cooperation as an alternative to competition, gradually becoming more favourably disposed to cooperation (Claeys 1987b), considering both systems to be mutually supporting.
2 The spell of money, Marx argued, is that it allows us to transcend our individual properties and powers. "Money's properties are my – the possessor's – properties and essential powers. Thus, what I *am* and *am capable of* is by no means determined by my individuality" (1844: 60). As such, Marx added in *Capital*, money is "the radical leveller that … does away with all distinctions" (1867: 86), yielding unlimited social power.
3 Appropriation, for Marx, is the process through which property arises as a socio-economic practice, evolving into a legal institution, by which the practice is legitimised. Although appropriation and property are of all times and places, their forms vary with the modes of production through which a community seeks to acquire its means of subsistence (see Cahan 1994/5).
4 To be sure, Marx meant something different by cooperation than the utopian writers. The latter had referred to cooperation as a system in which all work together for the

common good or interest, because people have learned that their interest and happiness is strictly tied to that of all others. For Marx cooperation simply is a form of labour in which "[a] great number of labourers working together, at the same time, in one place ... in order to produce the same sort of commodity under the mastership of one capitalist" (1867: 227).

5　An English translation of Marx's *Capital I* only appeared in 1887. Blaug is right to reject the argument that marginalism "was nothing but the bourgeois answer to Marxism". However, the further claim that "the new tradition had no knowledge of socialist thought" (Blaug 1980: 317) neglects the wide currency of socialist thought through the work of Owen, Thompson and others.

References

Arthur, C.J. and G. Reuten (eds) (1998). *The Circulation of Capital: essays on volume two of Marx's Capital.* Basingstoke: Macmillan.

Blaug, M. (1980). *Economic Theory in Retrospect.* Third edition. Cambridge: Cambridge University Press.

Cahan, J.A. (1994/5). The concept of property in Marx's theory of history: a defense of the autonomy of the socioeconomic base. *Science & Society*, vol. 58(4): 392–414.

Campbell, M. and G. Reuten (eds) (2002). *The Culmination of Capital: essays on volume III of Marx's Capital.* Basingstoke/New York: Palgrave.

Claeys, G. (1987a). *Machinery, Money and the Millennium; from moral economy to socialism, 1815–1860.* Princeton, NJ: Princeton University Press.

Claeys, G. (1987b). Justice, independence, and industrial democracy: the development of John Stuart Mill's views on socialism. *The Journal of Politics*, vol. 49(1): 122–47.

Claeys, G. (1989). *Citizens and Saints: politics and anti-politics in early British socialism.* Cambridge: Cambridge University Press.

Eltis, W. (1991). Marx on the unproductiveness of the financial sector and its tendency to grow. In: *Marx and Modern Economic Analysis Volume II: The Future of Capitalism and the History of Thought*, Caravale, G.A. (ed.), Aldershot/Vermont: Edward Elgar, pp. 129–46.

Engels, Friedrich (1844). *Outlines of a Critique of Political Economy.* Translated by Martin Mulligan, www.marxists.org/archive/marx/works/1844/df-jahrbucher/outlines.htm.

Fornäs, J. (2013). *Capitalism: a companion to Marx's economy critique.* London/New York: Routledge.

Goodwin, B. (1978). *Social Science and Utopia: nineteenth century models of social harmony.* Sussex: The Harvester Press.

Harvey, D. (2010). *A Companion to Marx's Capital.* London/New York: Verso.

Harvey, D. (2013). *A Companion to Marx's Capital, volume 2.* London/New York: Verso.

Heinrich, M. (2004). *An Introduction to the Three Volumes of Karl Marx's Capital.* Translation by A. Locascio. New York: Monthly Review Press.

Hirschman, A.O. (1977). *The Passions and the Interests: political arguments for capitalism before its triumph.* Princeton, NJ: Princeton University Press.

Hollander, S. (2011). *Friedrich Engels and Marxian Political Economy.* Cambridge: Cambridge University Press.

Hunt, E.K. (1979). *History of Economic Thought: a critical perspective.* Belmont, CA: Wadsworth Publishing Company.

Hunt, E.K. (1990). *Property and Prophets*. Sixth edition. New York: Harper & Row.

Jevons, William Stanley (1965[1871]). *The Theory of Political Economy*. New York: Kelley.

Luyendijk, J. (2015). *Among the Bankers: a journey into the heart of finance*. Brooklyn, NY: Melville House.

Marx, Karl (1844). *Economic and Philosophical Manuscripts of 1844*. Translated by Martin Mulligan, www.marxists.org/archive/marx/works/1844/manuscripts/preface.htm.

Marx, Karl (1857). *Grundrisse; Foundations of the Critique of Political Economy*. Translated by Martin Nicolaus, www.marxists.org/archive/marx/works/1857/grundrisse.

Marx, Karl (1867). *Capital: critique of political economy, vol. 1, the process of capitalist production*. www.marxists.org/archive/marx/works/1867-c1/index.htm.

Marx, Karl (1885). *Capital: critique of political economy, vol. 2, the process of circulation of capital*. www.marxists.org/archive?marx/works/1885-c2/index.htm.

Marx, Karl (1894). *Capital: critique of political economy, vol. 3, the process of capitalist production as a whole*. www.marxists.org/archive/marx/works/1894-c3/index.htm.

Mill, John Stuart (1857). *Principles of Political Economy*. Two volumes, fourth edition. London: John W. Parker and Son.

Mill, John Stuart (1963–1991). *The Collected Works of John Stuart Mill*. Edited by J.M. Robson. Toronto: University of Toronto Press/London: Routledge and Kegan Paul.

Muller, J.Z. (2003). *The Mind and the Market; capitalism in Western thought*. New York: Anchor Books.

Owen, Robert (1991). *A New View of Society and Other Writings*. Harmondsworth: Penguin Books.

Palermo, G. (2016). Power, competition and the free trader vulgaris. *Cambridge Journal of Economics*, vol. 40(1): 259–81.

Pankhurst, R.K.P. (1991). *William Thompson (1775–1833) Pioneer Socialist*. London/Concord, MA: Pluto Press.

Ricoy, C. (2003). Marx on division of labour, mechanization and technical progress. *European Journal of the History of Economic Thought*, vol. 10(1): 47–79.

Ryan, C.C. (1981). The fiends of commerce: Romantic and Marxist criticisms of classical political economy. *History of Political Economy*, vol. 13(1): 80–94.

Senior, N.W. (1965 [1836]). *An Outline of the Science of Political Economy*. New York: A.M. Kelley.

Shuklian, S. (1991). Marx on credit, interest and financial instability. *Review of Social Economy*, vol. 49(2): 196–217.

Taylor, K. (1982). *The Political Ideas of the Utopian Socialists*. London/Totowa: Frank Cass.

Thompson, William (1824). *Inquiry into the Principles of the Distribution of Wealth Most Conducive to Human Happiness*. London: Longman and Green.

Tinel, B. (2013). Why and how do capitalists divide labour? From Marglin and back again through Babbage and Marx. *Review of Political Economy*, vol. 25(2): 254–73.

7   The neoclassical turn and the fading-out of greed and pride

Political economy in disarray

The dinner at the Political Economy Club held on 31 May 1876 to celebrate the centenary of the publication of *The Wealth of Nations*, should have been the perfect occasion for complacency about the advances made in economic science. Instead, a taste was served up of the dissension about the direction in which political economy was to proceed. The meeting was chaired by former Prime Minister William Gladstone; some hundred members and guests attended, including six chairs of political economy (Winch 2009: 136). Dutifully Robert Lowe, chancellor of the exchequer under Gladstone, noted in his after-dinner speech that "the great work had been done" (Revised Report 1876: 21). He added, however, that although its past was reason for celebration, the future of political economy was to be regarded with gloom. At the same time that economics professionalised and turned into a field of study with its own university chairs and journals, it faced a crisis. In 1878 William Cunningham reported "a widespread tendency to look upon its [economic science] teachings with suspicion . . . The mercantile public are not swayed by it; working-class leaders notoriously disregard it, and foreign statesmen do not pretend to listen to its preachings" (cited in Reisman 1990: 61). Critics rallied and with reason. The principles of political economy had been coined in a profoundly different context. But the world had changed, and the principles and policy views of classical political economy were increasingly out of tune with developments in society. Real wages had risen, in contradiction to the predictions from the Malthusian population theory around which political economy had been erected. Mill's recantation of the wages fund theory knocked over another pillar of classical political economy, while problems of monopoly, big business, protectionism and competition proved too strenuous for the worn-out theories. The gap between theory and reality fuelled the idea that political economy was a representation of bourgeois ideology rather than a science. The after-dinner speech and the discussion that followed brought dividing lines to light between two contending perspectives. Both claimed they could rescue political economy from its declining state: marginalism and historical economics.

Marginalists disputed the principles and theoretical framework of classical economics, marching straight against its capital, value theory. They charged that classical economics had neglected demand. This was a serious flaw because the wants and desires of consumers make the economy go round. Repairing this omission, marginalists put economics on a new footing. They dispensed with practical concerns by developing economics into an exact, more abstract, value-free science. Historical political economy sought answers in the opposite direction. During the second half of the nineteenth century, social thought emphasised evolutionary, historical and collectivist forces in shaping society. Building on the evolutionist ideas of Darwin, Comte and Spencer, historical political economy argued that economic principles are relative to the conditions of time and place, so they should not be seen as invariable laws of nature. With Ricardo's lead, political economy aimed to formulate general principles by abstract, deductive reasoning, using simplifying assumptions to isolate economic phenomena. This method was rejected. Developments in production, growth and distribution cannot be understood in isolation from changes in social, religious, political and cultural structures. Economic phenomena are inseparable from social phenomena, so they can only be understood within their social context. Therefore political economy must gain knowledge about economic relationships by working in close collaboration with the other social sciences to discover underlying, general development patterns. Historical economists argued the need for inductive, empirical and historical research and emphasised the need to take the social and moral consequences of production and distribution of wealth into consideration.

These controversies over the scope and method of political economy cast their shadows at the centenary dinner.[1] In 1877, Francis Galton proposed to abolish section F of the Royal Academy of Sciences on the ground that economics was unscientific. In the preface to the second edition (1879) of his *Theory of Political Economy*, Jevons wrote: "Many would be glad if the supposed science collapsed altogether, and became a matter of history" (1965: xvi). Nobody cared much for economics. It was in this climate that Alfred Marshall was appointed at Cambridge in 1885. In his inaugural speech, *The Present Position of Economics*, he made a diplomatic effort to align conflicting views (Reisman 1990: Chapter 5). He agreed that economics was a branch of a generalised sociology. He argued that induction and deduction complemented each other: theory without facts does not make sense, but facts themselves are silent without a theoretical framework. Marshall granted Darwinists that society is a social organism and that human nature is variable in adapting to changing circumstances. He deplored the resentment against economics as a 'science of illth' rather than wealth, based on notions of interest rather than duty. The focus on material wealth, he insisted, was not to define wealth as an end in itself, but as the most promising way towards progress and altruism.

Although Marshall took economics as a moral science, he left no doubt that the first step was to build a new theoretical framework, updating classical economics with the new insights of marginalism. Many of Marshall's further steps were never taken in the development of neoclassical economics, underscoring the 'triumph' of marginalism. As a consequence, textbooks only deal sparingly with historical economics, while marginalism is said to have revolutionised economics. This chapter first deals with the emergence of neoclassical economics in the last decades of the nineteenth century. The next topic is how the concept of self-interest was redefined in the process. Then the chapter describes the vicissitudes of greed in this transformation. Being emptied out of the concept of self-interest, greed met the same fate as self-love or pride. The section that follows shows how Veblen constructed a contrasting view from these very ideas and concepts made redundant by the reorganisation of economic thought. A closing section concludes this chapter.

The neoclassical turn and the redefinition of self-interest

Much has been written on how, in the 1870s, three economists – Jevons in England, Walras in Switzerland and Menger in Austria – came up with similar ideas to reboot economics, independent of each other. Views still differ on the extent to which marginalism can be seen as a Kuhnian paradigmatic shift. Whatever the case, the rise of neoclassical economics is a fine example of a Hegelian dialectical process, in which an idea or thesis (classical economics) calls up and is challenged by an opposing idea or antithesis (marginalism), and the ensuing struggle results in a synthesis (neoclassical economics). So, what was this remake about (*History of Political Economy* 1972; Fisher 1986; Howey 1989; Steedman 1997)?

The big question in classical economics had been to explain how changes in the quantity and quality of resources would affect output and hence welfare in a system of private property and free competition. Key to the growth of output was capital accumulation, acting in concert with division of labour to increase productivity, output and demand. Changes in the profit rate and distributive shares of the three social classes in society were the pivotal variables in long-term trends. The 'new' economics after 1870, by contrast, assumed resources to be given, and focused its attention on allocating scarce resources to maximise satisfaction. The unit of analysis highlighted was the individual agent, household or firm aiming to maximise utility or profit. This new perspective was shying away from social aggregates like social classes and social structures, which had dominated classical thinking, Marx included.

Key in transforming the scope and method of economics was the application of the marginal technique as an analytical tool. Economics was all about decisions taken at the margin; about whether to have or produce one more unit of a commodity or not (instead of having or producing this commodity at all). Marginal analysis was used to construct a model of the market mechanism as a system of resource allocation. The whole idea is to have a system of economic organisation through which available resources are used for producing commodities in the quantities and qualities that match the wants of consumers. The essence of the system's functioning is the competitive market and its pricing mechanism. Disregarding the role of demand, the classical economists had been unable to explain this mechanism in a satisfactory manner. Although the first marginalists focused exclusively on demand, they gradually worked out the system as a two-way street. Neoclassical economists demonstrated the optimal allocation of productive resources if consumers maximise their utility by spending their income so that the marginal utility of each commodity bought equals its price, and if producers maximise their profit by increasing production so that the marginal cost of each commodity equals its price. The central idea is to push forward until any additional change results in a zero-sum change (equilibrium). As Blaug explained this 'equimarginal principle':

> in dividing a fixed quantity of anything among a number of competing uses, "efficient" allocation implies that each unit of the dividend is apportioned in such a way that the gain of transferring it to one use will just equal the loss involved in withdrawing it from another . . . The whole of neoclassical economics is nothing more than the spelling out of this principle in ever wider contexts coupled with the demonstration that perfect competition does under certain conditions produce equimarginal allocation of expenditures and resources.
>
> (Blaug 1980: 312)

Economics had always been about how to avoid zero-sum/negative-sum outcomes, but here the issue was framed anew. Instead of the interplay between institutions and passions mediated through the actions of self-interested individuals in a competitive market, the issue was treated within the abstract world of decision-making under constraints by isolated individuals. If all conditions of perfect competition were fulfilled, the neoclassical model showed the system to work perfectly efficient in allocating resources so as to maximise consumer satisfactions or so-called Pareto-optimality. Pareto-optimality or maximum welfare implies that productive resources are allocated and goods produced such that any rearrangement to benefit someone would harm someone else. Joan Robinson described the new version of 'Freedom, Equality, Property and Bentham':

> Everyone must be free to spend his income as he likes, and he will gain the greatest benefit when he equalizes the *marginal utility* of a shilling spent on each kind of good. The pursuit of profit, under conditions of perfect competition, leads producers to equate marginal costs to prices, and the maximum possible satisfaction is drawn from available resources. This is an ideology to end all ideologies, for it has abolished the moral problem. It is only necessary for each individual to act egoistically for the good of all to be attained.
>
> (Robinson 1978: 53)

The shift towards neoclassical economics implied a shift in the scope and method, boundaries, place and relevance of determining factors within the system of interconnected variables. After its prominent position in classical economics, distribution received a far less exalted place in 'new economics'. Distribution was seen as an appendage to value theory, primarily concerned with price determination of inputs in the context of market exchange between utility-maximising consumers and profit-maximising producers. Distribution did not give in without a struggle, however. The structure of demand presupposes that there is money to burn. Hence, income and the process of price determination are premised on an initial distribution of income. In classical economics, Dobb pointed out, "income-distribution is treated as being the result of social institutions (e.g. property-ownership) and social relations, whereas in the latter (modern approach) it is determined by the conditions of exchange" (Dobb 1973: 34). Although Marx had argued the social determinacy of distribution, questions of property ownership, class relations, power and conflict were relegated to outside the domain of economics.

The transformation of economics after 1870 also involved its methodology. In changing its ways, however, it did not give in to objections from Romantic writers or historical economists. Although Alfred Marshall, father of neoclassical economics, was careful not to thread on anyone's toes and argued that the most appropriate metaphor for economics was that of biology, he affirmed that

> the forces with which economics deals have one advantage for deductive treatment in the fact that their method of combination is, as Mill observed, that of mechanics rather than of chemistry. That is to say, when we know the action of two economic forces separately . . . we can predict fairly well their conjoint action, without waiting for specific experience of it.
>
> (Marshall 1961[1890]: 771)

The disenchantment with classical economics had produced competing views on the scope and method of political economy. In *The Scope and Method of Political Economy* (1973[1890]), John Neville Keynes contrasted two conceptions of political economy: the one as a positive, abstract and deductive science; the other as an ethical, realistic and inductive science. He duly noted that both approaches were complementary, but left no room for doubt that economics was to be a positive science. And if a positive science, then moral considerations also needed to be purged from economics. Eager to establish economics as a deductive science, Jevons argued the need for subdivision (recognising a separate branch of social science on a historical foundation) to rescue economics as a science from its state of confusion. Economics was to focus on theory – general principles on which all branches were founded, stating "the mechanics of utility and self-interest" – turning economics into an exact science, using mathematical reasoning and method "as self-evident as are the elements of Euclid" (Jevons 1965[1879]: 21), dealing with quantities "in matters of moral indifference" (*ibid.*: 27). Based on such views economics coagulated into an abstract deductive science, discarding contingent elements that defied economic relationships to be treated as universal, abstract and mathematical. Confronted with the spectacular advances made by the natural sciences, economics was to be modelled after the natural sciences to achieve similar success. Economic laws were assumed to have the same universality and objectivity as natural laws and, in the pursuit of this scientific ideal, historical and institutional influences, conflicts, property and class relations were relegated to outside its domain (Screpanti and Zamagni 1993: 149). Economics adopted the principle of methodological individualism in seeking to explain all phenomena from the propensities, beliefs and purposes of individuals. As Dobb commented:

> It treated individuals, their structure of wants and the choices and substitutions resulting therefrom, as the ultimate and independent data of the economic problem: these were the ultimate atoms of the exchange-process and of market-behaviour, beyond which analysis did not go (*e.g.* it did not, indeed could not, concern itself with the social conditioning or social interdependence of individuals' desires and behaviour-reactions).
>
> (Dobb 1973: 33)

Although starting from the "behavior of individuals without going into the factors that formed this behavior" (Schumpeter 1954: 889), the assumption of self-interest remained unimpaired as the moving principle in economic life. As Edgeworth wrote in *Mathematical Psychics*: "The first principle of Economics is that every agent is actuated only by self-interest" (1881: 16). Nevertheless, the concept of self-interest was (once again) tailored to the new formalisation. Studying the relationship between *given* ends and a *given* supply of means, economics inquired into the conditions under which the most could be made out of the available resources in terms of satisfactions. As the implications of the new approach were gradually worked out, it became apparent that the assumption of self-interest in its interpretation as the desire for wealth – part of a construction of economic reality to answer questions about growth and accumulation – sat uncomfortably with the new theory. Keynes (1973[1890]: 127–8) accepted the view of "the economic man as being actuated solely by self-interest", and still used it interchangeably with the desire of wealth.

Such confusion led Wicksteed[2] to open *The Common Sense of Political Economy* (1910) with the claim that many had not yet recognised the revolutionary impact on economics of the principle emanating from "the psychology of choice between alternatives" (1935[1910]: 2). This principle operates always and everywhere – there is no sharp line that delineates economic life – and allows us to dispense with economic motives as a way to isolate economic from other social phenomena as the subject of study of the economist. "We are not to begin by imagining man to be actuated by only a few simple motives, but we are to take him as we find him" (*ibid.*: 4). Especially the desire for wealth as economic motive meets with criticism. It makes no sense "to think of him [economic man] as only desiring to collect tools and never desiring to do or to make anything with them" (*ibid.*: 163). To make an end to all confusion, it should be clear that economics studies human behaviour and its consequences, only insofar as the human effort to satisfy wants involves the use of scarce means, whereby choosing one thing implies that we have to relinquish others. It is this economising aspect which defines economic science. Fitted for purpose in this new theoretical framework, the concept of self-interest takes on the meaning of rationality, rational decision-making, consistency etc. In this vein Jevons set out his theory of "the mechanics of utility and self-interest" (1965[1879]: 21) in terms of 'choice', 'calculus', 'maximisation', 'comparison' and 'measurement'. Marshall emphasised that modern life was characterised by "free choice by each individual of that line of conduct which after careful deliberation seems to him the best suited for attaining his ends" (1961[1890]: 5–6). Pareto distinguished between the logical and non-logical actions of men to separate economics from sociology. Economic analysis, he argued, dealt with the logical action of men, related to the self-interest of rational individuals. More recently, it was stated as follows in a microeconomics textbook:

> A key assumption of most economic analysis is that people act rationally, meaning that they act in their own self-interest . . . Rational people respond to incentives. When the pay-off, or benefit, from doing something changes, people change their behavior to get the benefit.
>
> (O'Sullivan et al. 2008: 10)

Wicksteed added that any qualification in terms of egoism and altruism with respect to the concept of self-interest, and by association economics, is entirely besides the mark, because rational calculation with a view to gain may serve the noblest objectives (as well as the basest ones). Making the most of one's resources, he continued, is the reason why people enter into economic relations. "Every man has certain purposes, impulses, and desires" (1935[1910]: 165), of whatever nature, and he needs the assistance of others to give effect to them: he cannot do it alone or expect it all from the benevolence of others (like the butcher, the brewer and the baker). "But by direct and indirect processes of exchange, by the social alchemy of which money is the symbol, the things I have and the things I can are transmuted into the things I want and the things I would" (*ibid.*: 166). So people enter into economic relations, creating "a system of mutual adjustment by which we further each other's purposes simply as an indirect way of furthering our own" (*ibid.*: 166). Entering into an economic relation simply means that each party has the possibility to transcend the limitations of their own resources in a way that is mutually beneficial, even if the other's benefit is not the first reason for such cooperation. Wicksteed emphasised that it is not selfishness, but non-tuism that characterises an economic relation: economic relations are impersonal, whereby decisions are unbiased by loyalty or humanity but simply based on rational calculation to get 'a good bargain'. "The reason why . . . there is no room for 'you' in my consideration is just because 'I' am myself already excluded from my own consideration" (*ibid.*: 175).

Together these economic relations constitute a machinery through which people can accomplish their own purposes by serving others: a system of inter-dependent relations which only comes to rest (equilibrium) when all possibili-ties for gain are exhausted. The whole focus is on exchange and the market. The market provides the individual with the information about preferences, expectations and the like of other market participants expressed as prices "which confront him independently of his own action, and which impose upon him the conditions under which he must make his selections between alternatives" (*ibid.*: 5). As individuals all act on the same principles, "the resultant of the sum of their individual actions . . . presents itself to each one of them . . . as an alien system imposed from without" (*ibid.*: 5). Wicksteed rejected the view that puts buyers and sellers into opposition with one another, explaining the operation of the market as the interplay of rival interests. Buyers and sellers are presented as a homogeneous group, all operating on a single principle, which allows each to maximise his benefits.

The concept of competition was accommodated to fit the new theoretical framework. Its meaning shifted from competition as a process to its effects in terms of ideal results reached on applying strict conditions (perfect know-ledge, large numbers of buyers and sellers, free entry, homogeneous goods and the like). "Competition came to mean, with the mathematical economists, a hypothetically realized situation in which business rivalry, or competition in the Smithian sense, was ruled out by definition" (McNulty 1967: 398). In similar vein, Marshall argued that a new term was needed to describe the characteristics of modern industrial life and to get away from the evil conno-tation that the notion of competition had acquired in being associated with selfishness. The characteristics of industrial life are better described in terms of self-reliance, independence and deliberate choice and forethought and Marshall settled on the term of economic freedom for this purpose (Marshall 1961[1890]: 5–10).

The fading-out of greed and pride in economics

In neoclassical economics, self-interest was reframed as 'getting the most from the least', bringing out its rational, maximising character. The formulation is Viner's and used by Kirzner to qualify 'the new economics' as "the science of avarice" (1976: 51). The view that all is greed, however, is misleading, as it harks back to motive (avarice or greed) to delineate economic phenomena in the new economics, while its representatives at the time did their utmost to put the idea out for the garbage collector. In fact, in the new framing greed drops out, and not only because of this decisive shift away from efforts to define economic relations with reference to economic motives. Greed also drops out as a consequence of the new framing of self-interest. If self-interest is reframed as rationality and greed is the excess of self-interest, greed is redefined as irra-tional. Rational self-interest helps us to enter into economic relations through which both giver and taker are blessed, although we only seek to further our own purposes, not those of others. There is nothing selfish in mutually benefit-ting from shared interests. Neither is there any danger of excess for the plain psychological fact that the more we have, the less we are prepared to strain ourselves to get more.[3] On this law, greed is simply irrational.

This was also seen to apply to money. Money, like other objects within the circle of exchange, is only a means to an end (satisfaction), but it is a necessary means. Wicksteed acknowledged that we are prone to transfer the urgency of securing a certain supply of things to satisfy desires to the items by which we secure these satisfactions "and regard the acquisition of money, or command of things in the circle of exchange, as characterised by a kind of intrinsic urgency" (1935[1910]: 156). Nevertheless, the law of diminishing utility applies here as well. Marshall was likewise dismissive. "Money is a means towards ends, and if the ends are noble, the desire for the means is not ignoble" (1961[1890]: 22). And although economists tend to focus on money, it is only because "it is the one convenient means of measuring human motive on a large scale" (*ibid.*: 22), not because they think that money is the main aim in life. Moreover, the money motive does not rule out other considerations in reflecting on advan-tages and disadvantages. In a footnote Marshall added: "We do indeed hear of people who pursue money for its own sake" but this inclination is attributed in particular to people "at the end of a long life spent in business" and there is the suggestion of its habitual or nonrational character ("the habit of doing a thing is kept up after the purpose for which it was originally done has ceased to exist") (Marshall 1961[1890]: 22 (n1)). Robbins similarly rejected the idea that money-making is the economic end of our conduct. He argued that money is a means to achieve whatever end; not an end in itself. "Only the miser, the psy-chological monstrosity, desires an infinite accumulation of money" (Robbins 1946[1932]: 31).

Greed is first and foremost an irrational aberration and as such does not fit the neoclassical model. It harms the individual who is guilty of greed in misallocating his resources and hence failing to maximise satisfaction, while perfect competition ensures that such behaviour does not harm others. As a motive greed is irrelevant, and as behaviour greed falls outside the domain of economics. In the meantime, self-interest had been dismantled and stripped of the influences of "social conditioning or social interdependence of individu-als' desires and behaviour-reactions" (Dobb 1973: 33). Without social condi-tioning, without all the fashioning Smith wrote about in *The Theory of Moral Sentiments* and on which account he could 'equate' self-interest with prudence, self-interest takes on a much more self-assertive meaning, capable of harming others. Self-interest as rationality is predominantly instrumental rather than a social construction that incorporates values like cooperation and trust.

Having rejected the relevance of egoism or altruism to describe economic action, and having claimed the moral indifference of economic principles, Wicksteed acknowledged that it will not do to claim the benign effects of self-interest operating in a competitive market. Throwing in some rhetoric, he asserted that this would be easy enough: "Do they [economic forces] not embrace all the world in one huge mutual benefit society?" (1935[1910]: 183). Ultimately, however, such benefit depends upon the nature of the individual's purposes, the purposes of others and the means to achieve them. Economic forces are indifferent in this respect. "It is idle to assume that ethically desirable results will necessarily be produced by an ethically indifferent instrument" (*ibid.*: 184). It may go either way. The system is not mutually beneficial by definition, if only because, given the interdependence in the provision of services, each individual has an interest in his service remaining scarce, while the things he desires are abundantly supplied:

> Thus every man whose desires are uncontrolled by social considerations will welcome any disaster that raises the relative significance of the thing he has or can do. Where there is an open competitive market, this desire for scarcity may remain a pious (or impious) wish, to which those who entertain it can give little or no effect.
>
> (Wicksteed 1935[1910]: 353)

Wicksteed emphasised the fact that the network of interchanges created and sustained by economic forces is absolutely indifferent, morally, socially and aesthetically. "Neither the urgency of his want nor the nobility of his purpose determines the extent to which a man may rely on economic forces to help him" (*ibid.*: 396). The apparent cosmos of the economic system that these economic forces bring about may well hide the moral and social chaos underneath. Nevertheless,

> We know that through the blind interplay of all these forces the collective means of forwarding human purposes steadily advance, and this shews that in point of fact the destructive and wasteful tendencies less than balance the constructive and conservative ones.
>
> (Wicksteed 1935[1910]: 397)

Advancement notwithstanding, it cannot be assumed that the best of all possible worlds will result from the spontaneous working of these blind forces. The better we understand these forces, the better we can control them. Wicksteed's views illustrate Medema's argument that, in the absence of a benign framework that absolves self-interest for its positive effects on social welfare, marginalism was accompanied by "a greater degree of suspicion about the effects of self-interested behaviour" (Medema 2009: 26). It could not be assumed that efforts to maximise individual happiness automatically benefit public welfare. The literature of the period shows a growing awareness of the existence of divergences (between individual self-interest and the interests of the community) that the market failed to coordinate. Medema (2009) described the process by which the classical faith in the system of natural liberty to harmonise self-interest and social interest and its concomitant distrust of government was substituted by the view that government intervention was needed in the face of market failures.[4] He showed that Mill and Sidgwick were central players in this evolution of the theory of market failure.

The Cambridge utilitarian philosopher and political economist Henry Sidgwick (1838–1900) reaffirmed the centrality of the motive of self-interest in political economy. It may be too much to presume that self-interest presents "the ideal condition of social relations and the final goal of political progress", but it "contains a very large element of truth" (1901: 402). Qualifications are necessary, not just the acknowledgement that self-interest needs to be checked by legal and moral limitations or is modified by other motives. Political economists were well aware that the pursuit of self-interest by economic man may fail to realise "beneficent and harmonious" results (1885: 3). Maximising individual wealth may fail to maximise social wealth or/and laissez-faire may fail to maximise wealth. The latter may be the case, Sidgwick suggested, because reality does not live up to the conditions characteristic of a system of natural liberty (1901: 40–03). Consequently, social and private interests may diverge. Sidgwick followed Mill in claiming that non-interference is the general rule, "so long as they [people] do not cause mischief to others without the consent of those others" (1897: 137n). If this is the case, the market system may have to be supplemented by government intervention. Such interference requires "a careful balance of conflicting inconveniences" (*ibid.*: 69) in any particular case, given that it is quite difficult to determine to what extent interference is appropriate.

Sidgwick and Marshall set the stage for Pigou. Focusing on changes in the national dividend, assuming that such changes would be reflected in changes in social welfare, Pigou (1912) built an analytical framework with the tools of marginal analysis. This framework was used to study market failures as divergences from the market optimum. And it was to derive conditions of optimality, analytically demonstrating the contribution of government to welfare. As Pigou summed up:

> the doctrine of the invisible hand evolving social benefit out of private selfishness has never been held by economists – certainly it was not held by Adam Smith – in that absolute and rigid form in which popular writers conceive it. All are agreed that many times the hand falters and fails of its aim. This fact justifies State planning in principle.
>
> (Pigou 1935: 115)

A world of difference becomes visible. Lowry Todd reminded us earlier that "[t]o be self-regulating, any system with contending elements . . . requires an internal limit to prevent any one of the elements from overwhelming the others" (1987: 20). In the eighteenth century, a framework of thought developed that built a theory of limits onto a concept of self-interest as (1) an internal balance between passions through processes of socialisation, in interaction with (2) an appropriate institutional environment, structuring incentives to meet the demands of law and morality. Within a network of mutual dependence, competition is a positive force through which a positive-sum society is created. As political economy developed and adapted its theoretical framework, however, the concept of self-interest was first tailored to fit 'economic man' and later redefined in terms of rationality. At the same time, the historical and institutional context of economic behaviour was narrowed down and came to be modelled as external constraints upon choice. Putting the new principles to work, the ideal model and its conditions were worked out under which individual maximising would lead to benefits for the group as a whole, or, in terms of interests, the pursuit of self-interest coordinated through the market would maximise the social interest. This framework of 'private maximisation, public benefits' first defined the healthy condition of an economic system. Next it allowed addressing 'health issues' as imperfections of or infringements upon the ideal model. Self-regulation of the system hinges first and foremost upon the prevalence of conditions of perfect competition. In such a conception, non-optimal results follow from market failures, implying that self-interest is out of step with social interest, or individual rationality out of step with collective rationality.[5] At the beginning of the twentieth century, these 'imperfections' preventing efficient results to come about were still hidden in future times. Attention focused on establishing the basic truth of 'private maximisation, public benefits'. Descriptions of the basics of the neoclassical framework included key terms like 'equilibrium', 'rationality', 'statics', 'scarcity', 'individual choice', 'allocation' and 'maximisation' in any preferred sequence or combination, moving away from analysis in terms of dynamics, institutions, historical and social circumstances, social classes, growth and distribution. Doing away with economic motives, neoclassical economics also severed the link between human psychology and choice (Rabin 1998). In his study on the fate of the conception of the individual in economics, Davis (2003) likewise argued that all psychological content has been emptied out of the neoclassical conception of the individual. It faded out greed in the process.

In the eighteenth century, greed was always discussed as paired with self-love, pride and vanity. It is no coincidence that the concept of self-interest sprang from both self-love and greed. So, if the concept of self-interest was detached from greed in the rise of neoclassical economics, did pride receive a similar treatment? As a matter of fact, the disappearance of pride behind the scenes in political economy was even more marked than for greed. After the amount of ink spent on pride and vanity in the seventeenth and eighteenth centuries, its demise after Adam Smith is quite remarkable (Hill 2012). Brennan and Pettit (2004) were perplexed by the failure of economics to deal with the topic of esteem. They offer three reasons for this neglect. First, esteem was associated with virtue, and esteem lost its appeal with the tendency to relegate moral issues to outside of economics. Second, given its link to the aristocratic notion of honour, esteem shared the fate of the aristocratic ideal. Third, the 'invisible hand' model offered a more attractive alternative for disciplining behaviour than the desire for esteem.

In classical economics, behavioural assumptions were narrowed down to the desire for wealth to isolate economic from social phenomena in order to arrive at natural laws governing economic phenomena, leaving other motives aside. Only Nassau Senior was prepared to pay more than passing attention to the desire for distinction. He repeated the focus on wealth for reasons of vanity, after Smith, and presented the desire for distinction:

> a feeling which, if we consider its universality and its constancy, that if affects all men and at all times, that it comes with us from the cradle, and never leaves us till we go into the grave, may be pronounced to be the most powerful of human passions.
>
> (Senior 1965[1836]: 12)

He acknowledged that beyond the most basic needs, 'appearance' is "the ruling principle of conduct" (*ibid.*: 12). Senior argued that superior wealth is the best (and best attainable) means to capture the admiration of one's fellowmen and is sure to encourage accumulation. He deals with the motive of distinction in a cursory manner though, and only in reference to influences of specific human behaviour on production, consumption, economic and population growth (Karayiannis 2001). The same goes for John Stuart Mill (Mason 1998).

Champion in the classical period was John Rae (1796–1872), a medical man from Scotland who emigrated to Canada and later moved on to the United States. He got interested in economics to argue the benefits of the colonial status of Canada. In 1834, he published his *New Principles on the Subject of Political Economy*. Its subtitle already announced that he was going to take Adam Smith to task for his fallacies concerning free trade. Later economists particularly appreciated his views on capital accumulation and innovation. Rae challenged the exact identity of individual and national interest, and of private and public wealth. He pressed upon his readers that although society may generate economic prosperity through capital accumulation and technological advance, counterforces may offset any such benefits. First among these counterforces was the drive of individuals for luxury consumption.

Accepting the need for expenditures suitable to one's social standing, Rae, a devout Presbyterian, took issue against the drive for vanity-driven consumption. "It gives no absolute enjoyment, it is all relative, as much as one is raised by it, another is depressed, the superiority of one man being here equivalent to the inferiority of another" (1964[1834]: 290). It is worse than a zero-sum game for the resources that are wasted in the process. Rejecting the mild tone with which Smith had portrayed this passion, he defined vanity as "a feeling that finds its proper gratification in merely going beyond others, without reference to the path taken . . . Its aim in all cases . . . is to have what others cannot have" (*ibid.*: 265–6). Free market conditions encouraged luxury consumption to gratify man's personal vanity. They depended upon the two countervailing forces – the intellectual powers and the social and benevolent affections – to restrain man's indulgence for vanity and allow the drive for accumulation to take the upper hand. Conspicuous consumption, if left unchecked, must inevitably lead to national economic decline by undermining the values upon which prosperity was built. It would first threaten social and economic stability, as the social and economic distance between classes would widen at the expense of social cohesion. This in turn would destroy all hope of upward mobility, turn away from accumulation and saving, increase status seeking, undermining family, work ethic, innovation etc. Material prosperity, *pace* Mandeville, goes hand in hand with thrift, hard work. These virtuous powers work to keep conspicuous consumption within manageable levels. The case of luxury consumption allowed Rae to demonstrate his main contention that individual and national wealth are not identical. While individuals can improve their social and economic status by increasing their relative share of existing national wealth, nations themselves have to secure increases in absolute wealth before they can become richer.

Marshall accepted that recognition was an important determining factor in consumption patterns, but criticised these expenditures to uphold social standing if they transgressed into forms of conspicuous consumption to satisfy vanity. Such display was a waste of wealth. Marshall was much concerned about "the tendency among commercial nations to think too much of wealth and to use it for the purposes of display" (1961[1890]: 245), but he hoped for moral sentiments to exert a correcting influence. He passionately argued that consumer patterns needed to serve higher purposes and emphasised the benefits if people would use higher income to raise their standard of life. At the same time he shared the view that economics as a science should make use of abstractions and could not include all social factors in the analysis. He was reluctant to incorporate status-driven consumption into his theory of demand. Neoclassical economics continued this point of view. It was only in the 1970s and 1980s that interest in status-led consumption was to return in economics (Hirsch 1976; Frank 1985).

David Hume had qualified the acquisitive passion as one of the strongest and most destructive passions of mankind. Rousseau had made similar claims about pride or the desire for distinction. And, as Mandeville had argued in his explorations of the paradoxical nature of commercial society, these passions combined in the pursuit of wealth and property. In commercial society, wealth and property were considered to be the means to achieve social distinction and esteem, aligning the acquisitive passion with man's efforts to gratify his vanity. Eighteenth-century thinkers were acutely aware that the desire for wealth was grounded in motives that set people up as rivals and was bound to trigger envy and conflict. The science of political economy was built on such ideas and considerations. And yet, at the end of the nineteenth century these essential building blocks of political economy had been put aside as economics matured and defined itself as a separate domain of knowledge, with its own scope and method, differentiated from other social sciences. On the neoclassical turn, economics moved beyond a class-based, dynamic account of economic life in which institutional structures, as products of the accumulated experience in regulating human passions, varied according to the stage of development of society. Mainstream economics developed a framework in which greed and pride had no place.

Veblen's pecuniary culture and invidious distinction

All of economics? No. It was in the United States that the son (and black sheep) of Norwegian immigrants settling in rural America, constructed a biting image of the culture of greed and pride of modern industrial society: Thorstein Veblen (1857–1929). Although his work was highly acclaimed for its sharp observations on economic and social life,[6] his way of thinking about economics went much against the tide (and the grain) in economics. Receiving his education at Carleton Minnesota, John Hopkins and his doctorate from Yale but unable to secure an academic position, he lived off his family at his father's farm, married and studied. In 1891 he finally managed to obtain a postdoc position with the economist Laughlin at Cornell, moving (with Laughlin) to the University of Chicago a year later. Despite the (international) fame his publications brought him, Veblen's extra-marital affairs, ill-adjusted behaviour, disdain for rules and regulations, and his sharp criticisms of mainstream economics did not win him any popularity contests and killed many of his career opportunities (Dorfman 1961; Seckler 1975).

Veblen took the economy as the outcome of a historical process of cultural change. Rather than static and universally valid principles to account for the value and exchange of material objects, the study of the economist should focus on evolving economic action (Veblen 1961: 72). Economics should study "the manner and degree in which the economic interest creatively shapes the general scheme of life" (*ibid.*: 177). One might think that Veblen started building his framework out of self-interest, but he had something quite different in mind. Economic interest, in Veblen's view, is itself a product of cultural evolution and institutional growth and needs to be explained. Along Darwinian lines, Veblen offered an updated version of the eighteenth-century conception of interest as passionate drive under the directive guidance of institutions, with society featuring as the historically evolved, cumulative outcome of the interaction and relationships between propensities of human nature and culture. He steered clear of methodological individualism and methodological collectivism (Hodgson 2004: 176). While he acknowledged that it is the conduct of individuals in a group from which institutions arise, "[t]he wants and desires, the end and aim, the ways and means, the amplitude and drift of the individual's conduct are functions of an institutional variable that is of a highly complex and wholly unstable character" (Veblen 1961: 242–3).

Adopting the habit-instinct psychology of William James, he started his explanation of human behaviour from instincts, biologically inherited traits like self-preservation, the need for esteem, emulation and so on. These instinctive drives are purposeful and the ways and means by which people come to pursue these goals Veblen termed 'habits'. Triggered by instincts, habits are shaped by material circumstances and their cultural environment through socialisation. People acquire culture-bound habits of thought and behaviour through a process of habituation (Hodgson 2004: 168ff). These customs and institutions evolve over time as society develops (Veblen distinguished between the savage, predatory, handicraft and pecuniary culture) with changing material and technological circumstances in which man has to provide for his needs. Only from the perspective of human evolution through evolving habits and institutions, can we understand human behaviour in contemporary society. Veblen (1) built his critique of economics on these views; and (2) constructed an evolutionary account of the inner tensions of the pecuniary culture of capitalism (Atkinson 2007).

Veblen argued that man acts with some goal in view and he likes his efforts to be effective, not futile (1979[1899]: 15). This instinct of workmanship is a necessary propensity in human evolution, which man employs to provide for his material needs. In the capitalist stage of society, however, a set of motives is favoured in selection processes that is at cross purposes with this want for useful, productive work. This creates a clash between pecuniary and industrial motives, between employments and institutions. Economics had failed to identify this basic conflict in capitalism, because it starts its reasoning from the given individual and given institutions, thereby shying away from explanations, and leaving basic characteristics of economic life out of its analysis. Economic man or the utility-maximising agent did not come out of thin air. Such views on human nature and agency need to be explained as the outcome of processes of human evolution.

Veblen, like Marx, criticised the fact that economics reasoned from some simplistic, harmonious surface-view of the economy without foundation in fact. In this manner economics takes the sting out of the self-regarding motive of pecuniary gain that rules economic behaviour. Understanding society as the sum of all individuals, "the interest of society is the sum of the interests of individuals", and consequently, "the sum of the individual gains is the gain of the society, and that, in serving his own interest in the way of acquisition, the individual serves the collective interest of the community" (Veblen 1961: 139). Moreover, in conditions of free competition, agents neither stand in each other's way nor play a zero-sum game, because all pay for what a thing is worth. These abstractions, described as the 'normal' or 'natural' condition, Veblen submits, tend to acquire a life of their own. They became ingrained in the perception and selection of facts by economists and coagulated into doctrine despite substantial changes in society and its institutions. Economics is castigated for its failure to include "a theory of genesis, growth, sequence, change, process, or the like, in economic life" (*ibid.*: 232).

It is equally inappropriate to picture man as "a lightning calculator of pleasures and pains", with "neither antecedent nor consequent" and "an isolated, definitive human datum" (*ibid.*: 73). Given the hedonistic psychology prevalent in economics, economic theory "can take account of conduct only in so far as it is rational conduct, guided by deliberate and exhaustively intelligent choice – wise adaption to the demands of the main chance" (*ibid.*: 235). Ideas like rationality, preferences or 'economic man' require explanation in terms of cumulative cause-and-effect relationships.

To Veblen it was a fateful misconstruction to reduce human nature to hedonistic calculus, and the institutional context to a few constants under which individuals make choices. If economics is concerned with human conduct in relation to the provision of the means of subsistence, it must necessarily study the dynamics of the development of the productive forces in society and the culture it engendered with the advance of industrial ability and technological knowledge. Any theory abstracting from all these cultural elements is inadequate. Institutions, like property, are the product of historical and cultural evolution and cannot be taken as inconsequential parts of the nature of things. Private property is a historical category, strictly tied to a culturally specific institutional setting in which everything is rated in terms of price. These pecuniary considerations ruling modern business life are like weeds in a garden, gaining strength and extending into non-economic spheres of life, including our tastes and sense of merit and demerit. "Pecuniary institutions induce pecuniary habits of thought which affect men's discrimination outside of pecuniary matters" (*ibid.*: 247).

From Veblen's perspective, economics had built itself *a world of illusion*, which may have been adequate in the time of Adam Smith but was now hopelessly outdated. Large corporations instead of small or single-owner enterprises inhabit the economy. Management has taken over from owners who, engrossed in the efforts to 'one up' others, run the companies in their absence. Workers are lured into the game by education and advertising, while financial or business capital has come to run the world rather than production capital. And on top of this, economists had adopted a methodology (individualistic, static, given individual, given institutions) that allows them to keep the world of illusion intact. Failing to appreciate this fact, the scientific inquiry into economic life is distorted as it mistakes economic life for an honourable activity to secure material life-support, seeking out the most pleasurable alternative. In the pecuniary culture of modern industrial society it is not. It is about the predatory tactics for pecuniary gain and its nasty consequences, not least because business interests conflict with the public interest. However, "any theory of business which sets these elements aside or explains them away", Veblen insisted, "misses the main facts which it has gone out to seek" (*ibid.*: 250).

These elements – cultural change, the money economy and credit, institutions, the predatory drive for pecuniary gain, invidious distinction, class – became the cornerstones of Veblen's theories. In *Industrial and Pecuniary Employments* (1961[1901]) Veblen argued that economic theory wrongly classifies the activities of business men as productive, and as such of service to society at large. Business men, and speculators in particular, are engaged in activities which "are lucrative without necessarily being serviceable to the community" (*ibid.*: 293). Veblen further developed these ideas in *The Theory of the Business Enterprise* (1958[1904]). In the modern industrial system, we provide for our needs by producing goods through mechanical processes: the machine process. The whole system is made up of interconnected detail processes in which each unit receives its supplies and turns over its output to others in a concatenation of industries, at the end of which consumers await to satisfy their wants. The system only works smoothly if all these different sub-processes are efficiently coordinated. Any degree of maladjustment in the 'interstitial coordinations' of this industrial process at large hinders its working, and the more sophisticated the system becomes, the more it is vulnerable to disturbances. Given the close interdependencies throughout the system, any disturbance is like a stone thrown in a pond, sending ripples through the whole system. The management and balancing of the processes are therefore essential to the welfare of the community. This task rests in the hands of the businessmen who organise production through the institution of the corporation, "a complex organism that lent itself to manipulation by passions and spirits that ran counter to the objective of its function in the economy" (Dorfman 1958: 5). However, Veblen claimed, "the motive of business is pecuniary gain" (1958[1904]: 16), not the efficient operation of the system to maximise satisfactions. Disturbances are opportunities at differential advantage and therefore the bread and butter of business. Economists are simply wrong to assume that, perhaps unintentionally, businessmen further the welfare of the community. Instead businessmen seek pecuniary gain by a "conscientious withdrawal of efficiency" (1921[1919]: 14) as Veblen wrote in *The Engineers and the Price System*. Like Marx, Veblen argued that businessmen are not interested in the use values of the goods they produce. "The vital point of production with him [the businessman] is the vendibility of the output, its convertibility into money vales, not its serviceability for the needs of mankind" (1958[1904]: 30). Arguing that there is no relation between the value and the price of a good (while the point of neoclassical economics was to explain how, in equilibrium, price equals value), Veblen contended that the gains of business have no relation to the value rendered to the community. It is like putting the fox in charge of the chicken farm.

Veblen argued that the businessman can improve his chances of gain by increasing the rate of turnover of his capital. The latter can also be increased by the of credit. As long as the profit rate exceeds the interest rate, credit adds to profit. Competition forces all competitors to have recourse to credit to deny others this differential advantage. As the use of credit becomes general practice, Veblen argued, it turns into a zero-sum or even a negative-sum game: although an enterprise may (temporarily) have a competitive advantage over others within the industry, total earnings or total output in the industry is unaffected, while the total of interest payments reduces aggregate profits from industry. Veblen extended his analysis to a business-cycle theory (Davanzati and Pacella 2014; Argitis 2016). The extension of credit allows competitors to bid up the price of material capital goods, increasing the value of the property (without adding to the material means of industry). The increased value of collateral property becomes the basis for further extension of credit, creating an ever-widening gap between the money value of the property and its expected earning capacity (given the growing portion of business capital barren of productive capacity). Neoclassical economics failed to distinguish between industrial capital and business or financial capital, missing out on the changing nature of business enterprise and its focus on monetary values, 'goodwill' and pecuniary expectations. This shift greatly enhanced the financial instability of the system. Veblen argued that cycles of depression and exaltation are endogenous to a system built on the quest for profits. He emphasises that such crises and depressions are phenomena of business, of prices and in the first instance a matter of psychology (Veblen 1958[1904]: 91). It is a game of finance and monetary values (business capital), affecting output and industrial capital as a spill-over effect when the fun is over. Liquidation and recapitalisation follow once this discrepancy between financial and productive values becomes apparent (*ibid.*: 55), creating loss of output, employment and income. It is a system in which most people are not invited to the party, but still have to suffer from the hangover.

Veblen described how society had advanced from a natural economy (distribution in kind) to a money economy in which the exchange of goods is organised through markets. While doctrines of political economy were built with such a money economy in view, the credit economy has established itself with the capital market calling the tune. Trading in capital has become prevalent with a class of professional traders seeking "pecuniary gain that is to be got through an advantageous discrepancy between the price paid and the price obtained" (*ibid.*: 75). The value of capital is determined by the expected future earning capacity of capital, which lends itself to 'embellishment' through manipulation, misinformation, fraud etc. Businessmen, "experts in prices and profits and financial manœuvres" (1921[1919]: 40), employ predatory techniques that inhibited the market to work in order to increase profits. Veblen likened their ways to sabotage, underlining that their interest is at variance with those of the community. Fraud becomes endemic to (financial) capitalism, which in Black's definition is "theft by deception: one creates and exploits trust to cheat others" (quoted in Henry 2012: 990). By manipulating vendible capital to boost money values, moreover, businessmen try to shift the risks involved unto industry. The credit economy engenders a *world of make believe*, inhabited by predators who play their prey by manipulation, deception and fraudulent practices. Not only is there a discrepancy between the business interest and the interest of the community, there are also discrepancies between the interests of the managers and those of the corporation (Veblen 1958[1904]: 78). Veblen criticised economics for its positive reading of competition as 'rival commercial interests', with rivalry seen as 'natural', normal and serving the common good. This narrow view neglects other strands of competition: the competition between businessmen and the community, and the competition between the captains of industry and the absentee owners. Veblen referred to "conspiracies between business men each seeking his own advantage at the cost of any whom it may concern" (1921[1919]: 128). With government representing vested interests at the expense of the public interest, it is ludicrous to suppose a solidarity of interests, working to the welfare of the community: "Having begun as an industrial community which centered about an open market, it has matured into a community of Vested Interests who vested right it is to keep up prices by a short supply in a closed market" (*ibid.*: 130).

Rather than developing this perspective into a class conflict between capital and labour, as Marx had, Veblen argued that, like weeds in a garden, all classes are infected with the pecuniary virus. Society even builds up cohesion with this emulative drive to outdo one another running through its ranks. Although vanity and emulation are of all times, modern industrial society and "the system of free competition has accentuated this form of emulation" (1961: 395) by its growth of output and cutting off other means of success. Given the increasingly impersonal nature of most of man's interactions, it is not enough to possess wealth; it must be displayed. This is the theme of *The Theory of the Leisure Class* (1979[1899]). In this book Veblen argued that in industrial society wealth and property are the modern equivalent of trophies and exploits of war by which men in predatory life sought to gain honour and esteem. By way of wealth and property, people put their success in evidence in order to compare favourably and gain esteem. Far from being reprehensible, "[i]t becomes indispensable to accumulate, to acquire property, in order to retain one's good name" (*ibid.*: 29). A certain standard is a necessary condition of upholding reputation. What is more, it is a matter of self-respect, and so identity is caught up in this emulation. Standards, as well as the classifications they bring along, rise with accumulation and prosperity, and individuals have to follow. If an individual is playing catch-up, he will live in "chronic dissatisfaction", and as soon as he reaches the going pecuniary standard, it "will give place to a restless straining to place a wider and ever-widening pecuniary interval between himself and this average standard" (*ibid.*: 31). So much for the diminishing marginal utility of wealth. In modern industrial society man's regard for reputation takes the form of "a striving to be, and more immediately to be thought to be, better than one's neighbor" (1961: 392), is competitive and it is pre-eminently economic success which counts: pecuniary achievement. According to Veblen, emulation by way of conspicuous consumption never yields lasting satisfaction, if any satisfaction at all, and has all the marks of a zero-sum game. Many feel dissatisfied in not being able to uphold their "standing in the esteem of his fellowmen" (*ibid.*: 392). As a consequence, the interest of the community no longer coincides with the emulative interests of the individual. The collective interest of any modern community centres on industrial efficiency. The individual is serviceable to the community by his efficiency in productive employments. This collective interest is best served by honesty, diligence, goodwill, absence of self-seeking etc. These traits by which collective interest is served are a hindrance to the individual in pursuing gain under the competitive regime:

> Under the regime of emulation the members of a modern industrial community are rivals, each of whom will best attain his individual and immediate advantage, if, through an exceptional exemption from scruple, he is able serenely to overreach and injure his fellows when the chance offers.
>
> (Veblen 1979[1899]: 228–9)

So Veblen argued that the machine process and the culture it generated tend to disintegrate the cultural tissues of society and the institutional basis of business enterprise. He perceived a growing tension between business and industry, between profit and welfare. The more the industrial system becomes "delicately balanced, more intricately bound in a web of industrial give and take, more sensitive to far-reaching derangement" (1921[1919]: 118), the more the captains of industry have the power and ability to derange the system, with dire consequences for society at large. Veblen noted a growing division of interests between the business community and the underlying population, calling forth "a certain division of sentiment and a degree of mutual distrust" (*ibid.*: 107), contending that "the régime of business enterprise is fast approaching the limit of tolerance" (*ibid.*: 119). The system's internal control mechanism – the business cycle – does not align instinctive drives and habits of thought with the common good. In fact, the system develops ever more violent oscillations, increasingly undermining the conditions – industrial efficiency, workmanship, productivity, useful labour – for the survival of the capitalist system. Crises, manipulation and fraud are no incidental excesses; they are systematic, given the system of ownership and control of corporate and financial enterprises. These practices will continue as long as the system remains intact and as long as a system of control does not change the structure of incentives. He rejected the Marxian claim that "the system of competition has proved itself an engine for making the rich richer and the poor poorer" (1961: 391). Undoubtedly, the system has improved material life. However, it failed to result in an equivalent increase in satisfaction. Indeed, despite advances in wealth, the system "does tend to make them [the industrious poor] relatively poorer, in their own eyes" (*ibid.*: 392). He believed that the emulation and jealousy inspired by wasteful and conspicuous consumption would breed dissatisfaction and unrest that may bring the institution of private property down. While remaining vague about the prospects of capitalism, property and socialism, Veblen offered the possibility that the engineers might seize control and bring the system around, once they started to resist the corruption and sabotage of the technological and productive opportunities they helped to create for the sake of pecuniary gain to the business class.

It may be argued that Veblen pushed the conflict between business and industry to extremes (Hodgson 2004: 203). There is no good reason to suppose that making profits and making goods to service the needs of society are incompatible or that business interests are always at cross purposes with the interests of society. This is as improbable as the assumption of the identity of interests he challenged. Criticising neoclassical economics for its unfounded faith in the beneficial outcomes of a market-driven society, Veblen erred similarly by focusing on the negative-sum outcomes of capitalism. Not only did he sketch how the quest for profits among businessmen degenerates in a zero-sum game or worse, but also how consumers in their quest for status are worse off by the waste of resources in efforts that do not give satisfaction. Emphasising the search for pecuniary gain at the expense of others, the notion of self-interest is coloured accordingly. If neoclassical economics interpreted self-interest anew in terms of rationality, Veblen emphasised that self-interest, adapting its colouring to that of the pecuniary culture, was the "concomitant of a predatory life" (1898: 194). In these terms he sketched how a pecuniary culture run on greed and pride arose with the rise of the credit economy, which increasingly undermined trust and cooperation, the basic conditions for the survival of the economic system.

Shading into sociology

Marx and Veblen fulminated against economics for the way the development of its theoretical and methodological framework had trivialised the fact that society is the scene of antagonistic forces at all times. Eighteenth-century thought was permeated with this idea of constructive and destructive forces operating in society. Attention focused on how to guide these forces, channelling man's passions by institutions, towards cooperation and trust. Economics learned to define itself by focusing on market exchange as a separate domain of knowledge differentiated from other social sciences with its own subject-matter, scope and method. The opposing forces were seen to be captured by the market forces of supply and demand to which agents react in their aim to maximise satisfactions and profits, lending itself to mathematical precision.

Veblen countered that one cannot start building on the third floor, assuming that the foundations and first two floors are securely in place. He provided a view of society in terms of the discarded elements from neoclassical economics: psychology, history, philosophy, sociology, Darwinism etc., focusing on institutions, culture, change, class, crises, telling the story of the two forces and their interaction in industrial society. That is the story of the growing preponderance of a pecuniary culture, in which economic behaviour is motivated by greed and vanity, shaped by emulation and manipulation, to gain at the expense of others. The economy had evolved into a credit economy, increasingly delinking finance from the real economy. With an ever-sharpening focus on financialisation to increase profits, the credit economy runs on corporate and personal greed and emulation, with fraudulent activities becoming systemic. A blinding world of illusion had been created, of spinning the wheel of Fortune, and juggling words, figures and bookkeeping, all for the good of the fat cats.

Veblen took economists to task for their belief in the rosy world they had created by their abstractions. Although the issues of business enterprise should be addressed by economists, "they do not raise those questions because such questions cannot be answered in the terms which the hedonistic economists are content to use, or, indeed, which their premises permit them to use" (1961: 249). These facts "are explained away as being aberrations" (*ibid.*: 249). As a consequence,

> Neoclassical economics depicted business people, under the guidance of the benign market, producing as much as they could and striving to lower

costs and bring the most cost-effective products to consumers. In Veblen's system this same group of business people would as soon sabotage production as enhance it, in order to obtain a financial gain.

(Cornehls 2004: 34)

Emphasising the incongruence between the two worlds, Veblen castigated neoclassical economics for presenting a comforting narrative in which references to the evolutionary, systemic and predatory nature of greed and pride in capitalism had been erased. Emphasising instead the mutual benefits, the equality and liberty, and promotion of the common good, economics choose to ignore the fact that this darker side is part of the very nature of capitalism. No wonder that economics failed to provide a proper theory of limits. Inquiring into the conditions by which centripetal forces achieve maximum results is not the same as setting forth a mechanism of self-regulation to prevent any of the forces to become dominant and upset the balance.

Veblen sketched a system that gets caught in a vicious circle as a culture shaped up that highlighted acquisitive and predatory incentives and habits of thought. Like Marx, he emphasised that the system undermines its own foundations, negating the optimism about commercial society with which political economy had started its career. Material advance would neither lead to a higher level of satisfaction for an increasing number nor bring about social and moral progress. However, their analyses came at a time when the frontier had already moved elsewhere and new challenges and tactics had come into use. Where greed and pride had no place.

Although dismissed by economists, greed was not left unattended. Sociologists took care of subjects like social change, institutions, social control, sociality and culture, including the topic of greed. Debates on changing society, human action and institutions were rerouted through the work of romanticists and historical economists to sociology. Actually, Marx and Veblen are often seen as sociologists first and economists second. The same goes for Max Weber (1864–1920). We owe to Max Weber's *The Protestant Ethic and the Spirit of Capitalism* (2005[1906]) the question of how the pernicious activity of money-making could have become a matter of spiritual calling. Trying to understand changes in society through the lens of ideas and beliefs, Weber traced the rise of capitalism to the protestant ethic as a set of beliefs and attitudes highlighting productivity, work ethic, innovation, thrift and frugality (Collins 1986). Weber referred to "the earning of more and more money, combined with the strict avoidance of all spontaneous enjoyment of life" as its *summum bonum* (Weber 2001: 18), and a sign of being among the elect. Capitalism is part of a process of rationalisation, focusing on calculation and efficient use of means, which infused western society with the Reformation. Although Weber acknowledged that the acquisition of wealth may become an end in itself, he strongly objected to the allegation that capitalism was unscrupulous greed. "Unlimited greed for gain is not in the least identical with capitalism, and is still less its spirit" (*ibid.*: xxxi). On the contrary, Weber notes that greed is far more prominent in countries where the bourgeois-capitalistic development has remained backward. The counterclaim Weber dubbed "the illusions of modern romanticists" (*ibid.*: 21). It is true that capitalism is characterised by instrumental rationality or "the tendency to calculate as carefully as possible the most efficient means, and to implement them methodically in order to achieve control over nature, society, and the self" (Muller 2002: 240). Nevertheless, capitalist economic organisation is the most efficient economic system to date. At the same time, Weber was ambivalent about its cultural effects. People may become "dominated by the making of money, by acquisition as the ultimate purpose of . . . life" (Weber 2001: 18) at the expense of happiness or personal utility.

Similar issues were discussed by Georg Simmel (1858–1918). In his work Simmel developed the notion of society as a complex web of the multifarious relationships resulting from interaction between individuals. Interaction features both integrative and antagonistic impulses and tendencies, within human nature, between individuals (consensus and conflict) and between individual and society (autonomy and regulation). This produces forms or patterns within which interaction between individuals takes place. Simmel called this process of social formation sociation (*Vergesellschaftung*). The family or economic organisations are examples of the coagulated forms of interactions between individuals. Taking forms of sociation to always involve centripetal *and* centrifugal forces, Simmel rejected the idea that competition only embodied destructive *or* constructive tendencies: "Modern competition is often described as the fight of all against all, but at the same time it is the fight of all *for* all" (1955: 62). Competition does involve rivalry and conflict, but it also forces people to reckon with others' sentiments, interests, reason to gain their attention and favour, and so it binds people together.

In *The Philosophy of Money* (2004[1900]) Simmel extended his analysis to money. With the advance of the division of labour and differentiation of culture, more steps need to be taken to realise final goals, creating a growing preoccupation with means. Consequently, modern man has developed a more abstract, more numerical and more calculating mind-set. The more diverse and remote ends are, the more man becomes engrossed in the pursuit of means. Money is the ultimate means. Linking people to flows of goods and services and to one another, money is the common thread running through economic relations. Money is the ultimate symbol of modern life, expanding into all social relations. It is a medium through which people associate and cooperate. Simmel emphasised that "the effect of money approaches that of a religious mood" (*ibid.*: 237). As absolute means, money

> becomes the centre in which the most opposed, the most estranged and the most distant things find their common denominator and come into contact with one another. Thus, money actually provides an elevated position above the particular and a confidence in its omnipotence.
>
> (Simmel 2004[1900]: 237)

At the same time, however, money may become an end in itself. We often transfer emotional value from end to means and end up aspiring the means as an end in itself. In the case of greed, people are transfixed upon the possession of money for the sake of ownership to the exclusion of others, instead of the enjoyment of its benefits and money "gains the power to reduce the other purposes to the level of means" (*ibid.*: 242).

Like Marx, Simmel pointed out that money, and especially credit, involves an element of trust, given that money only *represents* value. Trust in the economic realm is part of "the general trust that people have in each other" (*ibid.*: 177), a necessary condition to make society possible. Trust may partly be said to have been build up from experience, but it also contains an element of 'faith', reaching beyond reason and observation (*ibid.*: 178). Faith is about what it means to be part of a community. Trust and faith are assets of a social formation rather than individual properties and important resources in the production of the benefits of society. This has, more recently, been the message of Francis Fukuyama's *Trust: The Social Virtues and the Creation of Prosperity* (1995). The social virtues, i.e. the extent of trust, cooperativeness and solidarity in society, are essential elements in the creation of prosperity and the vitality of civil society and its political institutions. Social virtues, public benefits. Such ideas hark back to the eighteenth-century debate on social virtues and institutional control that underpinned the elevation of greed and the need for recognition on account of their positive-sum outcomes and the conditions and contextual factors that were gradually stripped down in the development of economic science.

Notes

1 Socialists presented schemes of reform to alleviate the economic and social consequences of capitalism, ideas which received a scientific basis in the writings of Marx. Notwithstanding socialist contributions, including attempts to accommodate Marxist views to marginalism (Steedman 1995), given that Marx is usually classified as the last of the classical economists (although he arrived at radically different conclusions), textbooks on the history of economic thought usually present two contenders.

2 Schumpeter described Philip Henry Wicksteed (1844–1927) as "the only Jevonian theorist of note". He observed that "this theologian, who was a lecturer on Dante, stood somewhat outside of the economic profession" (1954: 831–2). Schumpeter was much impressed by Wicksteed's benevolence, modesty and refinement.

3 As Marshall formulated the law of diminishing marginal utility: "The marginal utility of a thing to anyone diminishes with every increase in the amount of it he already has" (1961[1890]: 93).

4 Medema's monograph is the best source to follow the adventures of the concept of self-interest into the twentieth century, relating how with the development of the theory of market failure the invisible hand is seen to lose more and more of its magic touch and in need of the visible hand of government to deliver the goods.

5 One of the key issues in economic research after Marshall concerned such inefficient allocations of resources. Most accounts of such market failures include reference to imperfect markets, the nature of goods and incomplete markets. In the case of imperfect markets, the market power of agents violates the condition of perfect competition.

The nature of goods may also be a reason for markets to fail. Public goods are non-exclusive (defence) whereby non-buyers cannot be excluded from the benefits of their use; merit (demerit) goods are inadequately supplied because people under-estimate the benefits (healthcare) or costs (smoking) of their production. In the case of incomplete markets, there are transaction costs, informational failures or property issues, whereby resource allocation is non-optimal. Markets were also seen to fail to deliver benign outcomes in the case of strategic interactions. Especially game theory developed this line of enquiry, with the prisoner dilemma as its best-known example of a situation in which the optimal choice by the individual leads to a suboptimal outcome for all players. Behavioural economics has added yet another source of distortions: what if people are less rational than the model assumes.

6 In the United States a business class emerged that used its new wealth to compete for status and social prestige among themselves but in particular with the traditional elites. Wealth, rather than birth, became the ticket to success, status and power. It fuelled the acquisitive passion, while ostentatious and wasteful luxury consumption became a weapon in the battle for status (Mason 1998: 46ff).

References

Argitis, G. (2016). Thorstein Veblen's financial macroeconomics. *Journal of Economic Issues*, vol. 50(3): 834–50.

Atkinson, G. (2007). Pecuniary institutions: their role and effects. In: *Thorstein Veblen and the Revival of Free Market Capitalism*, Knoedler, J., Prasch, R. and Champlin, D. (eds), Cheltenham/Northampton: Edward Elgar, pp. 69–86.

Blaug, M. (1980). *Economic Theory in Retrospect*. Third edition. Cambridge: Cambridge University Press.

Brennan G.H. and P. Pettit (2004). *The Economics of Esteem: an essay on civil and political society*. Oxford: Oxford University Press.

Collins, R. (1986). *Max Weber; a skeleton key*. Masters of Social Theory, volume 3. Newbury Park: Sage.

Cornehls, J.V. (2004). Veblen's theory of finance capitalism and contemporary corporate America. *Journal of Economic Issues*, vol. 38(1): 29–58.

Davanzati, G.F. and A. Pacella (2014). Thorstein Veblen on credit and economic crises. *Cambridge Journal of Economics*, vol. 38(5): 1043–61.

Davis, J.B. (2003). *The Theory of the Individual in Economics*. London and New York: Routledge.

Dobb, M. (1973). *Theories of Value and Distribution since Adam Smith; ideology and economic theory*. Cambridge: Cambridge University Press.

Dorfman, J. (1958). Source and impact of Veblen. Veblen Centenary Round Table. *American Economic Review*, vol. 48(2): 1–10.

Dorfman, J. (1961). *Thorstein Veblen and his America*. Fifth edition. New York: Kelley.

Edgeworth, F.Y. (1881). *Mathematical Physics*. London: Kegan Paul & Co.

Fisher, R.M. (1986). *The Logic of Economic Discovery: neoclassical economics and the marginal revolution*. Sussex: Wheatsheaf Books Ltd.

Frank, R.H. (1985). *Choosing the Right Pond*. New York: Oxford University Press.

Fukuyama, F. (1995). *Trust: the social virtues and the creation of prosperity*. London: Hamish Hamilton.

Henry, J.F. (2012). The Veblenian predator and financial crises: money, fraud, and a world of illusion. *Journal of Economic Issues*, vol. 46(4): 989–1006.

Hill, L. (2012). Adam Smith in thumos and irrational economic 'man'. *European Journal of the History of Economic Thought*, vol. 19(1): 1–22.

Hirsch, F. (1976). *Social Limits to Growth*. Cambridge: Harvard University Press.

History of Political Economy (1972). *History of Political Economy*, vol. 4(2), fall: special issue on the marginal revolution.

Hodgson, G.M. (2004). *The Evolution of Institutional Economics; agency, structure and Darwinism in American institutionalism*. London/New York: Routledge.

Howey, R.S. (1989). *The Rise of the Marginal Utility School 1870–1889*. New York: Columbia University Press.

Jevons, William Stanley (1965[1871]). *The Theory of Political Economy*. New York: Kelley.

Jevons, William Stanley (1965[1879]). *The Theory of Political Economy*. Second edition. New York: Kelley.

Karayiannis, A.D. (2001). Behavioural assumptions in Nassau Senior's economics. *Contributions to Political Economy*, vol. 20 (1): 17–29.

Keynes, John Neville (1973[1890]). *The scope and method of Political Economy*. Clifton New Jersey: Kelley Publishers.

Kirzner, I.M. (1976). *The Economic Point of View*. Kansas City: Sheed and Ward.

Lowry Todd, S. (1987). The Greek heritage in economic thought. In: *Pre-Classical Economic Thought*, Todd Lowry, S. (ed.), Boston, MA/Dordrecht/Lancaster: Kluwer Academic Publishers.

Marshall, Alfred (1961[1890]). *The Principles of Economics*. Ninth (variorum) edition. London: Macmillan & Co.

Mason, R. (1998). *The Economics of Conspicuous Consumption; theory and thought since 1700*. Cheltenham/Northampton: Edward Elgar.

McNulty, P.J. (1967). A note on the history of perfect competition. *Journal of Political Economy*, vol. 75(4): 395–99.

Medema, S.G. (2009). *The Hesitant Hand: taming self-interest in the history of economic ideas*. Princeton/Oxford: Princeton University Press.

Muller, J.Z. (2002). *The Mind and the Market*. New York: Anchor Books.

O'Sullivan, A., S.M. Sheffrin and S.J. Perez (2008). *Microeconomics: principles, applications, and tools*. Fifth edition. New Jersey: Pearson/Prentice Hall.

Pigou, A.C. (1912). *Wealth and Welfare*. London: Macmillan.

Pigou, A.C. (1935). *Economics in Practice: six lectures on current issues*. London: Macmillan.

Rabin, M. (1998), Psychology and economics. *Journal of Economic Literature*, vol. 36(1): 11–46.

Rae, John (1964[1834]). *New Principles on the Subject of Political Economy*. New York: Kelley.

Reisman, D. (1990). *Alfred Marshall's Mission*. Basingstoke: MacMillan.

Revised Report of the Proceedings (1876). *Revised Report of the Proceedings at the Dinner of 31st May 1876, held at the Political Economy Club*. London: Longmans, Green, Reader & Dyer, internet site: http://scans.library.utoronto.ca/pdf/4/47/revisedreportofp00 poli/revisedreportofp00poli.pdf.

Robbins, L. (1946[1932]). *An Essay on the Nature and Significance of Economic Science*. London: Macmillan.

Robinson, J. (1978). *Economic Philosophy*. Harmondsworth: Penguin Books.

Schumpeter, J.A. (1954). *History of Economic Analysis*. Boston, MA/London/Sydney: Allen & Unwin.

Screpanti, E. and S. Zamagni (1993). *An Outline of the History of Economic Thought*. Oxford: Clarendon Press.

Seckler, D.W. (1975). *Thorstein Veblen and institutionalism: a study on the social philosophy of economics.* London: Macmillan.

Senior, N.W. (1965[1836]). *An Outline of the Science of Political Economy.* New York: Augustus M. Kelley.

Sidgwick, Henry (1885). *The Scope and Method of Economic Science.* London: Macmillan.

Sidgwick, Henry (1897). *The Elements of Politics.* Second edition. London: Macmillan.

Sidgwick, Henry (1901). *The Principles of Political Economy.* Third edition. London: Macmillan.

Simmel, Georg (1955). *Conflict and the Web of Group Affiliations.* Translated by K.H. Wolff and R. Bendix. Glencoe, IL: The Free Press.

Simmel, Georg (2004[1900]). *The Philosophy of Money.* Third enlarged edition. Edited by David Frisby. London and New York: Routledge.

Steedman, I. (1995). *Socialism and Marginalism in Economics: 1870–1930.* London: Routledge.

Steedman, I. (1997). Jevons's theory of political economy and the marginalist revolution. *European Journal of the History of Economic Thought*, vol. 4(1): 43–64.

Veblen, Thortsein (1898). The instinct of workmanship and the irksomeness of labor. *American Journal of Sociology*, vol. 4(2): 187–201.

Veblen, Thorstein (1914). *The Instinct of Workmanship, and the State of Industrial Arts.* New York: Macmillan.

Veblen, Thorstein (1921[1919]). *The Engineers and the Price System.* New York: B.W. Huebsch.

Veblen, Thorstein (1958[1904]). *The Theory of Business Enterprise.* New York: Mentor Books.

Veblen, Thorstein (1961). *The Place of Science in Modern Civilisation and Other Essays.* New York: Russell & Russell.

Veblen, Thorstein (1961[1901]). Industrial and pecuniary employments. In: *The Place of Science in Modern Civilization and Other Essays*, Parson, T. (ed.), New York: Macmillan.

Veblen, Thorstein (1979[1899]). *The Theory of the Leisure Class.* Harmondsworth: Penguin Books.

Weber, M. (2001[1906]). *The Protestant Ethic and the Spirit of Capitalism.* Translated by Talcott Parsons. London/New York: Routledge

Wicksteed, P.H. (1935[1910]). *The Common Sense of Political Economy.* London: George Routledge & Sons.

Winch, D. (2009). *Wealth and Life; Essays on the Intellectual History of Political Economy in Britain, 1848–1914.* Cambridge/New York: Cambridge University Press.

8 'It was the epoch of belief, it was the epoch of incredulity'

Ousting greed and pride

Greed had been marked as a deadly sin for ages. Greed, being one of the most dominant of passions, made for a destructive force in society. As Pierre Nicole wrote in his essay *De la Grandeur*: "men full of cupidity are worse than tigers, bears or lions. Each of them wishes to devour the others". So it was quite gutsy of seventeenth- and eighteenth-century philosophers to argue that such a destructive force could be enlisted for the good of all. To bring it off, greed was to be held on a short leash. Nicole continued: "yet by means of laws and police, these ferocious beasts are so tamed that one draws from them all the human services one might draw from the greatest charity" (Nicole, cited in Faccarello 1999: 31).

The rise of commercial society had much to do with this reputational make-over. As trade and commerce became the new basis of the health and wealth of nations, a reappraisal took place of the human passions and of the desire for gain and recognition in particular. Philosophers gradually built a new model of man and society that acknowledged social as well as selfish tendencies in human nature. The idea was brilliantly captured in Kant's happy phrase of "the unsociable sociability of man" (Kant 1997[1784]: 44). Based on these characteristics of human nature, society was the scene of integrative and antagonistic forces.

With the rise of commercial society, something shifted in the balance between these two forces. A positive-sum narrative emerged, which took the social and integrative tendencies in human nature into account, not least because in commercial society, as Smith put it, "[e]very man . . . becomes in some measure a merchant" (WN I.iv.1), and hence "stands at all times in need of the co-ordination and assistance of great multitudes" (WN I.ii.2). People are all in it together, so they better try to make the constructive forces prevail. Moreover, in commercial society, achieving one's own goals depends on servicing the goals of others: private gain was only to be realised by efforts beneficial to others as well. With the advance of specialisation and differentiation within an expanding network of exchange, greed had different consequences.

Cooperation and specialisation increased productivity and allowed for growth of output and income. The eighteenth century showed the gradual transition from the mercantile system, and its zero-sum logic of growth and rivalry in trade, to an economy of growth founded upon production, capital accumulation and increased productivity from which everyone was expected to benefit. Nevertheless, the idea that gain was only to be had at the expense of others proved persistent, and the ideas of greed, selfishness, zero-sum game and rivalry were often seen to imply each other. The reassessment of greed and pride was part of the rise of a framework of thought that disentangled these ideas, emphasising interdependence, cooperation and opportunities for mutual gain. Greed became part of a new world view. A model of society where greed, if properly managed, would be capable of producing beneficial effects for society. Nations as well as individuals would gain together. Trade and commerce, and their driving forces of greed, vanity and ambition, became part of a narrative of expanding cooperation and the exchange of goods, ideas, knowledge, practices and ways that would enrich people in the material and immaterial sense.

It sounds too good to be true. That is why philosophers discussed the conditions and limitations of these counterintuitive ideas, debating questions of sociability and rules of propriety, law and government, liberty and market competition. The terms and conditions on which greed could be agreed to be socially useful were discussed for more than a century. Sure enough, some were more outspoken in their adherence to the model (Hume) than others (Smith). Some were not persuaded at all and did not accept the positive-sum narrative of commercial society (Rousseau). Nevertheless, in the debate on commercial society, the following conditions were considered essential if greed and pride were to have social utility and as such be for the prevalence of constructive forces:

1   Philosophers developed an evolutionary account of how people learned to become sociable. Perhaps it was initially born out of need. But even if sociability was inborn, it had to be developed by practice. Greed was not a singularly operating incentive in human nature, but part of a wider set of interacting passions that all have their say. Man had social, unsocial and selfish inclinations and, being dependent on others, he learned how to balance the various tendencies to be able to meet his requirements. The principles of human nature were discussed. As were the ways these principles interacted to produce and maintain a social formation, and how rules and norms emerged to coordinate efforts to provide for shared needs. Learning the ropes of living in society, man became a socialised, disciplined being. These competences became ever more important in a society where advance depends upon cooperation and trust.

2   The directive force of (appropriate) institutions. In the process of learning to live together, man stumbled upon arrangements to make things work – institutions, rules, norms – encouraging some drives while restraining others. Given that interdependence is shaped within impersonal relations of exchange, these institutions are particularly important in commercial society.

3   Operating within a framework of interdependence, people must restrain their selfishness to continue and share the benefits of cooperation to keep everyone in a cooperative mood. Eighteenth-century thought came to recognise the benefits of the market as a system of control. In an exchange economy, the market informs people through price signals what to produce and in what quantities. Exploiting the desire for gain, the market pits self-interest against self-interest in such a way that when people pursue their own benefits and gain it is and cannot be other than beneficial to others as well. Competition is the *sine qua non* of this counterintuitive set of ideas. Intent on the same benefits and gains, people force each other through market competition to share the advantages of specialisation and cooperation. Infringements on the free operation of the market (market power or privileges through state intervention) distort incentives and the distribution of gains.

Based on these conditions, it was argued, the market does not create havoc in the rivalry between 'ferocious beasts', but effectively mobilises and coordinates private efforts at gain to the advantage of all. Regularities, observed in the operation of the market as a system of opportunities and control, were identified as natural principles through which Providence works its beneficent results of growth of wealth. A narrative emerged in which, fuelled by self-seeking passions, exchange of knowledge, goods, practices and manners created conditions of mutual gain, peace and trust.

If greed in its new setting was instrumental in producing the growth of wealth, knowledge and morals, 'greed' was greed no more. Indeed, the rise of the language of self-interest in the 'economic' context coincided with the revaluation of the destructiveness of greed. Self-interest, greed and self-love checked by considerations of need and utility was about balancing contrary passions and about being balanced by the directive influence of institutions to the mutual benefit of all. It was widely understood that the positive social function and beneficial outcomes of interest were contingent upon the conditions listed above, and therefore always precarious. Based on these conditions, philosophers constructed a conception of a positive-sum world from the idea of the social utility of pride and greed, remodelled as self-interest. In this sense, Smith linked self-interest (in *The Wealth of Nations*) to prudence and propriety (in the *Theory of Moral Sentiments*). On this basis, political economy took off as a distinctive field of inquiry. In the development of political economy, however, self-interest, originally the spin-off of greed and self-love or pride, got its own show, while greed and pride were side-tracked. What happened?

Well, perhaps it was too good to be true. The eighteenth century brought hope of progress and happiness for all. Such aspirations inspired the dismantling of the old ways and do things anew: liberty, equality and fraternity, grafted upon the unprecedented growth of production. However, things did not evolve as smoothly as expected. The question of going back to the old ways or pushing forward was hotly debated. It surely affected the new science of political economy, making it look for firmer ground to stand on. As the science of political economy shaped up, economists renovated their positive-sum narrative stripping it of its original ideas.

If the story started with a reassessment of the passions, political economy was now rid of the messy, contradictory and imprecise nature of human passions. The early socialists and romantics criticised political economy for defending the evil consequences of unjust institutions while helping to spread a spirit of calculating selfishness in industrial society. Conservatives, on the other hand, were disquieted by the agenda of reform that political economy pursued. Political economists were caught in the cross-fire between reformers and conservatives as revolutionary change hit society. So they tried to defend and define the scientific profile of their science. The subject matter was narrowed down (wealth, not happiness, virtue or civility) and political economy was given its own methodological approach (deductive science, reasoning from principles) to meet scientific pretensions. The concept of self-interest was refitted for purpose and redefined as the desire for wealth. Self-interest was assumed to be the sole motive in behaviour to explain the growth and distribution of wealth. So self-interest became a behavioural premise within an analytical model.

The variety of motives and impulses underlying human behaviour, as well as the institutions of society that shaped interactions, were set aside and with it the first two conditions on which greed had been conceptualised as self-interest. Reflections on the civilising process, manners and morals were gradually discarded from the science of political economy, narrowing down public benefits to the growth of wealth. Self-interest lost its eighteenth-century alter ego, prudence, when redefining self-interest as the desire for wealth blurred the distinction between self-interest and greed. Moreover, the ties that bound self-interest to pride were severed when other motives to explain economic behaviour were discarded.

Consequently, the burden of the argument of the positive social function of self-interest as disciplined greed was shifted unto the remaining condition: competition within a network of relations of interdependence. Classical economics propagated the superiority of free, competitive market forces to create prosperity. It aimed to uncover the natural laws that governed economic phenomena by abstract reasoning. Classical economics considered the principle of competition the key to its benign effects. Competition is the spur to industry and innovation. It coordinates behaviour and guides adjustment between desires and means, innovation and growth, from which everyone benefits. Many derided political economy for the absurdity of building a positive-sum narrative upon the principle of competition, because its rivalrous and injurious nature was so much at odds with the acclaimed benefits.

In his *Manual of Political Economy* (1865), Henry Fawcett complained about "the wide-spread error" of associating competition with "something almost criminal. Many . . . social philosophers attach to competition the stigma of selfish greed" (1865: 130). Weighted down by such ignorance, he explained once more that competition is beneficial to capitalists and labourers, buyers and sellers alike, exerting a tendency of equalisation. Charges against greed were countered by highlighting its positive function and beneficial tendencies. A fine specimen is Cliffe Leslie's essay *The love of money* (1862). The Irish (historical) economist inquired whether the love of money was a good or a bad quality in mankind. He answered, first, that it does not make much sense to blame (or applaud) money for the things you can do with it. Second, "there is a transformation in the moral character of wealth, and of the desires involved in the general love of money. For the most part, instead of representing wickedness, brutal delight, and idle pomp, or conquest, tyranny, and plunder, the wealth of Europe represents peace, culture, liberty, and the comfort of the many rather than the magnificence of the few" (Cliffe Leslie 1888[1862]: 8).

Despite such reassuring words that greed does not harbour disaster, socialists increasingly rallied against competition as a benign mechanism. Marx, helped unto this track by Engels, tried to prove the political economists wrong on their own terms. Forget about benefits for all from the free pursuit of self-interest in a competitive environment. Self-interest is predefined by property relations through which relations between labour and capital are determined. So self-interest is socially determined instead of socialised. Capitalism is not a system of economic organisation to provide for people's needs. It is a highly efficient system of exploitation, troubled by increasing inconsistencies within the system in which competition plays a pivotal role. Competition primarily facilitates the growth of capital at the expense of labour. Competition is the mechanism through which capitalism generates increasing inequality, as an ever growing share of wealth is concentrated in the hands of the ever smaller class of capitalists. Greed is a systemic feature of capitalism. The notion of society as a meeting-ground of constructive and destructive forces, and the optimism about the rise of a positive-sum society from which political economy started out in the eighteenth century, resulted in two separate narratives at the end of the classical era.

The reconfiguration of ideas in economics following the marginalist revolution did nothing to diminish the polarisation of both narratives. In the last quarter of the nineteenth century, political economy was remodelled as neoclassical economics. Analysis of the economy shifted from production to exchange, substituting capitalists and labourers for the perspective of producers and consumers to understand economic life. Attention focused on a theoretical account of individual decision-making in conditions of scarcity of means relative to desires, using the tool of marginal analysis. Again self-interest was reinterpreted to fit the new model. Rather than the desire for wealth, self-interest was redefined as 'getting the most from the least', bringing out its rational, maximising character. Reconceptualising self-interest in terms of rationality qualified greed as irrational. It was to be discounted from the model as an aberration, sharing the same fate as pride had earlier. Self-interest had gotten rid of its founding passions and now had its own show.

Belief in the positive-sum narrative

Although it would take another book to map out these developments, neo-classical economics built its own version of the positive-sum narrative, doing away with essential elements of the classical version. It fixated its theoretical development by resetting its theoretical framework. One expression of this lock-in effect was the development of mainstream, in separation of its opposing zero-sum narrative. Questions related to greed, cohesion, trust and sociality were emptied out of mainstream economics and passed off to sociology. For a long time the topic of greed only bubbled up within economics in the hands of economists with a sociological or philosophical bent, like Tawney or Keynes. Issues of sociality, the civilising process, morality and culture were removed from the neoclassical framework, and not for reasons of ethical neutrality alone. Perhaps more importantly, theoretical rigour demanded it. To be able to claim the social benefits of exchange, the economic world must be assumed to be inhabited by strangers dealing with one another strictly on the basis of rational self-interest. Social ties, loyalties, power and benevolence made for muddy waters that obstruct the glittering benefits from view. As Hirschman pointed out, allocative efficiency and welfare maximisation for all can only be claimed from the ideal competitive model (1982: 1473). Neoclassical economics built up a theoretically constructed positive-sum narrative in which markets lead to efficient outcomes. Improvements in technology, organisation, resources and laws are seen as welfare enhancing. Change is assumed to move the economy to a new equilibrium at a higher level of welfare (Stiglitz 2004). In a highly abstract model reflecting ideal conditions, free competition maximises welfare in society. Surely these ideal conditions are never met. And neither is it true that the more reality conforms to theory the more the benefits that theory predicts will be realised (Lipsey and Lancaster 1956). Yet, this ideal model is the point of reference. Market problems are seen as lapses from the ideal model. This way the theory of market failure developed, spelling out situations in which the market did not produce efficient outcomes. Welfare economics analysed infringements upon welfare optimality and sought to establish rules by which to decide when government intervention was called for.

In rewriting the classical version of the positive-sum narrative, neoclassical economics had no use for the elements on which the original classical version had been built in the eighteenth century. Stressing the instrumental rationality of human behaviour, passions were out. The concept of competition was turned upside down. "Competition means struggle, fight, maneuvering, bluff hiding of information – and precisely *that* word is used to describe a situation in which no one has any influence on anything, where there is *ni gain, ni perte* . . ." (Morgenstern 1972: 1171; italics in original). In general equilibrium theory, competition was used to describe a market form on the basis of a set of characteristics that effectively rule out competition in the older sense: "a mode of conduct, involving interaction amongst a number of individuals each of whom, identifying the others as rivals, strives to outmatch the others in the process of trying to attain a specified goal (or series of goals)" (Addleson 1984: 105). In order to maximise satisfaction, the market participant can only realise an optimum result by entering into a relation of exchange with others. Necessarily, his results will depend on the actions of these others. That is, unless it is assumed that no participant has any influence on events and that participants employ all kinds of strategies to outmatch others or cooperate to increase their advantages. As Morgenstern quipped: "It is *Hamlet* without Hamlet" (1972: 1174).

The classical idea of competition was antithetical to the determinism of the theory of equilibrium, in which outcomes are preordained by the conditions and structure of the model. Such determinism strikes at the roots of the idea of unintended consequences of human action and the invisible hand. The dynamics and instability of the balancing process of integrative and antagonistic forces are traded in for the static and stable character of the equilibrating forces on which general equilibrium theory relies. The invisible hand belongs to another framework of thought, one in which cooperation, competition and interests meant something quite different than in general equilibrium economics.

The introduction of game theory, as a new mathematical format to think through problems of individual decision-making, was an attempt to repair such shortcomings. In a way game theory reinstated competition in the older sense by reintroducing strategy, bargaining, exploiting information etc. Moreover, it acknowledged that "social phenomena are different [from physical phenomena]: people are acting sometimes against each other, sometimes cooperatively with each other" while "[i]nanimate nature shows none of these traits" (Morgenstern in Davis 1983: ix-x). Nevertheless, game theory assumes a formal framework inhabited by rational individuals pursuing their self-interest.

Despite these qualifications and limitations, the positive-sum narrative was the point of reference in theorising for a long time. In *The Acquisitive Society*, Tawney already noted, however, how much the notions of the invisible hand and the unintended social benefits of self-interest had become entrenched in conventional wisdom.

> The laborious refutation of the doctrine that private and public interests are co-incident, and that man's self-love is God's Providence . . . has achieved, in fact, surprisingly small results.
>
> (Tawney 1982: 30)

It did not help that at times even leading economists did their bit of preaching. In *Capitalism and Freedom* (1962), Friedman explained the liberty and benefits gospel, doing it all over again in *Free to choose* (1981):

> The key insight of Adam Smith's *Wealth of Nations* is misleadingly simple: if an exchange between two parties is voluntary, it will not take place unless both believe they will benefit from it. Most economic fallacies derive from

the neglect of this simple insight, from the tendency to assume that there is a fixed pie, that one party can gain only at the expense of another.

(Milton and Rose Friedman 1981: 5)

Competition is the great and benign regulator among rational, self-interested individuals. Other systems of control only mess things up. Even greed did not deter Friedman. Asked by Phil Donahue whether he had ever had any doubts about capitalism, its excesses and greed, Friedman responded:

Is there some society you know that doesn't run on greed? You think Russia doesn't run on greed? You think that China doesn't run on greed? What is greed? Of course, none of us are greedy, it is only the other fellow who's greedy. The world runs on individuals pursuing their separate interests. The great achievements of civilisation have not come from government bureaus.

(Interview in The Donahue Show, 1979)

The message is that greed is plainly a simple fact of life. Don't fret about it, because it has given us civilisation. The real struggle is between the evil forces of restraint, government and bureaucracy, and the good forces of liberty, the free market and trade. That is what decides between liberty and serfdom, and between wealth and poverty.

It was this positive-sum narrative that was widely adopted in the 1980s. On the other side of the crisis, Michel Camdessus, President of the IMF between 1987 and 2000, wrote that the consensus at the 2010 annual meeting of the IMF and World Bank was that the crisis originated in the "perversion, by a culture of greed, of a well-established model of market economy" (2012: 111). Under the spell of money, a cultural context emerged that produced "a collective blindness". He concluded that "there are three major failures that explain the origin of the crisis: the absence of necessary rules, the inadequacy of monitoring institutions, and very fundamentally, collective behaviors that result from this culture of having" (2012: 113). It reads like the 'don't'-list of the eighteenth-century philosophers who wrote the manual of the social utility of greed and self-interest. Considering "Men left to their own desires are worse than Lions, Bears, or Tygres", Pierre Nicole had good reason to warn that "[a]s soon as i'ts (greed) left to it self, it flies out and keeps within no bounds. Instead of being beneficial to human Society, it utterly destroys it. There is no excess it will not run into, if not held back" (Nicole *Moral Essays* 1696, vol. II: Of Grandeur, Part I, §30/29: 98). There is no positive-sum narrative distinct from a negative-sum narrative. Society is the scene of interacting forces, integrative and antagonistic, which somehow need to be balanced, in the full recognition that any balance is always temporal, tentative and never self-evident. Marx and Veblen offered a historical or evolutionary approach, accepting at one point in time the social utility of greed. However, the history of greed demonstrates that any claim about the social utility of greed is contextually determined. So is its disutility.

The quote from Dickens's *A Tale of Two Cities* as the title of the conclusion of this book is appropriate for yet another reason. Key issue in eighteenth-century debate was the idea that a society of rational self-interested individuals, held together by virtue of the advantages they derive from society, would not work. The cooperative strategy requires something more than a setting of shared interests to be sustainable. Hence the study of human nature, human passions, sociability, moral sentiments, rules, norms, and institutions. Self-interest alone is not up to the task. This has only become truer with the advance of the money economy, the rise of an extended credit-system and the ongoing processes of commercialisation, financialisation and globalisation. The economy increasingly runs on beliefs and trust built on a sense of mutual dependence. Within the intricate web of interconnected relationships of a highly advanced economy, gains cannot be taken in isolation of the network of interdependence by which they are realised. This gives rise to questions like: Can I still trust that we are in it together? That if I am dealt the bad risks and am among the losers, there will be more than instrumental rationality ('collateral damage') and the letter of the law? That I can rely on society and its institutions as a community to help me out? Greed violates this sense of mutuality and trust. It is no coincidence that the topic of greed resurfaced in economics in tandem with topics of trust and cooperation. Greed is real. It is alive and kicking. Economists cannot rely on the usual quick start guide to self-interest. Inquiring into the motivational springs and moral environment of economic decision-making and action to explore the differences between greed, self-interest and virtue, economists need to delve into the manual itself to study the operating instructions of self-interest as written by philosophers and economists in the past. If greed saps basic requirements to the functioning of modern economies as trust, cooperation, and justice, economics should be able to address greed within its own frame of reference.

References

Addleson, M.S. (1984). General Equilibrium and 'Competition': On Competition as Strategy. *South African Journal of Economics*, vol. 52(2): 104–13.

Camdessus, M. (2012). From a "Culture of Greed" to a Culture of Common Good. In: *Free Markets and the Culture of Common Good*, Schlag, M. and Mercado, J.A. (eds), The Netherlands: Springer, pp. 111–20.

Cliffe Leslie, T.R. (1888[1862]). The Love of Money. In: *Essays in Political Economy*. Second edition. Dublin and London: Hodges etc and Longmans etc.

Faccarello, G. (1999). *The Foundations of Laissez-Faire; The Economics of Pierre de Boisguilbert*. London and New York: Routledge.

Fawcett, Henry (1865). *Manual of Political Economy*. Second edition. Cambridge and London: Macmillan and Co.

Friedman, M. (1979). Interview with Phil Donahue in The Donahue Show, https://www.youtube.com/watch?v=Vpq3Cv5Wen8

Friedman, M. and Friedman, R. (1981). *Free to Choose – A Personal Statement*. New York: Avon Books

Hirschman, A.O. (1982). Rival Interpretations of Market Society: Civilizing, Destructive, or Feeble? *Journal of Economic Literature*, vol. 20(4): 1463–84.

Kant, Immanuel (1997[1784]). Idea for a Universal History with a Cosmopolitan Purpose. In: *Political Writings*, Reiss, H. (ed.), translated by H.B. Nisbet. Second, enlarged edition. Cambridge/New York: Cambridge University Press.

Lipsey, R.G and K. Lancaster (1956). The General theory of Second Best. *Review of Economic Studies*, vol. 24(1): 11–32.

Morgenstern, O. (1972). Thirteen critical points in Contemporary Economic theory: An interpretation. *Journal of Economic Literature*, vol. 10(4): 1163–89.

Morgenstern, O. (1983). Foreword to the first Edition of M.D. Davis, *Game Theory; A Nontechnical Introduction*. Revised edition. New York: Basic Books.

Nicole, Pierre (1684). *Moral essays*. Two volumes. London: Bartley/Magnes. https://books.google.com/books?id=PmR4znKlC1cC (09–05–2011).

Smith, Adam (1976[1776]). *An Inquiry into the Causes and Nature of the Wealth of Nations*. Edited by R.H. Campbell and A.S. Skinner. Oxford: Clarendon Press.

Stiglitz, J.E. (2004). Evaluating Economic Change. *Daedalus*, vol. 133(3): 18–25.

Tawney, R.H. (1982). *The Acquisitive Society*. Brighton: Wheatsheaf Books.

Index

For Product Safety Concerns and Information please contact our EU
representative GPSR@taylorandfrancis.com
Taylor & Francis Verlag GmbH, Kaufingerstraße 24, 80331 München, Germany

www.ingramcontent.com/pod-product-compliance
Ingram Content Group UK Ltd.
Pitfield, Milton Keynes, MK11 3LW, UK
UKHW020956180425
457613UK00019B/718

9 780367 666972